Strategies for Successful Acquisitions
in the United Kingdom

Strategies for Successful Acquisitions in the United Kingdom

Edited by Elizabeth Gray

Published by Euromoney Books

in association with

Box89
Denton Wilde Sapte
Fortis Bank
PricewaterhouseCoopers
Weil, Gotshal & Manges

Published by

Euromoney Books

Nestor House

Playhouse Yard

London EC4V 5EX

Telephone: +44 (0)20 7779 8155

E-mail: books@euromoneyplc.com

www.euromoneybooks.com

Copyright © 2003 Euromoney Institutional Investor

ISBN 1 85564 998 5

Typeset by Julie Foster

Printed in England by Cromwell Press.

Contents

Contents

Contents

Contents

Box89 Intelligence Services Limited
12, St. James's Square
London
SW1Y 4RB

Tel: +44 (0) 20 7849 6072
Fax: +44 (0) 20 7849 6300   *Contact:* David Hutchinson,
Email: Contact@Box89.com   managing director
www.Box89.com   *Email:* Hutchinson@Box89.com

Member of the British Venture Capital Association

◗ DENTON WILDE SAPTE

Denton Wilde Sapte
One Fleet Place
London
EC4M 7WS UK

Tel: + 44 (0) 20 7246 7000   *Contact:* Martin Kitchen
Fax: + 44 (0) 20 7246 7777   *Tel:* +44 (0) 20 7320 6692

Fortis Bank
23 Camomile Street
London
EC3A 7PP

FORTIS BANK

Solid partners, flexible solutions

Contact: Peter Hanratty, Acquisition Finance

Tel: +44 (0) 20 7444 8808
Email: peter.hanratty@fortisbank.com

PricewaterhouseCoopers
Transaction Services – United Kingdom/Global
1 Embankment Place
London
WC2N 6RH, England

Tel: +44 (0) 20 7583 5000
Fax: +44 (0) 20 7804 4907
www.pwcglobal.com/transactionservices

Weil, Gotshal & Manges
One South Place
London
EC2M 2WG

Tel: +44 (0)20 7903 1000
Fax: +44 (0)20 7903 0990
www.weil.com

Author biographies

Jonathan Andrew is a director in the Transaction Services practice of PricewaterhouseCoopers and specialises in assisting businesses maximise the return on their deals. ACA qualified, Jonathan works closely with management teams to provide tailored assistance with integration and transition planning in the periods immediately before and after deal completion. His focus is to maintain the performance of the underlying business and drive the realisation of synergy benefits in the shortest timeframe.

In 1999, Jonathan was seconded to The Arcadia Group to assist them with the integration of four Sears womenswear brands and the closure of the Richards brand. He subsequently set up and ran the Programme Office for the BrandMAX Programme – an extensive cost-cutting and brand-repositioning programme run over 18 months and affecting stores in 250 high streets across the United Kingdom. The successful implementation of the BrandMAX programme significantly contributed to the dramatic turnaround in Arcadia's performance reversing a loss of £8.5 million in 2000 to a profit of £53 million in 2001.

Jonathan has also been involved in integration and synergy review work with a range of leading UK businesses including Smiths Group, Penguin Books, Corus, HIT Entertainment and Pubmaster.

Paula Doyle is an associate within the intellectual property and technology department of Weil, Gotshal & Manges in London. She advises a variety of clients, including clients in the insurance, banking and technology sectors on a range of matters including software licensing, intellectual property protection, system procurements, outsourcing and data protection. Paula speaks on e-commerce related issues at seminars and recently contributed a section on Escrow and Disaster Recovery Agreements to the *Encyclopedia of IT Law*.

Juliette Enser is a competition/EU lawyer at Weil, Gotshal & Manges. She is experienced in advising European and US companies on the competition aspects of mergers and acquisitions and the formation of joint ventures, and has often assisted companies in complying with merger control regimes worldwide. Her experience also encompasses general compliance issues, and she has counselled major companies on the application of European competition rules to distribution and technology licensing agreements.

Juliette has worked for a range of clients including those active in the telecommunications, media, defence, construction and automotive sectors, and has regularly advised on the application of the European merger rules to complex transactions involving private equity funds.

Barry Fishley is a partner at Weil, Gotshal & Manges, specialising in IT, IP, E-commerce and telecoms.

He advises financial institutions, FTSE 100 companies, technology companies, government departments and start-ups on a range of transactions and issues including outsourcing, complex procurement exercises, strategic alliances, licensing, general commercial matters and IP/IT aspects of M&A. He also advises on data protection and privacy matters.

Nick Flynn is a corporate lawyer at Weil, Gotshal & Manges and specialises in environmental law, in particular dealing with environmental issues in mergers and acquisitions.

His experience includes a wide range of transactional work in both the general corporate and environmental areas. Amongst others, Nick has worked on Europe-wide joint ventures by major oil companies and a large-scale divestment programme by one of the world's largest chemical companies.

Elizabeth Gray is an editor at Euromoney Books and Institutional Investor Books where she has researched and written on corporate finance, banking and capital markets, alternative investments, portfolio management and risk management. Prior to joining Euromoney, Elizabeth worked as an editor in publishing for the defence and energy sectors, and has also edited a number of academic newsletters. For three years, she was an editor of the *Monash University Law Review*, Australia.

Elizabeth has qualified as a solicitor and worked for one of Australia's largest law firms, Corrs Chambers Westgarth, in Melbourne. Like many professionals in the late 1990s, she has dipped her toes into the cauldron of venture capital, but hastily withdrew them.

Elizabeth has a PhD in Social and Political Science from King's College, Cambridge, specialising in Soviet and post-communist Russia, and formerly taught Soviet and Russian history at the University of Melbourne. She maintains a keen interest in contemporary east and central Europe. Elizabeth is author of *The Fiction of Freedom. The Development of the Czechoslovak Literary Reform Movement* (Melbourne, Monash Publications in History 1991).

James Gubbins is a partner at Weil, Gotshal & Manges, specialising in corporate finance. He is experienced in a wide range of corporate finance transactions and joint ventures, including acquisitions, disposals, rights issues, fundraisings and flotations. He has particular expertise in advising companies in the biotechnology and pharmaceutical sectors.

Peter Hanratty has 23 years international banking experience. After graduating from the Sorbonne University, Paris and the University of Nottingham, Peter trained with Lloyds Bank International in Spain and completed several special assignments for LBI in Central and South America. In 1985 he joined the Bank of Montreal, graduating from their Management Development Programme in Toronto in 1986. After a spell in the Middle East, Peter joined The Industrial Bank of Japan in London, establishing the Acquisition Finance Group in 1987, and helped develop IBJ into one of the leading leveraged finance houses in the London market. In 1993 Peter set up a UK Mezzanine Fund as a joint venture with MeesPierson. When Fortis acquired MeesPierson, Peter developed the fund into a leveraged finance group which subsequently became part of the Global Acquisition Finance Group in Fortis with 50 staff in London, New York, Madrid, Paris, Brussels and Rotterdam – the centre of Global Acquisition Finance operations.

Fortis has recently established regional acquisition finance teams in Leeds, Birmingham, Manchester and Reading; the London team works closely with European Financial Sponsors in originating and financing UK and European acquisitions out of the London market.

Peter is a well-known speaker at conferences and business schools.

Chris Harrison is a finance partner in the London office of Weil, Gotshal & Manges with a broad range of experience in complex cross-border financing transactions. He has acted for financial institutions, sponsors and governments. His experience includes structuring senior mezzanine and bridge financings in connection with acquisition finance, debt restructurings, debtor-in-possession financings, telecommunications and other infrastructure projects on a secured and unsecured basis.

Chris's recent restructuring experience includes advising Citicorp in relation to a major debtor-in-possession refinancing and representing a major cable TV/telecoms company in relation to the restructuring of their senior and high-yield debt.

David Hutchinson has over 15 years investigative experience, having been based in Hong Kong, New York and London working for police, government and commercial groups. Whilst in the United States and Hong Kong, David advised financial institutions on performing due diligence and anti-money laundering enquiries, specialising across Central and South East Asia. In 1999 David returned to London and began working predominantly with the private equity community on the discreet checking of management within MBOs, MBIs and similar transactions.

David holds a degree in Geology and is a fluent Cantonese speaker. He has a wide range of experience within the intelligence and investigative fields – personally advising key players as well as conducting in-country operations.

David is the founder and managing director of Box89 Intelligence Services Limited, which is headquartered in St James's Square, London. Box89 is a member of the British Venture Capital Association, BVCA, and was created specifically to focus on providing high quality and extremely discreet referencing of people.

David is also contributing author in *The Private Equity Practitioner's Manual* 2001, entitled 'Management Referencing – People-Focused Due Diligence', and has spoken at a number of private equity forums.

Rosemary Jackson is a partner in the Corporate Group at Denton Wilde Sapte. Rosemary's practice focuses on all aspects of corporate advice for listed and private companies, both large and small, including acquisitions and disposals, joint ventures and investment agreements, including investment into and by venture capital funds. She also has a broad commercial practice. A significant element of her client base is in the media sector.

Martin Kitchen is a senior partner in the corporate department of Denton Wilde Sapte in London. He specialises in all aspects of corporate transactional work and corporate finance and has particular experience of takeovers, recommended and hostile, private acquisitions and disposals and joint ventures both in the United Kingdom and overseas, where he spent three years in the Middle East as managing partner of DWS's Dubai Office.

As a transactional lawyer, Martin's M&A sectoral experience reflects the strengths of the firm in energy, TMT, (publishing in particular) and banking and finance.

Evelyn McAdam is a senior solicitor in the London-based corporate department of international law firm Denton Wilde Sapte. She specialises in mergers and acquisitions and corporate finance, and has advised a number of high-profile clients in relation to domestic and international transactions. She graduated with a law degree from University College, Cork and obtained a masters degree in commercial law from University College, Dublin. She is admitted in Ireland and the United Kingdom and joined Denton Wilde Sapte in 1999 from leading Dublin firm Arthur Cox, where she worked in the commercial and corporate department.

Douglas Nave heads up the international competition-law practice in Weil, Gotshal & Manges' London office.

Doug, a US-qualified partner of the firm, has a broad regulatory practice focusing on EC and US competition and international trade law. He has a wide range of experience before courts and regulatory agencies in the EU and United States. He is specialised in government reviews of mergers, acquisitions and joint ventures, and has assisted numerous companies in complying with the requirements of merger notification laws around the world. Doug also advises leading industrial companies on distribution, technology licensing and related matters under the EU and national competition laws in Europe. He has acted on behalf of an international clientele in numerous anti-dumping and other international trade proceedings.

His clients represent companies in numerous economic sectors, from emerging technologies to consumer branded goods and public media.

Antony Rabar, principal, High Plains Investment group, is an entrepreneur and qualified lawyer, with an extensive background in corporate finance, commercial law and strategy consulting.

Tony has worked with some of the top corporate finance and investment houses, and recently with several of the United Kingdom's premier universities and research institutions leading and developing new ventures in a principal capacity, and advising others on commercialising promising new technologies. He established the High Plains Investment Group in 1997 as a specialist corporate finance and management group specialising in high-tech entrepreneurial ventures. In this role he successfully established and led a number of start-ups, raising considerable early-stage funding and managing their day-to-day operations during early stage commercialisation efforts. After leaving a career in strategy consulting, he also acquired and managed a number of traditional manufacturing and services companies.

Hugh Reynolds has been a director in the London Transaction Services practice of PricewaterhouseCoopers since 1997. He specialises in financial and commercial due diligence on both UK domestic and cross-border M&A transactions. Major corporate clients have included Unilever, Shell Chemicals, GKN, Deutsche Post and TI Group. Major private equity clients have included Cinven, Candover, ABN Amro and Texas Pacific Group.

Gary Richards is a corporate tax partner in the London office of Weil, Gotshal & Manges. His experience includes advising corporate and financial clients, both on domestic and cross-border transactions, on a wide range of issues including tax-efficient structuring of M&A transactions, business combinations and spin offs, innovative funding techniques, remuneration and compensation packages, and tax-related disputes. He also advises on VAT and stamp duty mitigation.

Gary provides cross-border transactional and structuring advice in conjunction with the WGM tax practices in Europe and the United States.

Philip Slater is a senior associate within the finance group of Weil, Gotshal & Manges in London. Prior to joining Weil Gotshal, Phillip worked as a finance lawyer with Latham & Watkins. Throughout his career, he has advised on a variety of project financing transactions providing both lender and sponsor representation. In Poland, Phillip continues to represent the arrangers (Deutsche Bank and Bank Handlowy) with respect to the ongoing administration of a project financing facility totalling DM600mm for Polkomtel, a Polish GSM operator.

Kevin Smith is an associate within the intellectual property and technology team of Weil, Gotshal & Manges in London. He represents a variety of clients primarily in the areas of hardware, software, media, biotechnology, electronics and telecommunications. Kevin has experience in a full range of transactions relevant to technology companies, including technology and intellectual property licensing, research and development collaborations, service agreements, information technology outsourcing arrangements, and intellectual property protection.

Nick Thody is a senior associate in the London office of Weil, Gotshal & Manges. He specialises in a wide range of corporate finance transactions, including mergers and acquisitions, flotations, takeovers, restructurings and fundraising. Before joining Weil Gotshal in 2001, Nick worked in the corporate department at Linklaters and previous to this at Hammonds Suddards Edge.

Neil Vickers is a senior corporate partner specialising in corporate finance and mergers and acquisitions. He advises corporates, institutions and banks on a wide range of transactions, both domestic and cross-border. Neil was educated at Durham and Cambridge Universities.

His expertise is, by choice, varied. He specialises in IPOs and other stock exchange transactions on the LSE and AIM. He advises on private placings and private equity deals. He has been involved in takeovers as well as undertaking private M&A transactions. Neil is active in the technology, media and energy fields, but has experience across a range of business sectors.

Neil regularly speaks at conferences in the United Kingdom and overseas (including the International Law Development Institute in Rome) on subjects of corporate law and practice.

Introduction

Elizabeth Gray

Mergers and acquisitions have become a principal method of corporate expansion and for the generation of shareholder value. The UK marketplace has always been buoyant due to a liberal corporate culture and regulatory framework that has made the country an attractive place to invest. As a result, it has become the home to a number of global corporate giants, as well as a key service provider to foreign companies (both in manufacturing and financial services). With the increasing homogenisation of global financial markets and integration among the members of the European Union, the country witnessed a phenomenal growth in M&A activity during the 1990s. This frenetic activity has now ended, and a cold sense of reality has struck the corporate world. Corporate valuations, financial structuring arrangements and takeover activity are all likely to remain conservative in the coming years. However, the United Kingdom remains a sympathetic environment for domestic and foreign acquisitions, and M&A will remain a key driver in any confident corporate strategy.

Any book devoted to the strategies for ensuring the completion of a successful merger or acquisition must not only itemise key legal and financial principles, but provide insight into the creative and intuitive structuring of negotiations, documentation, financing and post-merger integration. The financial arrangements for acquisitions have become more complex, the regulatory environment more imposing, and the liberalisation and globalisation of financial markets have opened more opportunities for corporates across borders. All of these factors outline the necessity for professionals to be cross-disciplinary in their approach to advising clients, and for them to work together across their professional and jurisdictional borders to ensure a smooth and successful completion.

In this book, we have asked the contributors to go this extra step, to provide the reader with both the structural details and the benefits of their experience in arranging and advising successful, and unsuccessful acquisitions in the United Kingdom. *Strategies for Successful Acquisitions in the United Kingdom* is designed to assist CEOs and CFOs in all stages of the merger and acquisition process – discussing the pivotal features of the UK market, and the cultural, regulatory, legal and financial environment for both the domestic and foreign acquirer. For those targeting or advising on M&A transactions, and for other stakeholders in the transaction, this book provides guidance on the best steps and strategies to be taken to ensure a successful completion of the deal.

The first two chapters of this book, *The climate for mergers and acquisitions*, and *Current trends in merger and acquisition activity*, provide a description of the environment for mergers and acquisitions in the United Kingdom, the sectoral trends which have affected the pace of acquisitions across the United Kingdom and by UK companies abroad, profile some of the prominent acquisitions of 2001 and 2002, and look ahead into 2003. These chapters also provide an economic and sectoral outlook for M&A in the United Kingdom in the short and medium term.

Critical to the success of any M&A transaction are the financial arrangements in place for the deal. The stock market collapse, accounting scandals of 2002 and ongoing concerns over corporate governance have changed the landscape for acquisition finance. While the recipe for a successful financing may not have altered, many of the key ingredients have: some of the more exotic options have lost flavour with more conservative financial palates; some raw staples are now in short supply. Chapter 3, *Acquisition methods*, discusses these methods, and how these have been adapted through a number of acquisitions across different industry sectors. The discussion of financial structuring has been expanded in Chapters 4, *Acquisitions of unquoted companies*; 5, *Acquisition finance: the relationship between senior debt and private equity*; and 6, *Financial structuring of corporate acquisitions*. Through these chapters, the authors discuss some of the financing methods in use in the current marketplace and the impact that recent events have had on financial structuring, the changing nature and origination of acquisition finance, valuation, due diligence and practical steps for negotiating the purchase.

The steps taken toward effecting a smooth acquisition are the subject of Chapters 7, *Negotiation tactics and strategy* and 8, *Financial and commercial due diligence issues*. Chapter 7 itemises the methods and steps taken to ensure a smooth acquisition of a private or public company in the United Kingdom, including privatisations of public services and businesses. Chapter 8 considers the role of due diligence in ensuring a successful acquisition in the United Kingdom, including both the techniques essential to obtain access to the relevant information, and the steps relevant to ensuring that this information is assessed and acted upon in a timely and integrated manner. It is only when each of the components and personnel involved in financial and commercial due diligence (as well as those involved in financial structuring, tax planning, human resources issues, insurance and regulatory compliance discussed in other chapters of this book) act in concert, that acquirers can ensure both a successful acquisition and a smooth post-acquisition management or integration of the target company.

Core to structuring a successful acquisition and ensuring the long-term viability of the target company post-acquisition is personnel. In the words of the author of Chapter 9, *The key people – a background investigation*, companies are run by people, staffed by people and owned by people. The investigation of key personnel has traditionally been a rather ad hoc affair, and this chapter highlights the steps needed to ensure that the due diligence of personnel is undertaken in a systematic and professional manner.

One of the oft-quoted advantages of the United Kingdom as an environment for mergers and acquisitions is the sophisticated, yet encouraging laws and regulations which govern changes of ownership in UK companies. In Chapter 10, *Legal issues*, the reader will discover those issues relevant to M&A in the United Kingdom, including the different rules governing public-to-public and public-to-private transactions, share versus asset deals, and critical information on due diligence, measures to protect the purchaser such as warranties and indemnities, and particular issues concerning restructurings and insolvencies. This legal discussion is extended in the following chapter, Chapter 11, *Intellectual property and information technology*, to these key assets of the modern company. Chapter 12, *Regulation issues*, likewise considers the important regulatory regimes affecting mergers and acquisitions – the competition law and environmental issues which are increasingly relevant to would-be acquirers.

The taxation environment for any transaction is a critical factor in structuring the deal, and Chapter 13, *Tax issues*, describes the UK taxation environment with respect to corporation tax, capital gains and income tax, and social security contributions. The discussion of the taxation implications of financial structuring for vendors, purchasers and shareholders is peppered with instructive examples of the effects of different financial engineering options.

The final chapters of this book are concerned with the results of acquisitions. Chapter 14, *Post-merger integration – maximising the return on your deal*, as its name suggests, discusses post-merger integration, and strategies for ensuring the best possible result from the transaction. With anywhere between 60 and 85 per cent of deals failing to complete, ensuring that those that do are stabilised and integrated quickly, and that focus is centered on the vital value drivers, is critical to ensuring a successful acquisition. For investors, focusing on exit strategies at the outset of the acquisition is critical for obtaining long-term value, particularly in the private equity markets. Chapter 15, *Exit strategies*, discusses these exit options and their relevant merits, focusing on each of the steps which will ensure the most successful disposal.

Many may question the wisdom of publishing a book on mergers and acquisitions in the United Kingdom at a time in which acquisitions have dropped to decade-low levels, corporate confidence has been bruised, and the drought in deal activity has parched the investment landscape. Yet in a time of financial and corporate uncertainty, the skills required to successfully effect a corporate acquisition become more pronounced than at the height of bubbling acquisition-compulsion which we saw through the late 1990s. As we enter the new century, corporates, investors, financiers, lawyers, accountants and regulators are reassessing the landscape for corporate and professional activity, and, in the sober light of falling equity markets, are striving to rediscover the core principles of successful investment strategies. This book is a testament to the confidence of its contributors: these are no fair-weather sailors, and we thank them for sharing with us their experience of and advice for successful acquisitions in the United Kingdom for the coming years. I would also like to thank my colleagues at Euromoney Books, in particular to Jacqueline Grosch Lobo for her encouragement and professionalism in the collation and editing of this text.

1

The climate for mergers and acquisitions

Elizabeth Gray

Introduction

Mergers and acquisitions in the United Kingdom have waxed and waned during the growth and then slump in the global economy. UK companies, and those investing in the United Kingdom, have benefited from a liberal economic and regulatory culture, and in recent years from the high-tech and stock market boom. Since the beginning of 2000, however, changeable and then lethargic markets have depressed both the number and the value of acquisitions in the United Kingdom, and the activity of UK companies acquiring targets abroad. Initially, this stemmed from the bursting of the so-called dotcom bubble, the falling of equity markets and thus of company valuations. However, the accounting scandals in the United States, the slowing global economy and the resulting cautious approach to corporate financial structuring from company boards and lenders have taken their toll on corporate and investor confidence. Throw in the near certainty as at the beginning of 2003 of a war in the Middle East, and all the indications point to a continuation of this stagnant period for M&A at least for the first half of 2003. Yet many UK companies are well placed to take advantage of any indications of economic change: they have undertaken, or are in the process of undertaking, the structural changes which they hope will give them the capacity to do so, and the United Kingdom remains a favourable jurisdiction with a positive climate for mergers and acquisitions.

This chapter provides an overview of the environment for acquisitions in the United Kingdom. It begins with a discussion of the political and economic structures which have shaped the development of the UK M&A market and are affecting its response to what has been termed the current M&A recession. The chapter then examines the corporate and investment culture that continues to provide sustenance and hope for corporate acquisitions, and looks at the legal and regulatory environment which has provided the basis for industry consolidation. The chapter ends with some different perspectives on the short and long-term outlook for mergers and acquisitions in the United Kingdom.

The political and economic climate for M&A

The political, economic and also regulatory environment for mergers and acquisitions in the United Kingdom is one of the most mature and well developed in the world. This has come about as a result of a combination of historical accident, calculated regulatory and policy decisions, and a liberal legal culture. With the world's fourth largest economy, the United Kingdom is strategically well placed to exploit both its special relationship with the United States – politically as well as economically – and its, at times, contradictory one with the rest of Europe. Sharing language and cultural links with the United States, strategically situated in the arc of the 'blue banana'[1] of European industrial and commercial might stretching from East Anglia to Lombardy, and retaining economic and investment links with the Commonwealth of Nations, the United Kingdom has been able to carve out an enviable economic and political position which its corporates have not been slow to exploit. UK companies have always been international investors and traders, and this has only been strengthened and compounded by the increasing political and economic integration of European countries, and the globalisation of world markets. As a result, there are few significant M&A deals in the United Kingdom that do not involve an international acquirer or target.

Despite what appears to be uncertain financial prospects, the UK economy is expected to grow by 2.4 per cent over 2003, almost matching that of the United States (an estimated 2.5 per cent) and significantly better than the euro area, at 1.3 per cent.[2] As at the beginning of 2003, sterling remained strong against the euro, and had strengthened further against the dollar, in particular during the second half of 2002. Interest rates, set by the Monetary Policy Committee of the Bank of England, have been reduced to 3.75 per cent in February 2003, despite an escalation in personal debt and a four-year boom in the housing market, particularly in the South East, which only in the first quarter of 2003 was showing signs of tempering.

Inward investment in the first six months of the 2002–03 financial year was stable on the year before,[3] although the trend toward investment in smaller projects employing relatively fewer people in the service industry and in research and development, rather than in high-volume manufacturing, is encouraging the trend toward job losses in the manufacturing sector. While the United Kingdom's abstention from entry into the euro area and the strength of sterling against the euro remains a problem for UK manufacturing competitiveness, it does not appear to have interrupted the capital inflow.

The United Kingdom continues to enjoy low unemployment – 5.2 per cent at October 2002, with little change over the previous 12 months. This is lower than both the euro area rate of 8.4 per cent, and that of the United States at 6 per cent. However, the collapse of the e-business phenomenon, the events of 11 September 2001 and the continued lack of confidence in the financial sector has, as at the beginning of 2003, disproportionately affected the financial community. Lay-offs and redundancies in the financial sector have been perhaps the largest amongst financial professionals since the 1929 crash.

While it is difficult to precisely estimate job losses by professionals in the financial community, it is clear that 2002 has been the worst in many years among investment banks, with estimates that 10,000 financial services jobs were lost globally in October 2002 alone, and that there will be another 10,000 reductions in the City of London through 2003, as corporate finance houses and investment banks continue to reduce staff to match declining deal volumes. The Centre for Economics and Business Research has used data on the number of people passing through Bank Underground station on an average weekday to illustrate the attrition from the City. At the peak of the market in 2000, nearly 79,000 people used the station on an average weekday. In 2001 that figure fell 2.5 per cent, to around 77,000. In 2002, it fell a further 8 per cent, to less than 71,000.[4] Many of those affected have not figured in official statistics, but they have contributed to the general perception of economic gloom among the financial community, and thus also to confidence of capital arrangers and providers in fueling new acquisitions. Moreover, as the cuts continued into early 2003, it was clear that the investment banks did not expect to be considerably busier in the near future.

Europe and the euro

Despite the prediction of many, the introduction of the euro has neither caused Frankfurt to supplant London's financial predominance in Europe (on the contrary), nor undermined the political and economic stability of the European Union (EU). Remaining outside the euro area, the UK's currency has remained strong against the euro. This has enabled UK companies to adopt strategies of expansion into continental Europe – especially companies supported by the strong performance of the United Kingdom's service sector, and entering into newly liberalised markets. Examples include Vodaphone's acquisition of Mannesman, Kingfisher's acquisition of Castorama, and BP Amoco's acquisition of Veba Oel.

Yet the strong pound has had the commensurate disadvantage of reducing the competitiveness of UK exporters and negatively affecting the levels of inward investment. This is evidenced in the current account deficit, which in the third quarter of 2002 was at its lowest since a surplus was recorded in the third quarter of 1998. A clear result of the highly valued currency, at the end of the third quarter 2002, the £3 billion deficit with EU countries was the highest at any time since 1990.[5] Exports from the United Kingdom to the EU are continuing to fall and imports to rise. The strong pound is clearly continuing to hamper large corporates in raising equity and debt capital, despite low interest rates. French and German companies have been able to hold their own and the euro has positioned them in many ways more strongly than their UK competitors to weather current economic climate. French M&A activity actually increased over 2001, rising more than 13 per cent.[6] This has also been evident in French and German acquisitions in the United Kingdom, particularly of UK utilities, discussed further in Chapter 2, *Current trends in merger and acquisition activity*.

Whether the United Kingdom is likely to join the European Monetary Union (EMU) remains hotly debated. A poll released by the British Chambers of Commerce in January 2003 suggested that even amongst the country's business leaders, support for adopting the euro remains mixed.[7] Only 35 per cent of those polled supported adopting the euro by the end of 2004, by which time the Labour government has promised a nation-wide referendum on the issue, providing its five economic tests have been met and the government supports entry. These tests are to determine:

- sustainable convergence between the United Kingdom and the economies of a single currency;
- whether there is sufficient flexibility to cope with economic change;
- the effect on investment;
- the impact on the financial services industry; and
- whether or not it is good for employment.

Only 32 per cent of those polled had made preparations for using the euro as a possible future currency in the United Kingdom. As one of the government's economic tests asks whether joining the single currency would: 'create better conditions for firms making long-term decisions to invest in Britain', the health of the UK M&A industry is not far from the core of the euro issue. Significant for primary issues affecting M&A with respect to taxation, competition and labour law, 54 per cent of respondents believed that the regulatory and tax burden of UK industry would increase with joining. The poll does suggest that while British industry is keeping an open mind on EMU (only 13 per cent believed that entry should be ruled out forever), change is moving at too slow a pace for the government to be confident of business support were it to recommend joining.

Corporate and investment culture

UK companies have also benefited from a corporate and investor culture which has given company boards a considerable degree of latitude in pursuing their corporate strategy, and acquirers a great amount of certainty with respect to successfully completing the transaction. This has led to considerable liquidity in the M&A market. There are a number of aspects of the UK corporate culture that have contributed to this situation (as far as generalising about the culture of any country is possible as personnel become more global and mobile).

Major equity investors in the United Kingdom have traditionally been institutional investors – pension, insurance and mutual funds – rather than individuals or corporations. These equity investors have tended toward passivity, as a kind of trade-off between the primacy of shareholder value and the principle of the accountability of management to shareholders. This has allowed management the freedom to pursue mergers and acquisitions as a tool for increasing shareholder value provided they are prepared to report responsibly on corporate strategy to shareholders, the wider financial community, and the press. Yet this hands-off approach of investors is likely to change as sophistication and improvements in management and productivity continue to accelerate. Laggards will be punished as financial investors sell their shares, and with less valuable shares they lose the ability to exploit opportunities and make the very improvements and strategic decisions they require. As the vicious cycle continues, the companies become targets. Pension funds impose their discipline by voting with their feet. If a company is satisfying their performance expectations, it is rewarded. If not, then the market will move quickly to make its displeasure apparent, leaving it open to changes in management, vulnerable to takeover and so on.

A concurrent factor improving the transparency of the UK corporate environment is that few large UK companies are retained or controlled by individual families and there are rarely cross-shareholdings of the continental European type. Bearer shares are also rare, which means that establishing the identities of the equity investors in a company is a matter of record. These features are combined with the principles of open and substantive financial reporting to ensure an encouraging corporate environment for M&A in the United Kingdom.

The legal and regulatory environment

Legal principles

There are a number of different legal jurisdictions within the United Kingdom: England and Wales (one jurisdiction), Scotland, Northern Island, the Isle of Man, and the Channel Islands. The jurisdiction of England and Wales is by far the dominant (both numerically and economically), and the legal discussion in this chapter, and through the remainder of the book is directed toward this jurisdiction, unless otherwise noted.

Mergers and acquisitions in the United Kingdom are subject to less statutory governance than those in civil law countries, which has resulted in a more liberal acquisitions environment, but with the concurrent effect of lengthening and complicating the documentary process. 'Caveat emptor', let the buyer beware, governs most dealings between parties. Unlike Civil Codes which will often oblige the parties to negotiate in good faith and make a full disclosure, English law places the burden on the acquiring party to fully investigate the asset under negotiation. A corollary principle is that a buyer can only acquire such title as the seller can pass. The result of these principles is that, historically, the due diligence, documentation, warranties and indemnities in UK transactions, as with those in the United States, are considerably more of a burden than in continental European jurisdictions. These issues are discussed more thoroughly elsewhere in this book, particularly Chapter 8, *Financial and commercial due diligence issues* and Chapter 10, *Legal issues*.

Taxation

The United Kingdom remains a relatively low taxation economy, which in the past has helped encourage the liberal climate for acquisitions and disposals. The full rate of corporation tax in the United Kingdom is 30 per cent. Capital gains tax is applicable mainly to an individual's disposal of shares, investment assets or business assets (at an upper limit of 40 per cent with taper relief down to a rate of 10 per cent). The most significant transactional charge affecting the vast majority of share and asset purchases in UK acquisitions is stamp duty. For the sale of shares, stamp duty is payable at a rate of 0.5 per cent of the consideration, and on a sliding scale for other types of assets, to a maximum of 4 per cent for consideration of £500,000 or more. For a more comprehensive view of the impact of taxation on M&A structures, see Chapter 13, *Tax issues*.

Changes to UK and European competition law

Another regulatory factor particularly affecting large acquisitions in the United Kingdom is competition law. The activities of UK companies and foreign companies seeking to acquire UK targets are subject to the oversight of the UK domestic Competition Commission, the Office of Fair Trading, and to the jurisdiction of the European Competition Commission on significant deals which involve a pan-European dimension. These authorities have fallen under some scrutiny, the earlier for the perception of political interference and the latter for a series of decisions which have been highly criticised by industry participants. With the cross-border nature of UK M&A activity well entrenched, both the UK and European regulatory environments have become essential to the success of significant mergers and acquisitions. Nowhere is this more the case than with competition law.

Reflecting the new transatlantic desire to keep a closer regulatory hand on corporate governance and activities, the Labour government's new Enterprise Act came into law on 7 November 2002. The new law criminalises cartels, provides stricter penalties for failing to comply with the Competition Commission's request for information or for non-compliance, and introduces procedures to ensure that certainty and consistency is achieved in how the powers and penalties will be applied in particular instances. The Competition Commission and the Office of Fair Trading will be expanded, and the Commission, rather than the Secretary of State, is to have the final decision to approve mergers. The test for disallowing mergers and acquisitions has also changed – from the supremely malleable 'public interest' test, which has been criticised in the past for subordinating commercial interests to political expediency, to the application of a more objective test of 'significant lessening of competition', the same test as applied in the United States.

The UK authorities have tended to be less interventionist than some of their European counterparts, and certainly less than the EU's Competition Commissioner, Mario Monti. As with other European countries, there is a two-tier system of monitoring threats to the competitive environment in the United Kingdom. Where transactions have the potential for a significant effect on competition across the EU, they must be referred to the European Commission. Transactions subject to the 'file and wait' system of the Merger Control Regulation of the EU are those between parties with a combined worldwide turnover of at least €2.5 billion and which have a substantial competitive presence in the EU. The test for mergers which pass the threshold for referral to the European Commission is that of 'market dominance' in the EU. The EU's Competition Commissioner, Mario Monti, has come under significant criticism for a number of rulings against potential mergers.

The first of these was the decision to block the attempted £950 million merger of the two travel companies, Airtours and First Choice in 1999, which was reversed in court in mid-2002 – too late for Airtours to renew the offer following the dramatic change in the travel market since late 2001, but heralding a new climate for European decisionmaking over competition issues moving into 2003. The second was the planned merger between the two US companies, GE and Honeywell, scotched by the European Commission in June 2001 on the basis, according to Mario Monti that: '[it] would have severely reduced competition in the aerospace industry and resulted ultimately in higher prices for customers, particularly airlines.' The merger had been cleared by the US authorities, and the Commission's decision was widely condemned. The United States was critical of the perception that the Commission had placed too much weight on the interests of competitors rather than those of consumers, and there were murmurs in Washington of retaliation against the Europeans. Thus, there is change, too, on the horizon in Europe, with a Green Paper issued by the European Competition Commissioner in December 2002 to debate both procedural and evidential issues in the Commission's working practice.[8] The

European Commission is also working on a new takeover directive which is designed to provide transparent, pan-European rules on the conduct of takeover bids to benefit shareholders, employees and all interested parties.

Cross-border issues and the European company

Another development demonstrating the integration of European markets and the place of UK companies within them is the proposal for the introduction of a European Company, to be known by its Latin name of *Societas Europaea*, or 'SE'. The SE will give companies operating in more than one member state of the EU the option of being established as a single company under European law. As a consequence, an SE will be able to operate throughout the EU with one set of rules and a unified management and reporting system, rather than (as at present), under the different national laws of each member state where the company may have a subsidiary. The legislation is due to enter into force in October 2004 and will break down the legal and administrative costs associated with cross-border mergers and acquisitions in the EU.

The changing nature of financing acquisitions

One of the results of both low interest rates and a depressed stock market has been a surge in the number of private acquisitions of publicly listed companies, usually referred to as public-to-private (PTP) transactions. Usually these acquisitions are by way of a management buy-out (MBO) funded by a private equity house. Private equity has become an asset class in its own right, and the M&A market continues to see aggressive private equity acquisitions in the United Kingdom (as has been seen in the case of KKR, Cinven, Texas Pacific and Philip Green/Arcadia, which were all in the bidding for Safeway, as at February 2003). This feature is discussed further in Chapter 3, *Acquisition methods*.

Outlook for the UK market

A clear outlook for the UK M&A market is contingent on a break in the clouds to the country's west and peace in the Middle East. Critical for the turnaround of the market is consumer and investor confidence. Economic globalisation has integrated the UK M&A market, especially with its closest trading partners, continental Europe and the United States. On the domestic front, the UK financial and corporate communities have largely avoided the allegations of corruption, conflict of interest and scandals that have so tarnished the US investment environment. Yet as long as the economic powerhouse of the United States continues to shudder, the global and thus the UK outlook for M&A remains temperate.

One important factor continuing to affect investor confidence is the prospect of war in the Middle East, which as at February 2003 appeared a real and present danger. The United Kingdom seems well placed to cope with any macroeconomic impacts, even if the war against Iraq is 'prolonged and disruptive'.[9] However, rising oil prices (the price of Brent crude hit a two-year high in January 2003 at US$31.80 per barrel) are bound to affect business confidence, as well as increase the possibility of a brief recession similar to those following previous conflicts in the Middle East region. Analysts appear confident that the UK economy is in a stronger position to absorb the economic disruption of the war than its European partners, although consumer spending would need to remain stable. Nevertheless, the London stock market has continued to twitch at the increasingly belligerent tone from Washington and Downing Street, and until and unless the situation is resolved, equities could continue their three-year downward march.

Investor confidence could well be restored with a new feel-good factor following a swift and decisive resolution to the US–Iraqi impasse. If so, the structural and macro drivers are in place to speed a revival in the UK M&A market. Critical will be the recovery of the IPO market (described further in Chapter 4, *Acquisitions of unquoted companies*), as taking subsidiaries public has been a favoured method of generating cash for new acquisitions. In the vicious circle of M&A, this too relies on corporate and investor confidence. Yet low interest rates, which are expected to be maintained into 2003, will continue to keep the cost of capital low. Companies in many sectors which have survived the downturn through reducing their investment in capital goods are in a significantly better position to take advantage of the recovery when it comes. Finally, after the corrections in the stock markets, corporate valuations are more attractive to new investors. If global economic conditions stabilise, therefore, the outlook for UK mergers and acquisitions in the latter part of 2003 and into 2004 is bright.

[1] The concept of the 'blue banana' was created in 1989 in France by Roger Brunet as a description of the active/passive zones in Europe. Brunet based his concept on a study about the European cities, according to which this area comprises 40 per cent of the EU-population as well as the most important European industries.

[2] *The Economist*, 11 January 2003.

[3] Invest-UK, January 2003.

[4] The Centre for Economics and Business Research and *Financial News*, 6 January 2003.

[5] Office of National Statistics Economic Indicators, Q3, 2002.

[6] Thomson Financial.

[7] Reported in *The Financial Times*, 9 January 2003.

[8] See *The Economist*, 6 June 2002, 13 June 2002 and 19 September 2002.

[9] Oxford Economic Forecasting Report, quoted in *The Financial Times*, 13 January 2003.

2

Current trends in merger and acquisition activity

Elizabeth Gray and

Tony Rabar, High Plains Investment Group

Introduction

The impressive increases in deal activity that were seen in the UK market between 1994 and 2000 are now far behind us. Acquisition levels have continued to shrink quarter-on-quarter as a result of low equity markets and shaken investor confidence following the bursting of the dotcom bubble, the events of 11 September 2001, accounting scandals and reports of analysts conflicts of interest in the United States, and continued uncertainty over the global situation. That significant deals in the UK M&A market involve international interests is highlighted by the commensurate retardation in global M&A activity.

This chapter looks at M&A deal activity in the United Kingdom, particularly over 2001 and 2002, since the deflation of the high-tech market accelerated towards a general downturn in the global economic outlook. The chapter then analyses the volume and types of M&A deals both in the United Kingdom, and by UK companies abroad, and examines the sectoral trends in M&A activity. Illustrative case studies are provided to help draw some conclusions from deal flow about what factors have contributed to make a successful acquisition in the United Kingdom in this uncertain climate. This provides the reader with some guidance as to future acquisition strategies. The chapters following this expand on these issues to give further guidance from professionals in their individual fields of financial and legal speciality.

Number and total volume of deals
The United Kingdom versus global M&A activity

Global M&A activity, including also activity in the UK market and by UK companies abroad, reached its peak at the beginning of 2000. In 2000, there was US$1,078 billion

(£674 billion) of European M&A activity. The year-on-year increase in both the number and volume of mergers and acquisitions was fueled by a number of factors. The liberalisation of capital markets and the concurrent deregulation of key industries (particularly in Europe) during the last decade of the 20th century enabled easier cross-border movement of capital and new opportunities for business growth and development. The introduction of the euro as a single European currency gave European companies comparative cost advantages and arguably stimulated M&A activity by both European and US investors in the euro area. To this, add the emergence of the Internet as it changed familiar patterns of production and distribution, and accompanying technological progress in telecommunications and computer equipment. These technological changes marked new possibilities for corporate expansion into new sectors, and for the swifter integration of new acquisitions. Finally, of course, the now infamous dotcom bubble represented by escalating stock markets and investor confidence provided the financial and cultural impetus for expansion.

By mid-2000, the growth in M&A activity had stalled, then nose-dived sharply, and by mid-2001, pundits were describing the situation as effectively an 'M&A recession'.[1] By the end of that year, M&A activity had more than halved, to US$533 billion (£333 billion). By the end of 2002, only a further US$481 billion (£300 billion) of transactions were announced in western Europe.[2] Nevertheless, Europe has fared well next to other continents, surpassing activity in the Americas in 2002, and taking an estimated 44 per cent of global M&A.[3] Activity in the United Kingdom has dropped in line with the European average of 18 per cent: the German mergers and acquisitions market has particularly suffered over 2002, with total deal value down 28 per cent. The French and Italian markets, however, have grown over the same period, by 13 and 17 per cent respectively.[4]

M&A in the UK market

By the third quarter of 2000, both the volume and the number of all acquisitions in the United Kingdom and by UK companies abroad began to drop. In 2000, there were 814 acquisitions in the United Kingdom, 72 per cent of these by UK companies. In 2001, there were 654 acquisitions, 75 per cent of which were by UK companies. The total value of these deals had fallen from £171.5 billion to £53.4 billion – a 69 per cent drop. UK companies searching abroad had been similarly cautious over this period, with 557 acquisitions in 2000, and only 371 in 2001, a drop in overseas expansion capital of 77 per cent (£181.3 billion to £41.5 billion). The year 2002 continued the downward trend. By the end of the year, UK companies had made 389 acquisitions in the United Kingdom, at a value of £24.9 billion[5] (a 40 per cent drop from the same time in 2001). Exhibit 2.1 illustrates this situation.

A selection of notable domestic mergers and acquisitions over 2001 and 2002 is shown in Exhibit 2.2.

Exhibit 2.1: Acquisitions in the United Kingdom by UK companies, 2000–02

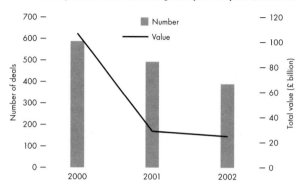

Source: Office of National Statistics.

Exhibit 2.2: Notable domestic M&A activity, 2001–02

Acquirer	Target	Value	Date
Persimmon Plc	Beazer Group Plc	£560 million	Q1, 2001
Taylor Woodrow Plc	Bryant Group Plc	£556 million	Q1, 2001
Bass Plc	Posthouse hotels	£810 million	Q2, 2001
BHP (merger)	Billiton	£10.6 billion	Q2 2001
Innogy Holdings Plc	Yorkshire Power Group Ltd	£509 million	Q2, 2001
Halifax (merger)	Bank of Scotland	£10.4 billion	Q3 2001
WPP Group	Tempus Group Plc	£383 million	Q4, 2001
Bridgepoint Capital (Venture Capital)	Virgin Active Holdings Ltd	£110 million	Q1 2002
Enterprise Inns Plc	Laurel Pub Partnerships Ltd	£845 million	Q2, 2002
Parking International Ltd	National Car Parks (NCP)	£820 million	Q2, 2002
Gamma Four Ltd	Subsidiaries of Thistle Hotels Plc	£600 million	Q2, 2002
Johnston Press Plc	Regional Independent Media Holdings Ltd	£560 million	Q2, 2002
Shell Resources Plc	Enterprise Oil Plc	£3.5 billion	Q2, 2002
Charterhouse Development Capital Ltd	Coral Eurobet Ltd	£860 million	Q3, 2002
Easyjet Plc	Go-fly Ltd	£345 million	Q3, 2002
BHS, Philip Green	Arcadia	£810 million	Q3, 2002

Source: Office of National Statistics.

The picture is similar with acquisitions in the United Kingdom by foreign companies. The number of such acquisitions in 2000 to 2001 dropped by 39 per cent, from 227 to 162. By the end of 2002, there were 113 acquisitions, down 30 per cent on the previous year. Deal size was also down – £16.5 billion from £24.4 billion – a 32 per cent drop. The decline in UK acquisitions by foreign companies is represented in Exhibit 2.3.

A selection of foreign acquisitions of UK companies which gave some buoyancy to the market over 2001 and 2002 is shown in Exhibit 2.4.

Exhibit 2.3: Acquisitions in the United Kingdom by non-UK companies, 2000–02

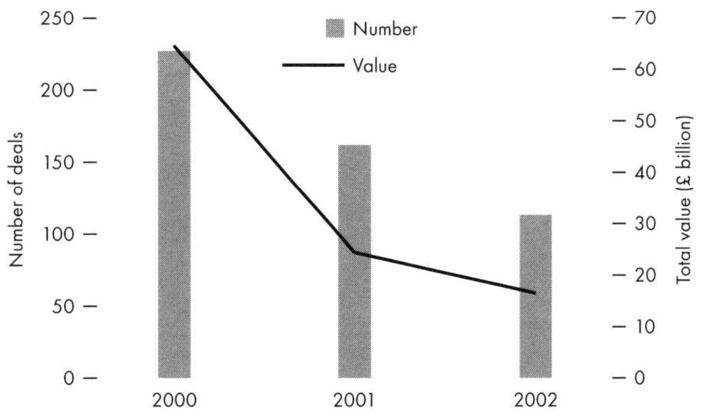

Source: Office of National Statistics.

Exhibit 2.4: Notable foreign acquisitions of UK companies, 2001–02

Acquirer	Target	Value	Date
Eni SpA	Lasmo Plc	£2.7 billion	Q1, 2001
France Telecom	Freeserve Plc	£1.65 billion	Q1, 2001
Etex Group SA	pipe systems division of Glynwed International Plc	£786 million	Q1, 2001
Vaillant GmbH	Hepworth Plc	£692 million	Q1, 2001
C&N Touristic AG	Thomas Cook from Carlson companies Inc	£550 million	Q1, 2001
Schlumberger Investments	Sema Plc	£3.6 billion	Q2, 2001
Degussa SKW Co	Laporte Plc	£1.4 billion	Q2, 2001
Lafarge SA	Blue Circle Industries Plc	£2.1 billion	Q3, 2001
Euronext NV	Liffe (Holdings) Plc	£555 million	Q4, 2001
Dynegy Inc	BG Storage Ltd	£421 million	Q4, 2001
Skandia Forsakrings AB	Lynx Group Plc	£210 million	Q1, 2002
Electricite de France	EPN Distribution (from TXU Corporation)	£560 million	Q1, 2002
Sempra Energe	Enron Metals Ltd from Enron Corporation	£102 million	Q1, 2002
RWE AG	Innogy Holdings Plc	£3.1 billion	Q2, 2002
YTL Power International Bhd	Wessex Water Ltd from Enron Corporation	£545 million	Q2, 2002
E.ON AG	Powergen Plc	£5.15 billion	Q3, 2002
Electricite de France	Seeboard Group Ltd	£670 million	Q3, 2002

Source: Office of National Statistics.

Finally, the same trend continues to unfold with acquisitions abroad by UK companies. The 77 per cent drop in the value of overseas acquisitions mentioned above by the end of 2001 was mirrored the following year, with only 225 transactions, with a value of £26.5 billion, again, a 36 per cent drop from the previous year (see Exhibit 2.5).

Selected significant UK companies' acquisitions abroad over £500 million in 2001 and 2002 are shown in Exhibit 2.6.

Exhibit 2.5: Acquisitions abroad by UK companies, 2000–02

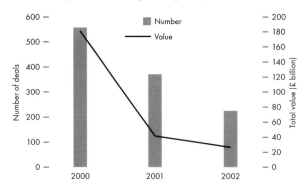

Source: Office of National Statistics.

Exhibit 2.6: Significant UK companies' acquisitions abroad (£500 million+), 2001–02

Acquirer	Target	Value	Date
British Telecommunications Plc	Viag Interkom GmBH	£4.4bn	Q1, 2001
Billiton International Services Plc	Reynolds Australia Alumina Ltd	£1 billion	Q1, 2001
Shell International plc	Fletcher Challenge Energy	£715 million	Q1, 2001
Vodafone Group Plc	Eircell 2000 Plc	£2.6 billion	Q2, 2001
Shire Pharmaceuticals Group Ltd	Biochem Pharma ltd	£1.8 billion	Q2, 2001
Hilton Group Plc	Scandic Hotels AB	£612 million	Q2, 2001
Reed Elsevier Plc	Harcourt General Inc	£3.2 billion	Q3, 2001
TI Automotive Ltd	automotive systems division of Smiths Group Plc	£940 million	Q3, 2001
Royal Bank of Scotland	retail arm of Mellon Financial Corporation	£2.1 billion	Q4, 2001
Gallaher Group Plc	Austria Tabak AG	£661 million	Q4, 2001
National Grid Group Plc	Niagra Mohawk Holdings Inc	£2.1bn	Q1, 2002
BP Amoco Plc	Veba Oel business of E.ON	£1.2bn	Q1 2002
Innogy Holdings Plc	Yorkshire Power Group Ptd	£509 million	Q2, 2001
Imperial Tobacco Group Plc	Reetsma Cigarettenfabriken GmbH	£3.5 billion	Q2, 2002
Man Group Plc	RMF Investment Group	£571 million	Q2, 2002
South African Breweries Plc	Miller Brewing Company	£2.1 billion	Q3, 2002
HSBC	Household International (US)	£8.75 billion	January 2003

Source: Office of National Statistics.

A sectoral view of UK M&A activity

Overview

The overall story told from the sectoral analysis shows the effect of the across-the-board slump in the economy and stock markets. Total deal value, not unexpectedly, has fallen from the peak year of 2000 when, aided by a number of massive deals in healthcare, finan-

Exhibit 2.7: Total deal value by sector, 2000–02 (£ million)

UK M&A ranking by sector	2000	2001	2002
Consumer products and services	21,716	3,984	4,991
Consumer staples	12,374	4,949	3,638
Energy and power	52,440	29,577	46,694
Financials	77,158	25,130	8,919
Government and agencies	6	46	1
Healthcare	84,419	2,651	2,501
High technology	18,440	9,180	4,196
Industrials	22,288	23,647	26,200
Materials	22,180	25,090	2,264
Media and entertainment	31,714	13,247	14,335
Real estate	23,978	12,348	9,734
Retail	33,944	8,038	15,754
Telecommunications	45,238	12,610	1,374
Industry total	**445,894**	**170,496**	**140,695**

Source: Thomson Financial.

Exhibit 2.8: Total number of deals, 2000–02

Number of deals	2000	2001	2002
Consumer products and services	605	500	362
Consumer staples	201	171	140
Energy and power	125	90	91
Financials	298	269	261
Government and agencies	1	1	3
Healthcare	88	87	87
High technology	655	369	249
Industrials	454	399	338
Materials	273	206	157
Media and entertainment	446	364	303
Real estate	324	104	93
Retail	259	194	174
Telecommunications	93	73	54
Industry total	**3,822**	**2,827**	**2,326**

Source: Thomson Financial.

cials and telecoms, it reached £445 billion. However, after the market's sharp reaction, the momentum was not maintained in 2001 and 2002. Deal flow fell to £170 billion in 2001 and £140 billion in 2002 (see Exhibit 2.7).

Although the headline figures may appear gloomy, there is considerable reason to remain upbeat when the numbers of concluded deals are examined. From this it is clear that while the mega-mergers may have been the headline grabbers back in 2000, the backbone of the M&A marketplace – the midcap market – has remained active. Total deals undertaken in 2001 and 2002 remain relatively high at 2,827 and 2,326 respectively (see Exhibit 2.8). The peak of 3,822 in 2000 was definitely substantial, but there is reason to believe that the market retains its perspective and maintains its belief in the underlying rationale for acquisitions. Certainly, if M&A professionals were asked to comment on the last two years of activity in contrast to normal turnover during the rest of the 1990s (and ignoring the binge that was 2000) many would be entirely happy with the market's current status.

The good, the bad and the mired

A number of stand-out examples can also be examined. Although financials, healthcare and telecoms accounted for a disproportionate amount of the totals in 2000, the market has been buoyed by energy and oil, industrials, media and entertainment and retail through 2002 and into 2003. Not surprisingly, the market for strong cash-flow rich, defensive and non-cyclical sectors has remained steady through the turmoil and, as will be examined later in Chapter 3, *Acquisition methods*, companies with good creditworthiness and continued support of the funding markets have continued to make acquisitions.

The sectors currently suffering the worst have been the financial, healthcare and telecoms sectors. The slump in healthcare can be readily understood. Much of this sector had already been consolidated in the mid-1990s with the GSK merger capping the list in both size and impact on the sector. Meanwhile, stock prices are being marked down over longer-term uncertainty and future earnings. Most of the healthcare companies are presently contending with the small bugbear of what to do with an ageing portfolio of drugs and few new blockbusters in the wings. The emerging biotech sector is still very small in comparison and is unlikely to have a significant impact on the healthcare sector, comparable with the old guard of the pharmaceutical industry, for another decade or more. In any event, it is presently difficult to see how any of these large pharmaceuticals companies could get much larger or what argument could be mounted for further merger.

The financial sector

The financial sector has been similarly characterised, with many of the mega-mergers occurring in the mid-1990s coinciding with the majority of the building societies converting to plcs. The merger of Halifax with Bank of Scotland in 2001 followed fairly quickly after other benchmark deals, including Royal Bank of Scotland's acquisition of NatWest. Operationally, the sector has done reasonably well during this current downturn to protect itself from worse ravages, with strongly defended retained earnings and sensible and foresighted provisioning during the last few years. Rather than one massive, possibly debilitating blow, the sector has taken the pain in annual bite-size pieces and overall, with the exception of the insurance industry which is still undergoing substantial adjustment, the majority of the financial sector is now in rude good health and benefiting well from the low interest rate environment.

Unsurprisingly, given the erosion of the financial climate and the low confidence of the financial professions, the prominence of financial institutions themselves in M&A activity had fallen to a decade-long low by the year-end 2002. Acquisitions within the UK financial sector fell from 17.3 per cent of the total market share of M&A in 2000 to 6.3 per cent in 2002. Although the number of deals did not drop dramatically, the size of these deals fell sharply – from £445 billion to £140 billion (2000–02), a drop from 3,822 to 2,326 individual deals (2000–02).[6] Given the results of the astounding internationalisation of the banking industry over the course of the last two decades, the story of the financial sector is probably better told through a European-wide narrative. There, the financial sector makes up 15 per cent of mergers and acquisitions in 2002 and the total value of deals involving a European financial target was £44 billion, just over half the level of the previous year.[7]

The telecoms sector

This sector poses more of a problem. Following the sale of the third-generation (3G) licences and the acquisition mania that possessed the industry in 1999 and 2000, the industry has been doubly stricken. First, it emerged that 3G licences were not the profit panacea that all the hype had prophesied them to be. Then, with companies still trying to work out how to write-off multi-billion pounds against these assets, the market bubble burst, and new orders and profits quickly disappeared, leaving most companies with rotting inventory to boot. Vanishing revenues and low interest in investing in new infrastructure and upgrades from existing rump commercial customers and massive provisioning and write-offs of poor paid investments have sucked all the wind from the sector's sails. The sector is now stuck in the doldrums facing a lengthy period of pain and it is unlikely to re-emerge for another few years until confidence returns and commercial customers begin to invest again.

Media and entertainment

Some of the gloss has come off 'new media' with the bursting of the bubble. Dotcoms and internet companies have not disappeared but have had to face up to a period of realigning themselves with more conventional commercial strategies and operations. Much of the overblown hype about consumers' changing leisure patterns has been blown away and the older wisdom and accepted truths have re-established their currency: consumers have a finite amount of leisure time, and it has proved devilishly hard to change or disrupt entrenched leisure pursuits and activities. Rewards are likely to be greater for those who seek to fit into the existing matrix than to players trying to redefine it. Accordingly, the focus has shifted back to traditional media and entertainment companies, whose market positions and revenues have proven to be mercifully more durable and predictable through all the recent tumult. Declining advertising revenues aside, this sector is likely to attract more attention in the coming years.

The proposed £2.5 billion merger of Carlton Communications and Granada media, the two main ITV television-franchise holders, to create a single ITV company is likely to be one of the most significant transactions of 2003. The two companies had failed to agree in the past on how to accomplish the merger, but announced they were once again in discussions in October 2002. The merger raises significant competition law issues: although the companies share only one quarter of the viewing public between them, they account for over half of UK TV advertising.[8] Some relief to the companies came when advertisers cautiously welcomed the merger, believing that the price structures in a united TV sales operation may not be uncompetitive.[9] The merger has been referred to the Competition Commission, and (as at February 2003) was awaiting clearance. Despite the competition issues, both industry and the government expect it to go ahead in 2003. If it does not occur, it is more likely to be due to the effects of the decline in advertising revenue and strong competition for audience from satellite and cable TV operators such as Rupert Murdoch's BskyB affecting both companies' share prices.

The airlines

Although minute in the overall scheme of acquisitions, one of the most successful acquisitions of 2002 was the budget airline easyJet's acquisition of its rival Go. In an industry struggling to come to grips with the decline in business following 11 September 2001, the rise of low-cost airlines has been a positive and faith-giving story. Although the clear market leader, Ryanair had managed to resist the urge to acquire until the beginning of 2003 (and that was only a £15 million splash-out on Buzz), it is now worth considerably more than the national flag carrier, British Airways (whose most valuable asset is its interest in QANTAS), and is still growing strongly, based on its existing business strategy of point-to-point flights to secondary, low-cost and regional airports.

British Airways, still reeling from the effects of 11 September 2001, on top of its existing operational difficulties and cost structures, has kept its course and is working hard to right its fortunes. The opening (in theory) of the European skies did not play to British Airways – the strongest of the large European carriers at the start of the 1990s – but to the low-cost airlines that picked the trends and redefined the industry. BA is refocusing its operations and strategy. On 8 May 2002, British Airways entered into an agreement with easyJet for the option to buy Deutsche BA, its subsidiary which flies exclusively in Germany, by 31 March 2003. The deal is potentially worth between £18.3 million and £28 million, dependent on when the option is exercised.

Retail

In the more subdued post-boom environment, focus has quite naturally shifted back to solid high-quality cash flow businesses, and the retail sector stands first in line for attention. The UK marketplace was refocused on this fact by the further purchase, by the entrepreneur Philip Green, of the Arcadia group in October 2002 following fairly soon after his successful privatisation of BHS. Attention is now firmly focused on the sector and considerable scrutiny is given to the major players and their possible pairings.

The unfolding story of mergers and acquisitions in the retail sector is the battle (ongoing as at February 2003) for control of Safeway supermarket. In January 2003, UK retailer, WM Morrison Supermarkets, closely followed by its rival, J Sainsbury, each bid for the company at a price of around £2.5 billion in various combinations of cash and stock. US retailer Walmart also entered the fray with an all-cash bid, as Tesco did later, the UK's largest supermarket chain. Several private equity firms, Texas Pacific Group, Cinven, CVC Capital Partners, and Kohlberg Kravis Roberts also entered the bidding for the company as, inevitably, did Philip Green. Any of these private equity deals transpiring would be of great significance to the financial structuring of mergers and acquisitions, as this would rank as Europe's largest public-to-private transaction to date and would have continued to have a significant impact on UK retail sales and the overall economics of the sector.

The Office of Fair Trading is likely to refer any transaction involving Safeway to the Competition Commission for a full enquiry, particularly that of Walmart, which through its Asda supermarkets controls around 16.6 per cent of supermarket retailing in the United Kingdom, or J Sainsbury (with 17.2 per cent). The acquisition of Safeway's 9.8 per cent market share by either of these companies would move them into direct competition with the leading supermarket chain Tesco, which controls 25.8 per cent.[10] This is especially the case if the acquirer planned to break up the Safeway chain, as this would strengthen the hands of the large chains as the only likely purchasers of the stores. The bid for Safeway is of particular interest, not only for watchers of the UK retail sector, but also as a concurrent effect of government planning policies. As planning constraints make building new stores more difficult, Safeway's 485 stores are themselves a significant strategic acquisition for retailers.

Utilities

Following from privatisation, the unravelling narrative of the power and energy sector has seen acquisitions from abroad, particularly from aggressive European power and water companies. Indeed, by far the most buoyant sector for M&A activity in the UK has been that of energy and power – accounting for over 33 per cent of total M&A market share in 2002.[11] It is estimated that more than half of UK households now receive their power from foreign-owned companies, most notably Electricité de France and E.ON (Germany).[12] Foreign firms have also been active in the water sewerage markets. This has been the result, less of bashfulness amongst UK utility companies, than the nature of UK privatisation which parcelled up a number of small companies and guarded them closely against their domestic competitors on grounds of competitions, thus providing discrete but strategically weakened units ripe for the picking by overseas hawks.

Conclusion

The years of 2001 and 2002 have been troubled for the mergers and acquisitions market. After the difficulties engendered by the collapse of equity markets in 2001, there was some cause for optimism that the following year would have brought postponed deals back to the table. However, the drawn-out unfolding of corporate scandals, falling asset prices and uncertainty with respect to global security continued to dampen corporate enthusiasm and investor confidence throughout 2002. In this respect, the globalisation of the mergers and acquisitions market has been undeniably in evidence, as the United Kingdom has been buffeted by the trailing arms of the cold transatlantic winds.

So what acquisitions activity is the weary investor likely to see emerging from the mists over the next few years? The early betting is that, absent any undue protraction in or fall-out (pardon the pun) from a likely war in the Middle-East, we will see more of the same for the coming one to two years. The view of many market commentators is that there are some pent-up deals that will possibly emerge if the war-oppressed western economies begin to look less unstable, especially with the new impetus given by the Bank of England's recent quarter per cent interest rate drop in February 2003. However, with continued flatness in top-end economic drivers such as R&D spending, investment in new capital equipment and infrastructure, cautions on new business development and the continued fragility of consumer confidence, much of the market is likely to maintain a close but wary approach to making expansive and flamboyant gestures such as new acquisitions. This is likely to last for at least another 12 to 18 months through to mid-2004. However, that is not all to say that the market will be in hibernation until then. As we have seen above, if we were to discount the brief and extravagant excursion that was 2000, overall acquisitions activity has not, by any means, been disappointing in an historical sense.

We will look for a continuation in activity in the energy and oil, utilities, and retail sectors. All sectors that can demonstrate strong and stable earnings and revenues will likely maintain a healthy appetite for acquisition – so long as the justification is strong enough to convince their investors. Also, there is likely to be resurgence in deal-making among biotechnology and technology sectors as cash and access to cash drives many players into alliances in order to survive the current market impasse. Further, by the end of 2003 some of the technology and manufacturing sectors should also begin to show signs of renewed life in deal-making as they tentatively begin investing in R&D, capital equipment and business development again after a three-year pause. The need to show continued and steady improvements in trade and productivity during 2004, after three years of internal repair work, or the small gains from cost-cutting and efficiency improvements have been exhausted, will force many of these boards to consider more expansive moves again.

[1] Stephen Barrett, vice-chairman of KPMG Corporate Finance quoted in *The Economist*, 12 July 2001.

[2] Dealogic.

[3] Thomson Financial.

[4] Thomson Financial.

[5] Source of all M&A data, unless otherwise stated, Office of National Statistics. In producing this chapter, the authors have relied on data provided by both the Office of National Statistics and Thomson Financial for the total numbers and value of transactions in the UK and abroad. Some readers will notice there is a considerable difference between the values reported by each of the agencies and this apparent inconsistency needs to be explained. The Office of National Statistics only collates its data from transactions reported in the financial press, specialist magazines, company and financial websites and, where necessary, supplements these with direct inquiries to the businesses. Accordingly, this results principally in data on listed companies or their subsidiaries. The ONS states that this reliably accounts for 90 to 95 per cent of all deal flow by both value and number and is sufficient for its own statutory purposes. Thomson purports to collect data on all transactions by registered UK companies and attempts to ensure the accuracy of its data with follow-up where appropriate. As a result, Thomson reports significantly higher deal numbers than the ONS, although the values of the total transactions are not considerably different. Simple time series analysis of the two data supports the ONS' assertion that reported acquisitions are relatively stable over time in both value and number.

[6] Thomson Financial.

[7] Thomson Financial.

[8] *The Economist*, 17 October 2002.

[9] *The Guardian*, 14 November 2002.

[10] Market share in January 2003, according to Taylor Nelson Sofres. Morrison brings up the rear with 6 per cent of market share.

[11] Thomson Financial.

[12] *The Financial Times*, 17 January 2003.

3
Acquisition methods

Tony Rabar, High Plains Investment Group

Introduction

The slump in the public markets during 2001 and 2002, falling share prices and low levels of business confidence have all had a substantial influence over the types of M&A deals and activity that have taken place. In addition, in the wake of the corporate scandals that principally racked the US markets, there has also been much closer scrutiny of acquisitions and acquisition accounting, particularly post-acquisition accounting for consolidated earnings, which has in turn influenced the types of methods and financing that have been used. Finally, the changing landscape of Wall Street, which for the purposes of this chapter means the corporate finance and advisory sectors, and the kinetic upheavals that swept through the various markets since the stock market slump and the events of 11 September 2001, have also left their indelible stamp on the types of deals that advisers have been promoting.

During most cyclical readjustments and downturns, some sectors manage to keep relatively clear of the storm while others get swept into its path. Not this time. Many observers have compared this cycle with the 70-year flood, or the perfect storm. Advisers, companies and markets have all realigned: some being caught in scandals, others being dragged down through an irrational loss of confidence, others by simply losing revenue. In early 2003, little else can conveniently be identified as the cause of Europe's greater stock market slump, given the extremes of US corporate behaviour, other than broad loss of confidence. Total M&A activity in the United Kingdom fell from 3,822 deals (worth £446 billion) in 2000 to 2,326 deals (worth £141 billion) in 2002.[1] However, in any period of change there is opportunity and profit for those who hoard their freedom to act.

This chapter sets out the basic acquisition methods but then moves on fairly quickly to discuss the factors that have affected each category in the last few years. It is assumed that most readers will be acquainted with the basics of M&A: stock consideration transactions, cash transactions funded by debt financing, and various private equity transactions. In-depth and specific information on acquisition methods is highly case specific, flavoured by the sector and prevailing market conditions. Consequently, this chapter breaks out the main types of method and examines the main drivers and market forces influencing each. It looks broadly at the major types of acquisitions by type of acquirer and analyses the type of methods that they are now employing, and why these have changed.

Acquisition drivers

Method is driven by motivation, and the basic rationale for M&A activity has not changed much in recent years (see Exhibit 3.1). Emphasis may have shifted between the various factors, and within different sectors the emphasis may change again. If M&A during the boom of the late 1990s can be likened to a land grab during a gold rush, the environment in the post-boom period is more like the Darwinian opportunism exhibited by animals in a drought. The strong resort to their strengths or develop new options and will survive.

Financial structuring and acquisition methods are largely driven by broader trends in the financial economy, and by financial technology and market confidence. As a result, we would expect to have seen substantial changes in the M&A marketplace during 2001 and 2002 since the stock market slump and economic slowdown, and indeed there have been a host of near seismic shifts in the market.

Exhibit 3.1 demonstrates that, while the basic motivators behind acquisition have remained the same, the emphasis on each has changed. The drive to remain at the vanguard of one's sector, and fear of ceding the future to one's rivals, have been replaced by the motivation to rebuild shareholder confidence in one's own company by focusing on basic business: stability and profitability. The future is becoming more familiar once again: no more talk of disruptive technologies and underlying business paradigm shifts. The future is more similar to the past and the basic business principles and the eternal truths are still there – they always were. However, for very good reasons, most companies participated and adopted boom-time behaviour (no matter how irrational it seemed). If they did not, they were marked down by investors and targetted by their rivals. Investors discounted their stock, making it more difficult to operate freely in the more expensive environment, and rivals looked greedily at the laggards making them easy prey. By not participating, the particular segment's agenda and direction were usurped and this made it even more difficult to remain relevant as a viable participant. This led to a prisoner's dilemma for many boards and executives. In the end it proved to be a Gordian Knot that could only be undone by dismantling the illusion, which is what happened.

Exhibit 3.1: Acquisition drivers and risks in rising and falling markets

Boom time issues	Acquisition drivers	Current post-slump issues
Price often very high. Cost/benefit must be analysed	Opportunistic acquisition	Bargain hunting. Inexpensive addition to cash flow and profit
Grow or die. Need to outpace rivals. Build synergies. Acquire rivals	Barriers to growth of current operations	Non-acquisition growth is hard to find. Chance to reduce costs and boost profits
Leveraging equity spreads between acquirer and target	Management team and shareholder concerns	Realign and restructure management for current needs: cash flow
Focus on main strategic units. Improve trading multiples	Non-core sale	Focus on profitable units. Improve returns to equity. Reduce debt
Use equity to build position before the tide recedes, then discard non-core/non-strategic	Consolidation	Only occurs where there is a good opportunity to build strategic position that outweighs costs of acquisition
High price expectations	Succession planning	Pressure on earnings. Good time to hand over
Necessary component to enable equity recycling and increase liquidity in the company's stock	Planned exit	Gap created by slowing equity markets and less acquisitive companies
Boom time issues	**Acquisition risks**	**Current post-slump issues**
Always a fear but using equity as consideration off-set and disguised many poor deals	Overpaying	Problem is with widening buyer/seller expectations spread
Volume of acquisitions made integration rushed and poorly executed, but worth it relative to the risks of not acting	Post-merger integration	Increased importance in lower growth and profitability environment
Business cycle shrinkage. Changes to market made short half-life for each opportunity	Failure to deliver on expectations	Can mean risk of insolvency or business closure
Momentum for growth was high. Strong views backed by incentive scheme distortion	Management clash/culture/vision	More preparation required for execution
Spurred by technology and financial shifts	Tectonic market shift	Less likely as market slows

The key drivers are based on the need to realign operations to current imperatives, and to overcome some of the problems with which the market has been left. In the first instance, some management teams geared to the boom-time models are now clashing with shareholders over post-boom strategy. Shareholders want a return to more conservative and defensive operations, and in many cases are forcing changes on management to ensure that this occurs. The United States has not been alone in replacing large numbers of CEOs and executives; the United Kingdom has done the same. The complaint, if any, has been that companies are returning to more conservative, accounting-led management styles. In other instances, management is looking at the landscape that emerged once the tide receded and is deciding how to position itself for the future ahead. Dramatic revenue growth is difficult, so consolidation through acquisition makes sense but financing this can be problematic. Profitability is again the core focus and non-core disposals and opportunistic acquisitions can be attractive, at the right price.

Another dilemma is how to deal with the disappearance of much needed liquidity in secondary markets. Investors are still holding investments that they need to realise if they are to mend their balance sheets or restructure their operations. Until they can do this they are caught in a vicious cycle with their own unforgiving investors and market. There is a pent-up stock of companies and assets acquired or developed specifically with planned exits and resale in mind. The market swung around before many players could complete. Particularly affected have been the venture capital and some private equity sectors, although many of the large acquisitive multi-nationals have also found themselves burdened with too many assets.

The penalty for mismanaging acquisitions is substantially higher in the current environment, both for the individual managers and for the companies themselves. Recourse to safety nets is weaker, and lenders and investors are unbending in their condemnation of failure. Fewer management teams are willing to take the risk. Mishandling a post-merger integration or failing to deliver on anticipated savings or growth can mean the hastened end of the acquiring company. Many are opting to wait and see what the market will bring. Others are seizing the opportunity.

Acquisition methods

The years 2001 and 2002 saw a change in the types of financial structures employed in acquisitions. The emergence of PIPEs (private investment in public entities) and other instruments have largely been in response to the changes in the market after the boom ended. PIPEs reflect the fact that many of the organisations that do have funds for investment are not the traditional investors in publicly listed vehicles. Private equity investment in listed businesses is emerging as an important source of funding while other markets, such as new equity or bonds, remain closed. A recent example has been Alchemy's investment in Regus Holdings, a property group. However, as before, the main methods of acquisition have not changed markedly, although the weighting has altered.

There are broadly only two types of financing method used in M&A, with countless variations and hybrids in between. The first is the stock consideration transaction in which the acquiring company issues its own stock to the shareholders of the target company in exchange for their shares in the target. This depends greatly on the target company's shareholders being satisfied with the valuation of, not only their own company, but also with the proposed value of the shares that they will receive in the acquirer. In the post-boom environment, it is therefore not surprising that it is harder to convince targets that the stock which is being used to pay for the acquisition is not only worth what the acquirer says it is at the time, but that it will retain its value in the near future. It is useful to note that AOL used its own stock to acquire Time Warner, but that AOL's shares are now worth only a fraction of their peak value. Many Time Warner shareholders feel that they have been deceived about the value of the consideration they were receiving.

The second type of financing method is cash. Cash can, and has traditionally, been used to acquire everything from multi-national companies to washing machines. The source of the cash is another matter. In many instances, companies making an acquisition will have a hoard of cash from existing operations that they may use. However, they may also raise additional funds by borrowing from banks specifically for the purpose, establishing a general line of credit upon which they can draw for whatever purpose, and also by issuing bonds or other interest-bearing securities into the markets. Different countries will place different emphasis on the origin of the funds, and this may be tax related or market structure dependent. In early 2003, for instance, it is more difficult to raise funds in the United Kingdom in the bond markets because of the general perceived risk, whereas individual lenders may be more enthusiastic because of their greater in-depth knowledge and familiarity with the borrower and its business.

Acquirers will typically try to structure their purchase consideration in such a way that the target's shareholders get good value if the transaction proceeds well and provides solid benefits afterward, but that in the event that the transaction does not bring the anticipated advantages, that the consideration will not be as generous. This can be achieved by offering some portion of one's own stock as part of the consideration. If the deal succeeds then the benefits will accrue to all shareholders. Over the last decade, and particularly the last few years, more hybrid forms, some extremely complicated, have been introduced. Bonds have been issued by borrowers seeking to make an acquisition with the proceeds, but which have been made more interesting with a bonus linked to the performance of the issuer's stock. If the acquisition and acquirer continue to go from strength to strength, the lenders who bought the bonds are rewarded with some upside, not just with interest payments. Conversely, this has made it easier for lenders to accept the risks of lending money if they can see a possibility of making a higher return from a successful acquisition. Such instruments that blend equity-like characteristics with debt instruments, and debt-like characteristics with traditional equity instruments (such as preference shares) can span the spectrum.

Exhibit 3.2 below, breaks out the market into four headings and broadly defines the four major participants. Although this is somewhat of a simplification, each is sufficiently different from the others, in both motivation and structure. Listed companies find themselves in a very changed economy and investment environment. Those companies that have the freedom to think acquisitively are slowly finding support in a market that is still largely wary of strategies redolent of the boom-times. Rationale for acquisition has to be well prepared and presented, and even then funding is difficult and expensive. In addition, acquisitive companies are still finding it difficult to locate targets in their own sectors. Companies in sectors that have performed poorly (such as TMT) are not thinking acquisitively but defensively, with perhaps a view to a defensive merger, otherwise they have gone

Exhibit 3.2: Acquirer segments and acquisition structures

Acquirer	Common transactions	Most common financial structure
Listed plc	Acquisition Spin-off MBO Privatisation	Equity issues (rights, warrants, new stock) Debt issue (bonds, equity-linked debt, prefs) Cash
LBO fund	Buy-out Privatisation	Private equity with appropriate capital structure Performance-based equity Syndicated debt and bond issues
Private equity fund	Buy-in Buy-out Acquisition	Private equity with appropriate capital structure Equity-linked debt PIPEs Performance-based equity Debt
Private company	Acquisition MBO	Cash Equity and debt placement Bank debt

quiet and are likely to remain so until they have repaired their operations and some measure of confidence returns to investors in their sectors.

However, those companies in solidly performing sectors that have the ability and willingness to make acquisitions are currently finding potential targets are either well-priced, making an opportunistic swoop difficult to justify, or hard to find. The major types of transactions will depend more on disposals or spin-offs by companies that need to offload divisions and assets to improve their own operations. Acquirers are having to wait for these opportunities to appear.

One aspect that is becoming more evident is the return to less complicated debt instruments for funding. Equity and index-linked instruments are simply less attractive in a flat market more focused on profitability than on growth and stock appreciation.

Private companies are finding it particularly difficult in 2003. Without access to the public funding markets and dependent upon bank financing and private equity, their alternatives are somewhat straitened. Banks are more conservative, especially when faced with a bold acquisition by a client, but they have been willing to lend where the proposition is compelling. Private equity is also available but differences in opinion over pricing and valuations are still nagging. It is probably true that private equity firms, based upon their own investment criteria, are taking a slightly tougher stance on valuations and price. However, the companies are also probably not too-far wrong in their own views on valuation based on their sector's performance and current attractiveness. The differences in viewpoints have made private equity transactions harder and longer to conclude. Private companies, on the other hand, have probably more patience and can afford to wait. This is also supported by Exhibit 3.3, which indicates that private firms have been successful in raising

Exhibit 3.3: Syndicated finance raised by UK private non-financial corporations (PNFCs), 1997–2002 (US$ billion)

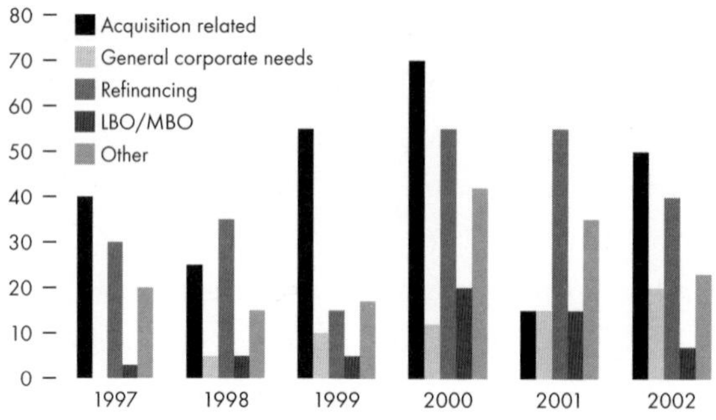

Legend:
- Acquisition related
- General corporate needs
- Refinancing
- LBO/MBO
- Other

Sources: Dealogic and Bank of England.

substantial funds through syndication and while restructuring remains important, loans for acquisition has grown markedly in 2002.

The other two groups in the exhibit are the LBO firms and private equity firms. Although they have different funding and techniques, these groups have risen to greater prominence in the current climate. With solid long-term funding in place, these players are well placed to wait for opportunities or to actively seek them out. Their liquidity and ability to make substantial placements or to undertake mid-market transactions increases their power and leverage. It is relevant that a number of LBO firms, including KKR, Cinven and Texas, are front-runners and presenting extremely viable alternatives in the struggle to gain control over Safeway. Traditional bidders such as Morrisons will have substantial difficulty in financing and completing such a transaction against the strengths that the financial investors bring.

Financing method

Stock consideration acquisitions

On a macro level, both in the United Kingdom and Europe, and across the Atlantic in the United States we have seen a continued slow weakening in the equity markets. Many technology-heavy sectors trading at barely 10 to 25 per cent of their boom-time levels – for those companies that managed to survive – their once favourite weapon (high stock price) has lost its potency. The booming stock markets monetised company stocks and together with the inexplicable and indefensible price multiples, the all- or partial-stock acquisition became a much used method. Some companies, such as AOL, managed to convert their new-economy shares into mergers with old-economy companies such as Time-Warner.

Stock acquisition was an appropriate tool for those peculiar economic circumstances. One overvalued company using its stock to acquire another, similarly overvalued company (usually in its own sector) was probably the best method available, and fallout should have been fairly limited to direct participants in the sector with modest effects (relatively speaking) flowing through the pension and insurance sectors to the otherwise uninvolved public. Discussions of whether this situation, operating hermetically sector-by-sector, largely prevented cross-contamination from one sector to another is now moot although the very wide gaps in sectoral performance indicates that financially the effects were relatively well ringfenced. The raft of court actions brought against AOL concerning the pricing of the acquisition consideration will tell its own story. To a greater or lesser extent, it was obvious that most of the market suffered from gross over-valuation, and that M&A using stock consideration was widespread across all the sectors in the United Kingdom and the European Union.

The disappearance of this method has had a substantial impact on the massive fall in M&A activity in the United Kingdom. Indeed, examining briefly the sectoral equity indices performance in Exhibit 3.4 the worst-performing sectors have been IT, media and telecommunications falling by 77 per cent, 66.7 per cent and 70.2 per cent respectively. It is hardly surprising that with the bursting of the bubble, so few companies in any of these sectors have made any recent acquisitions. Almost all companies in these sectors were hit by massive collapses in their revenues and all currently have dramatic profitability issues. Credit ratings agencies and lenders responded by sharply raising their interest rates to these would-be borrowers. With equity markets closed, costs of borrowing rising sharply and no immediate prospect of revenues picking up, all these sectors are busily focused on major repair works to their balance sheets. Asset sales have been used to pay down overhanging debt, and massive write-offs have been announced. Until consumer confidence begins to return, it is difficult to see how any of these sectors will stage a return to more aggressive, and outwardly focused, growth and acquisition strategies. It is likely that in the coming years, the main players who will be picking through these segments for opportunities will be the financial investors (LBO and private equity firms) who, being well cashed-up, will wait patiently for opportunities to arise.

There have also been more positive stories: from the same exhibit we can see that several sectors including consumer non-cyclicals, oil and gas, and pharmaceuticals have all largely passed through the slump with only modest declines. These sectors, to which we can add banking and insurance, have benefited from steady consumer demand and strong cash flows. Banking and insurance have been assisted by continued low interest rates, consumer spending, low unemployment and inflation and, in the United Kingdom in particular, a healthy dose of prophylactic provisioning and stored-up retained earnings. While it is true that the insurance sector, exposed as it is to the equity markets, is now undergoing considerable turmoil, aggressive (if unpopular) measures have been taken to manage their

Exhibit 3.4: Sectoral equity indices performance, from June 2002 to December 2003

UK sector	Market value change since June 2002 Review (%)	Market value change since June 2002 Review to total market low[a] (%)	Change since total market peak[b] (%)
Total market	-10.7	-23.2	-43.2
Airlines	-16.1	-29.4	-28.4
Autos	-13.1	-24.7	-30.4
Banks	-11.4	-26.4	-15.6
Consumer cyclicals	-11.4	-23.8	-29.6
Consumer non-cyclicals	-7.0	-10.6	-2.0
Diversified industrials	-11.1	-24.3	-50.2
Information technology	-6.7	-35.6	-77.0
Insurance	-14.0	-27.9	-17.9
Investment banks	-5.3	-28.5	-46.2
Media	-22.2	-34.9	-66.7
Oil and gas	-13.0	-17.5	-5.4
Pharmaceuticals	-1.2	-10.1	-17.9
Retail	-12.6	-23.8	-22.6
Telecom services	-0.5	-20.3	-70.2

[a] Low between June 2002 Review and 27 Nov 2002.

[b] Peak in total market price index (27 Mar 2000).

Source: Thomson Financial Datastream.

risks. Data shows that since 2000, UK life insurance companies have realigned their asset holdings, with corporate and government bond holdings rising substantially, while equities have declined some 25 per cent.[2]

It is in the non-financial sectors mentioned, such as in retail, that the lion's share of recent UK acquisition activity has taken place. While access to new equity has been closed to most of the troubled sectors, and together with limited access to increasingly expensive debt (discussed below), companies with sustained revenue and profitability levels have produced some bold acquisitions over the last two years. The signal Castorama acquisition by Kingfisher in the retail sector took place and was relatively well priced and well accepted by its investors. The rationale for its intended acquisition was sound and well presented. Nonetheless, it is clearly indicative that the advisers suggested a rights issue and a cash consideration driven structure rather than an equity consideration method.

Debt funded acquisitions

Corporate debt markets have also had their fair share of fallout and the result is that these markets are closed to most companies, other than those that have maintained their good ratings, which would seek to use them to raise finance for acquisitions. Most companies, as noted above, are too busy repairing their own balance sheets to have much time expanding through acquisition.

Although UK corporate profitability has recovered modestly, through reduced dividends and deferred capital expenditure, the weakness in the equity markets has pushed gearing up, as measured against market value. Together with a general feeling of unease about corporate profitability, fuelled in part by lingering indigestion from the WorldCom and Enron scandals, analysts' profit forecasts continue to show signs of pessimism for the near term. Credit rating agencies responded by downgrading European companies 10 times more often than upgrading them during 2001–02.[3] Despite the efforts of corporations to strengthen their balance sheets and stabilise their earnings, credit spreads have widened with weaker companies and the more exposed sectors facing much harsher borrowing conditions. This is also the case in the United Kingdom where, unlike in most of the European economies, corporate liquidation and credit default risk have been well managed, with corporate liquidations in 2002 rising by a modest 5.2 per cent above 2001 levels.[4] Most companies seeking to raise funds have had to look elsewhere and it is therefore not surprising that most used the equity capital markets. It has been rights issues that largely accounted for the slight increase in equity raisings in 2002 over that of 2001, with most companies issuing deeply discounted or underwritten investments only to meet their immediate commercial funding needs.

One of the biggest drivers of fund-raising has been the liability gap that many companies have been developing in their pension fund liabilities. In a sample of 83 FTSE-100 UK companies taken in November 2002, in which they were asked about their net pension liabilities under accounting rules FRS 17, all but 15 estimated that they had pension fund deficits. Forty-six of these were relatively minor (less than 5 per cent of market capitalisation), but in six cases the deficit exceeded 20 per cent of their then current market capitalisations, which in many cases is still under some threat of further softening before the markets stabilise.[5] Seventeen rate their deficit between 5 and 20 per cent. The pressures this has caused have added to the corporations' more general, and pressing, financial requirements for their day-to-day operations. A substantial number of the fund-raisings were instigated by the need simply to shore up their pension positions.

On the whole, debt interest payments have fallen by a further 11 per cent in the United Kingdom in 2002 which, on an income-gearing basis, is the lowest it has been for three years.[6] This suggests that there are large portions of the UK economy which a few years ago took the threat from narrowing liquidity levels very seriously, but which are now in fine shape. Those forward-looking companies, and those in the defensive sectors and non-

Exhibit 3.5: Capital and income gearing of UK PNFCs, 1970–2000 (%)

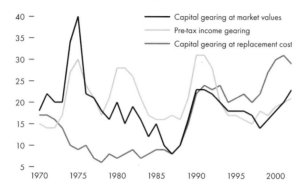

Source: Bank of England.

Exhibit 3.6: European PNFCs income gearing,[a] 1988–2002 (%)

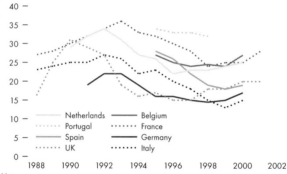

[a] Gross interest payments over gross operating surplus.

Sources: ONS, Eurostat.

cyclical sectors, are now getting into much better financial form and this will come in very useful in the coming years.

This stands in sharp contrast to the rest of Europe where income gearing has, on the whole, been rising steadily since the relative low-point of 1998–99. This is reflected in the increasing levels of corporate liquidation in the major economies. When coupled with the greater pessimism in the equity markets and generally poorer debt market environment, it is unlikely that corporate bond markets will feature heavily in the European market for acquisitions over the next few years.

In the United Kingdom, among the worst performing sectors has been the telecoms sector, which has been single-handedly responsible for a third of credit downgrades in 2002; seven of the eight private company credit defaults were made by telecoms companies. Coupled with average profit margins of -10 per cent in 2001, it is unlikely that much activity in bond issuance will occur in this sector in the coming years other than as purely defensive issues, at heavily discounted levels, to prevent collapse or further deterioration.

However, it is far from doom and gloom in the equity and debt markets. As noted above, the general trend in the UK commercial sector in addressing balance sheet vulnerability, through debt reduction and cost elimination, has left many sectors in relatively good shape at the beginning of 2003. The United Kingdom has seen particular activity in retailing, utilities, and services with a number of very interesting and high profile deals through 2002. Many of these have been funded with proceeds from rights issues. While prohibitively costly for poor performers in more vulnerable sectors, rights issues have been deemed good value by others. At least, the deep discounts have been viewed as acceptable in exchange for the strategic advantages from the anticipated acquisition.

Rights issue funding

Kingfisher staged its bold £2 billion underwritten rights issue on 19 July 2002 to provide funding for its €5.1 billion acquisition of the remaining minority stake in France's Castorama retail chain. The rights issue allowed Kingfishers' shareholders to acquire new shares at a 50 per cent discount to its pre-announcement share price. The remaining €2.4 billion required for the transaction was provided through a syndicated loan. Apart from the 2001 BT £5.9 billion rights issue, this has certainly been the largest UK acquisition-focused fund-raising in recent times. Kingfisher has argued that costs savings will amount to £40–55 million per year as a result of the merger. This is quite attractive and it clearly ameliorates some of the dilution pain from the rights issue itself. In a market where cash and market positioning are once again paramount, many other companies are also turning to rights issues for their funding needs. Indeed, data on primary issues on the London market during 2002 showed that rights issues accounted for £10,526 million, nearly 50 per cent of all equity funding raised during the year (see Exhibit 3.7).

A further sectoral analysis of the rights issues in 2002 (see Exhibit 3.8) indicates that rights issue activity was relatively confined with the top three segments accounting for 60 per cent of all rights-related funding. Kingfisher accounted for 30 per cent of the total single-handedly, and consequently further distorts the overall figures.

Financial investors

An emerging force in the current economy has been the purely financial investor. Often compared with the industrial conglomerates of the 1970s and 1980s, the modern financial

Exhibit 3.7: Value of rights issues, 2000–02 (£million)

Rights issues – LSE (£ million)	2002 UK-listed	2002 International	2002 Total	2001 Total	2000 Total
New companies	5,374	0	5,374	10,168	18,279
Further issues					
Public offer	495	0	495	3,882	437
Placing	3,821	1,353	5,174	6,263	10,121
Placing + public	1,215	10	1,225	1,399	1,883
Rights	6,434	4,091	10,525	7,241	3,705
Other	50	0	50	43	96
	17,389	5,454	22,843	28,996	34,521

Source: LSE Dec 02 Primary Market Fact Sheet.

Exhibit 3.8: Sectoral analysis of UK rights issues (£ million)

General retailers	2,005
Chemicals	850
Life assurance	805
Engineering and machinery	373
Leisure and entertainment	300
Transport	277
Media	226
Support services	150
Other	1,448
	6,434

Source: LSE Dec 02 Primary Market Fact Sheet.

investor is dressed as a private equity fund or as an LBO fund. Although the sector has been building its presence since the early 1990s, it is arguable that it is under the current market conditions that these investors will gain their most important role. During the boom, buoyant equity markets, strong liquidity and short transaction cycles from acquisition/investment to resale/float gave the financial investment community the ideal conditions in which to grow and become established. A number of UK groups became very experienced deal-makers and turned their groups into major money-makers for their parent companies and limited partners. Guy Hands' activities at Nomura made regular headlines and made it the most profitable unit in all of Nomura's group. Recently, Alchemy's acquisition of MG from BMW put private equity firmly into the public spotlight and made its financier/deal-maker managing director into a national folk hero.

The market into 2003 is considerably more troublesome in many ways. Confidence is down, and exits and IPOs are difficult. The increased time for which investments are now expected to be held, and the associated increase in business risk, have placed considerable pressure on sellers' and investors' price expectations. Deals are harder to find and, when they are identified, they are taking longer to close. Three to six months was the norm in 2000. Two years on, it could take as long as nine to 12 months,[7] and many deals will collapse at the final hurdle over irreconcilable differences about price. Many private equity firms have had a very poor 12 to 18 months since the middle of 2001, with barely 20 to 30 per cent of the deal turnover as in those years immediately prior. However, this statistic taken on its own means relatively little except that trade sales and corporate acquisitions have fallen by even more, IPOs are virtually non-existent and new equity investors are much scarcer. As a result, private equity (and their related LBO sisters) transactions have become much more prominent in the market and much more important in providing a bridge for companies needing the sale or the investment.

Worldwide, although the total value of private equity backed transactions fell 11 per cent in 2002 over 2001, with deals falling by 17 per cent, the actual weighting of private equity as a proportion of all acquisition transactions has risen from 2 per cent during the peak of the M&A cycle to 6 per cent. This result is reflected in the UK marketplace.

In many circumstances, private equity firms are the only groups that can provide liquidity or an outlet for some acquisitions. In instances where there is clear shareholder motivation for a sale or acquisition, perhaps driven by dissatisfaction with current management, private equity firms can gain a foothold and receive backing from one of the key stakeholder groups to resolve an impasse. In some cases, the private equity firm is the necessary mechanism needed to bring about change, or to act as the catalyst for substantial overhaul in operations, coupled with new funding. The acquisition of MG cars by Alchemy is a good example of such a transaction.

In other instances, private equity is the necessary escape hatch for companies needing to make a sale of a non-core asset, or for companies that need to effect an exit for their current investors. The closing of the IPO market has forced many companies and their investors to look for alternatives routes to staging liquidity events. Entrenched investors, as well as larger companies, need to recycle their investments and rebuild their capital structures. With the decline of other corporate acquirers and the disappearance of the public IPO market, the private equity and LBO firms have found themselves shouldering considerably more responsibility in the market. Indeed, by value, it is telling that the middle-market MBO transactions of £100 million or less have held up quite well in the last two years while the larger deals have disappeared.[8] Total transaction volume for all UK MBOs whose values were over £10 million summed to 120 transactions with a total value of £14.6 billion. The top two deals (Southern Water £2.05 billion and Voyager Pubs £2.01 billion) accounted for 28 per cent of this value. It is likely that with the ebb in liquidity and fall in the number of participants in the secondary market for companies and acquisitions, that financial investors will be rewarded for their willingness to step in and that the next few years in this environment will prove to be extremely profitable ones for them.

---

[1] Thomson Financial.
[2] Standard & Poor's, Bank of England.
[3] Moody's Investor Services.
[4] Department of Trade & Industry.
[5] Bank of England.
[6] ONS and Bank of England.
[7] HSBC Private Equity interview.
[8] KPMG Corporate Finance, 6 January 2003.

Acquisitions of unquoted companies

Evelyn McAdam, senior solicitor, Denton Wilde Sapte

Introduction

The purpose of this chapter is to look at the preliminary commercial issues to be considered when acquiring an unquoted company. In the United Kingdom an unquoted company is a private limited company or a public limited company which is not listed on a recognised investment exchange such as the London Stock Exchange or AIM.[1]

This chapter looks at the following general areas:

- target identification;
- valuation; and
- negotiation.

Target identification
Reasons for the acquisition

Prior to giving any consideration to the actual identity of the target, a purchaser should first consider its reasons for the acquisition. This will serve to narrow down substantially the number of suitable companies.

Expansion

A purchaser may want to expand its business by acquiring a company which is well established in the United Kingdom, has longstanding relationships with customers and suppliers and, in some cases, has an identifiable brand and substantial goodwill associated with its product or service offering. An example of this would be the recent US$375 million acquisition by Microsoft Corporation of British games developer Rare. The advantages of acquiring a ready-made business may outweigh the cost of establishing a new business in the United Kingdom and the time required to develop it. The opposite is also true: the acquisition of an established business can lead to post-acquisition integration problems. Much will depend on the purchaser's own circumstances and what it intends to do with the target post acquisition. If the purchaser has a strong brand, issues such as the branding of the target and the associated goodwill may be less important than the fact that the target has an established market for its goods or services. The purchaser may simply intend to rebrand the target and continue to trade in the usual way.

Diversification

The acquisition may be a step towards implementing the purchaser's diversification strategy. Diversification is often used as a way of spreading business risk. A company which has a limited product offering or customer base is particularly exposed to changes in consumer trends or the introduction of a competitor into its marketplace. Diversification may be geographical or product/service based. If geographical, this involves selling the product or service to a wider customer base thereby limiting the company's exposure to a particular geographical market. Diversification at a product or service level usually involves identifying existing customers and offering them either related or unrelated products. If the retail customer currently buys newspapers, then he may also buy magazines, telephone cards or lottery tickets.

Consolidation with suppliers or customers

Many companies have a consolidation strategy which can be effected vertically, either upward by integrating with suppliers or downward by integrating with customers and distributors, or horizontally by acquiring a business similar to that of the purchaser. An example of an upward vertical acquisition would be the acquisition of a main supplier. By integrating the supply aspect into its own business, the purchaser eliminates the supplier's profit margin thereby reducing the cost of the product or service. Likewise, by acquiring a business which is at the same stage in the production cycle as the purchaser, both parties immediately benefit from the expertise developed by the other party, such as marketing and research and development, and this generally leads to cost savings. Both parties could also benefit from the enlarged customer/client base to which they can cross sell other products/services. This type of acquisition also enables the purchaser to take advantage of the economies of scale afforded to a larger enterprise. A recent example of horizontal consolidation was the £1.39 billion acquisition of energy company Seeboard by London Electricity (owned by Electricité de France). This acquisition enabled London Electricity, amongst other things, to consolidate its position in the UK energy market and achieve critical mass by increasing its customer base to about 5 million customers.[2]

While certain acquisitions may be opportunistic, for example, a suitable target may be in financial difficulty and the owner may be seeking a quick sale, many purchasers will have given thought to their acquisition strategy and how a target will fit into their medium and long-term strategic objectives. Many purchasers will have a detailed acquisition strategy and will be compelled to comply with that. At the very least, a purchaser should create a highly detailed profile of the ideal acquisition including:

– the size of the target;
– its geographic location;
– its product/service offering;
– growth potential and, if applicable, turnover of customers;
– a price range within which the purchaser can negotiate;
– approved funding;
– a risk analysis exercise including to what extent (if at all) certain risks may be absorbed;
– any human resources issues;
– whether an acquisition of the entire share capital is required or whether a majority interest will suffice; and
– whether the acquisition will give rise to competition issues.

Once a purchaser has identified the reasons for the acquisition and the general profile of the ideal target, it must then commence the investigation of potential target companies. Depending on how sophisticated the purchaser is, this is generally done with the assistance of an investment bank or, where a business is very specialised, a boutique corporate finance house. However, a sophisticated purchaser with a developed acquisition strategy may carry out its own investigations. In the United Kingdom there are various opportunities for identifying target companies including various websites which list a number of acquisition opportunities. This method of acquiring a company may not be sufficiently proactive or focused for a purchaser seeking to make a strategic acquisition within an established timeframe but it is a useful source of information and will allow for a level of comparative analysis.

Alternatively, the purchaser may prefer to engage a corporate finance house with sector expertise. This has a number of benefits not least of which is that it can approach a target on behalf of the purchaser and on a confidential basis. This will enable the purchaser to establish whether the target would be interested in discussing a possible sale and whether the owners are prepared to enter into negotiations. This is particularly useful if the target is a competitor. When appointing an external adviser, the purchaser should shop around for an adviser who displays a clear understanding of the needs of the purchaser, the market in which it operates and the UK market generally. Investment banks are often engaged on a monthly retainer plus a success-based contingency fee payable on completion of the acquisition.

Valuation

Ultimately, the value of any business is what a potential purchaser is willing to pay for it. If the target company has been put on the market by the vendors, the vendors may have already conducted a valuation exercise and come up with a preliminary valuation of their own. This will generally establish the context within which the vendors will be willing to negotiate. If, on the other hand, the target company is approached by a purchaser, the vendors may not have considered the issue of valuation and the purchaser may be afforded an opportunity to value the target.

Having identified the reasons for the acquisition, this will have some influence over what a purchaser is prepared to pay for a business. If the purchaser is acquiring a similar business, the effect of which will be to eliminate a competitor or enable the purchaser to take advantage of the economies of scale afforded to the enlarged group, these factors will enhance the value of that particular target to that particular purchaser.

Although the purpose of the acquisition will have some influence on the ultimate valuation of the company, there are certain established principles of valuation which apply to the acquisitions of companies in the United Kingdom and it is important that the advisers are aware of the basis of valuation at the outset as this may have an impact on issues such as the warranty and indemnity protection sought later on in the process.

A prospective purchaser will usually engage a professional adviser, such as an accountant or an investment bank, to carry out a full investigation into the company's financial affairs and to report on this. Depending on the nature of the relationship between the purchaser and the target and any sensitivity issues surrounding the acquisition, the information may initially have to be derived from public records. UK companies generally file their annual report and accounts at Companies House within 10 months from their year-end. Therefore, assuming the company has not taken advantage of certain exemptions or is not in default of its filing obligations, historical financial information should be available from Companies House. This information will rarely be current and should be supplemented by management accounts and other up-to-date financial information.

Valuation methods

A detailed analysis of the principles of valuation used to arrive at the value of an unquoted company is outside the scope of this publication. The purchaser will generally come up with a valuation by taking the financial information available on the target and applying an appropriate valuation method to that information to establish an initial value. The purchaser may then add a premium to that value to reflect the enhanced value of the target to the purchaser or discount that value to reflect any issues of concern arising from its investigations of the target's business and affairs.

The main principles of valuation applied to unquoted companies in the United Kingdom are:

- the multiple of earnings principle;
- the discounted cash flow principle;
- the net assets principle; and
- the return on capital (dividends) principle.

It may be the case that only one of these methods is appropriate, for example, if the company is insolvent, the break-up value of its assets may be the only relevant factor. Alternatively, a combination of these methods of valuation may apply. A valuer may apply all of these methods and then weight them appropriately having regard to the type of business and the size of the shareholding to be acquired. For example, in the case of a service company (such as an advertising agency) the net tangible assets may be insignificant and the valuer will be more concerned with earnings, whereas in the case of a property investment company, the value of the net assets in its property portfolio will be paramount.

In the United Kingdom, the most common methods of valuation applied to unquoted companies are valuations based on a multiple of earnings and valuations based on discounted cash flow. The net assets principle is generally applicable only when the target has substantial tangible assets. In practice, dividend yield is more likely to be relied upon as a method of valuing quoted companies, as unquoted companies do not always pay dividends.

Multiple of earnings

In simple terms, this method of valuation involves applying an appropriate multiple to an estimate of the future maintainable earnings of the target company. The main consideration for the valuer will be the extent to which earnings of the target should be taken into consideration. It is in the interest of the vendors to enhance this figure whereas the purchaser will want to adjust this figure downwards to take account of any extraordinary income. There may be some negotiations between the parties as to what should constitute earnings, and adjustments should be made for items of a non-recurring or exceptional nature reported in the most recent results of the target company. These may include the following:

- extraordinary or exceptional items such as business integration costs following a recent acquisition or merger by the target;

- one-off and non-recurring items such as a litigation claim or the sale of an asset by the target;
- reduced income as a result of discontinued business (eg, sale of a division);
- additional income from new business (eg, the acquisition of a new division);
- exceptional employee remuneration packages; and
- income associated with non-arm's length contracts.

Earnings must then be capitalised by applying the appropriate multiple and the valuer will generally have regard to publicly available information on comparable companies. In relying on reported multiples, a potential purchaser should note the fact that these are multiples of adjusted earnings and adjustments can be subjective from deal to deal. Therefore, while useful for comparative analysis, reported multiples should not necessarily be the final determinant of price. There are sources of information available on private company values and these tend to be comparative analyses carried out by accountants and financial institutions based on reported private company sales in the United Kingdom. A purchaser should consult its financial advisers regarding the reliability of publicly available information.

Discounted cash flow

This method of valuation determines the present value of the target company based on the future after-tax cash flows expected to be generated by the company. The earnings method of valuation calculates an annual figure and assumes that figure will be maintained whereas the discounted cash flow method forecasts earnings for a foreseeable future period such as five to 10 years. The net present value of future cash flow is then calculated by applying an appropriate discount to each year. The discount applied to the future cash flows is known as the risk-adjusted rate of return and operates on the principle that, if the risk is high, the expected cash flow should be worth less in terms of today's cash. In other words, the greater the risk, the greater the discount applied to the future cash flows. A value is attributed to the residual value of the company at the end of the future cash flow period and this is added to the net present value.

As this method focuses on cash flow generation, it is particularly attractive to investors as an indicator of future performance. Additionally, it focuses on the cash flow generation of the particular target company concerned and is therefore more focused. One issue for negotiation is the extent to which future cash flows should take account of costs or savings arising as a result of the acquisition. Arguably, if the purchaser expects to reduce the costs of the business thereby enhancing cash flow, the vendors should not benefit from this by achieving a higher price for the target. The corollary is also true: the vendors will expect that the post-acquisition costs associated with business integration should not be reflected in the cash flow figures to reduce the value of the business.

This is an appropriate method of valuation to use where future cash flow can be calculated with relative certainty, for example, rental income under long-term leases granted by the company. This is a complex method of valuation which requires the input of an expert valuer, particularly in relation to the calculation of the appropriate discounts to be applied.

Dividend yield

This may not be the most appropriate method of valuation for unquoted companies which do not always pay dividends. Many private companies grow quickly and reinvest profits into the business. Additionally, as they are often owner-managed, the owners tend to extract payment by way of high remuneration and benefits packages rather than dividends.

Net asset value

An assets-based valuation is more commonly used on a sale of assets than on a company sale, as a valuation based on assets may not always represent the full value of the target company as a going concern and most purchasers will be more interested in the sustainable earnings of the target. This method of valuation is, however, appropriate for certain types of company. In the case of an insolvent company or a company which has no sustainable earnings, the purchaser may only be interested in the break-up value of the company's assets. Net asset valuations are also commonly used to value companies holding property and other investments.

Valuation on an assets basis depends on the value of each individual asset of the company either on its own having regard to the value of the business as a going concern or, if appropriate, the value of the asset if it was sold on the open market. In the case of a building, this would be the market value of the building for its current use assuming vacant possession. Certain adjustments may be appropriate to take account of matters such as tax liabilities or realisation costs. For example, if the current business use of a property is specific, the marketability may depend on certain modifications and an adjustment may be required to take into account the cost of this.

The method of valuation used will have implications for the transaction, both in terms of the information sought by the purchaser as part of the due diligence process and in terms of the warranty and indemnity protection required. On a net asset valuation, the purchaser would seek warranties in the share sale agreement regarding the assets, their identity, accounting treatment, depreciation and so on. However, regardless of the method of valuation applied to the target company, the ultimate price payable for the target is usually a negotiated figure arrived at following a detailed investigation of the target and its business.

Investigations by the purchaser

As the price paid for the target and the structure of the payment are often ultimately influenced by the investigation process, it is worth addressing the issue of due diligence at this stage. The extent of the investigations carried out by the purchaser and its advisers will depend on a number of issues including timing and the approach taken by the vendors to the sale process. For example, in an auction sale, the acquisition timetable is often tight; the vendors make limited information available to the potential purchasers and are not generally disposed to entertain detailed queries raised by the purchaser and its advisers. If the purchaser has concerns, it will generally seek indemnities from the vendors but, if these are not forthcoming, it may seek to offset the perceived risk by making a downward adjustment to the value of the target.

The purchaser's reasons for the acquisition will also have some bearing on its approach to due diligence. For example, if the purpose of the acquisition is to expand its existing business, the purchaser will be familiar with the business sector into which it is buying and may therefore have a clearer understanding of the risks at the outset. On the other hand, an acquisition in furtherance of a diversification strategy may be a foray into the unknown for the purchaser. The resultant nervousness can lead to an exhaustive investigation into the business and affairs of the target, particularly from a financial and operational perspective.

The due diligence process

The investigations carried out by the purchaser generally occur on three levels: financial due diligence is undertaken by either or both of the purchaser's financial team and its accountant; commercial or operational due diligence is undertaken by the purchaser's business and operations personnel; and legal due diligence is carried out by the purchaser's lawyers. The purchaser may also need to consider whether other specialists should be instructed, for example, actuaries, insurance brokers, environmental consultants, trade mark or patent agents or even private investigators. The due diligence process needs to be managed carefully so as to ensure that:

- the due diligence team is aware of the acquisition timetable and the key deliverables;
- a complete record of all information disclosed is maintained;
- no area of the target's business is overlooked, eg, the purchaser's financial team may believe that a matter is being investigated by the accountants and vice versa; and
- any issues arising out of investigations are collected and disseminated to the appropriate negotiating team.

The purchaser should identify at the outset which investigations are most critical and allocate these appropriately between its internal specialists and external advisers. In addition, it should appoint a project manager to oversee and coordinate the process. Although the advisers will typically be delivering a written due diligence report, it is often helpful to receive regular updates during the process. This means that issues can be raised during negotiations rather than at the end of the process. This can be a costly exercise for the vendor and it is therefore important that it extracts full benefit from it. In practice, what this means is that if an issue is revealed and cannot be remedied by completion of the acquisition, the purchaser should benefit from an appropriate downward adjustment to the purchase price.

Financial due diligence

This is dealt with in detail in Chapter 8, *Financial and commercial due diligence issues*, however, it is worth reflecting on this briefly in this chapter as it may have an effect on the ultimate valuation of the target. The purchaser will generally engage a UK accountant to carry out a detailed investigation of the financial affairs of the target company. The accountant will prepare a report for review by the purchaser. The financial due diligence will often comprise a number of aspects including:

- reviewing the historical accounts;
- reviewing the up-to-date management accounts;
- reviewing business plans and profit forecasts;
- advising on the appropriate valuation methods; and
- advising on the tax implications of the acquisition and suggesting structures to avoid or defer liability.

This investigation will usually involve site visits and can be costly for the purchaser but also distracting for the management of the target company. The purchaser will not usually want to incur extensive costs until it has reached agreement in principle with the vendors (this is discussed further below under 'Negotiations'). Therefore, it is usual for the purchaser and its accountant to carry out a preliminary investigation based on publicly available information such as accounts filed at Companies House. It may also engage in high level discussions with the executives of the target company although the target company may have confidentiality concerns and will also be anxious not to narrow the field of potential purchasers. This initial review should, however, enable the purchaser to come up with a preliminary valuation of the target to enable it to make an offer. Generally, any agreement reached in principle will be subject to the purchaser carrying out a satisfactory investigation of the target.

Commercial due diligence

The various features of commercial due diligence are considered in more detail in Chapter 8, *Financial and commercial due diligence issues*. It is worth mentioning in the context of valuation as the outcome of the commercial and operational analysis may ultimately have an impact on the price paid for the target. Operational investigations can uncover issues 'on the ground', which would not necessarily emerge from the financial or legal investigations. Examples include post-acquisition costs associated with the integration of the business and the integration of the information technology of the purchaser and the target. The vendor may be reluctant to allow what it considers to be normal business integration costs to impact on the value of the target, viewing these as a matter for the purchaser. The purchaser on the other hand may be of the view that the costs result from the peculiarities of the target's business or inefficient management and should therefore be absorbed by the vendors by way of a reduction of the valuation.

Legal due diligence

The purchaser will need to appoint UK counsel who will be involved with all aspects of the acquisition. One of the first tasks the lawyers will undertake is a detailed investigation of the legal affairs of the target. They will then prepare a legal due diligence report for review by the purchaser.

It is important that the purchaser agrees with its lawyers and other advisers the scope of the investigation at the outset. For example, the purchaser will need to consider whether it wants a full legal audit to take place (using auditing techniques) or whether it wants the legal team to focus on particular aspects of the target's business, such as material contracts with customers and suppliers or the ownership of intellectual property rights.

The scope of the legal due diligence will vary depending on the nature of the business, however, the following areas are generally reviewed:

– material contracts;
– intellectual property/information technology rights;
– human resources;
– environmental; and
– property.

Material contracts

The review of the material contracts of the target with its suppliers and customers will include issues such as:

– the right of the contract counterparty to terminate on a change of control of the target;
– the pricing and payment mechanism and price increase provisions;

- duration of the contract and whether it has or is about to expire;
- exclusivity (eg, if it is an exclusive supply contract, this may affect the purchaser's plans to use its own suppliers going forward);
- restrictive covenants or other limitations on the target's continuing business;
- other liabilities and onerous obligations of the target under the contract;
- retention of title provisions;
- termination penalties; and
- confidentiality (material contracts are often withheld on the basis that they are confidential).

Intellectual property/information technology rights

As the day-to-day operation of most businesses is now often dependent on information technology, it will be no surprise that this area should receive particular scrutiny. Whether the software used by the target is bespoke or licensed, the purchaser will want to ensure that the rights of the target to use the software are unassailable. Therefore, licences will often be subject to the same level of review as material contracts. As bespoke software is often written by employees or external contractors, the purchaser will want to be satisfied that the target owns the intellectual property rights to this software. In general, the position in the United Kingdom is that intellectual property created by an employee in the course of his employment belongs to the employer. This is subject to express agreement to the contrary between employer and employee and also a number of other exceptions. Therefore, investigation will be necessary to ensure that none of the exceptions apply and that no agreements exist in this regard.

Practically, the legal due diligence team are not necessarily in a position to identify what information technology is vital to the business. It may therefore be more effective for the purchaser to carry out an operational review at the earliest possible opportunity to identify what information technology is vital for the operation of the target's business. The lawyers should then be instructed to carry out a legal review to ascertain whether the target's intellectual property rights are adequate.

Human resources

The purchaser will want to ascertain the cost of the existing workforce, including wages, pension arrangements, share options schemes and other benefits, and include these in the cost of the acquisition. If the purchaser does not need the target's entire existing workforce, it will also want to factor the cost of redundancy into its valuation. The legal due diligence should include a review of the target's standard employment contracts, employee handbook and policy documents (safety at work, healthcare and so on), share options schemes and pensions documentation.

Environmental

The United Kingdom has a complex and sophisticated regime for environmental protection, including the recently introduced contaminated land regime[3] pursuant to which owners can be liable for historical contamination. This area is dealt with in more detail in Chapter 12, *Regulatory issues*, however, in this context, it is important to note that environmental issues can not only reduce the value of the property (and therefore the target) but can lead to additional liability for remediation costs and damages for personal injury. Additionally, enforcement of the UK regime is largely by way of criminal prosecution. For these reasons, some form of environmental due diligence investigation should take place in the case of every acquisition to assess the risk associated with acquiring that target, even if this involves deciding that a thorough environmental audit is not necessary. The risk will vary: the acquisition of a manufacturing or industrial company may necessitate the commissioning of an environmental assessment report, whereas the acquisition of a financial consultancy business may simply necessitate some general environmental questions supported by appropriate warranties. In each case, however, the purchaser will want to identify the likely impact that contamination or non-compliance with UK environmental legislation will have at the outset. If the risk is unquantifiable, this may affect the viability of the whole transaction. Generally, however, any risk identified will be reflected in the valuation and covered by appropriate indemnities from the vendors.

The purchaser should keep a detailed record of all information received from the target company through either its advisers or its management. This is important as the target company may seek to disclose all information released to the purchaser at a later stage in the transaction. This is, however, subject to the requirements for fair disclosure discussed below.

Negotiations

Before embarking on negotiations with the vendors, the purchaser should have a clear view of its reasons for making the acquisition and have carried out sufficient investigations to enable it to have established a preliminary view on valuation. This is important to enable the purchaser to define the parameters within which it will negotiate. The price ultimately agreed between the parties will also depend on commercial considerations such as the state of the market, the outcome of the pre-acquisition investigations carried out by the purchaser and the relative negotiating positions of the purchaser and the vendor. For this reason, it is advisable for the purchaser to have some understanding of the vendor's reasons for making the disposal before any approach is made. Vendors may have numerous reasons for selling a company and these could include:

- distressed sale where the target is insolvent;
- implementation of a non-core business divestment strategy;
- existing owner managers seeking to retire;
- trade sale to facilitate strategic exit by private equity investors; and
- opportunistic sale following unsolicited approach by the purchaser.

The purchaser will want to formulate a negotiating strategy at the outset and this will depend on both the purchaser's and the vendor's reasons for doing the deal. If the target is distressed, then the vendors will be anxious to sell and the purchaser will have a stronger negotiating position. On the other hand, if the purchaser has identified positive synergies between its business and that of the target and has made an unsolicited approach, the purchaser's negotiating position will be weaker.

Who should negotiate?

Following the identification of one or more targets, either by the purchaser itself or with the help of an acquisition strategist such as an investment bank or corporate finance house, the next step is to approach the target. A purchaser may decide to do this directly if it has a direct contact within the target company or, alternatively, it may choose to rely on its advisers to approach the target. In the case of a share acquisition, negotiations take place between the purchaser and the owners of the company rather than the company itself although the management of the target company, being those closest to the business, will generally be involved in this process. In smaller private companies, the distinction between shareholders, managers and directors may be blurred as the company may in fact be owned and controlled by one individual, or a small number of individuals, who fulfil all of these roles. It is important that the person acting on behalf of the purchaser has negotiating authority as this will avoid repetition of issues already discussed and also give the target company the impression that the purchaser is taking the negotiation seriously.

In the case of the target company, the negotiations will often be controlled by the majority shareholder in conjunction with the senior management of the company. However, it is worth noting that UK companies, particularly those financed by private equity investors, commonly have complicated shareholder arrangements. It should not be taken for granted that a deal with a majority shareholder means a deal with all shareholders. Shareholder arrangements can include complicated veto rights and rights of first refusal on share transfers which are triggered by the sale of shares in the target by any shareholder. It is important to identify at the outset whether the purchaser will find itself negotiating with several parties or more importantly, having gone to the expense of investigating the target and brokering a deal, whether a minority shareholder could frustrate the process. Often this manifests itself in the form of a demand for extra cash from a minority shareholder. The purchaser should therefore specify that the price payable is capped. This means that, if any issues arise as between the shareholders, it will be up to them to allocate the agreed consideration between them, including allocating more to a particular shareholder if necessary to secure the sale of the target shares. It should not fall to the purchaser to pay more for the target.

A purchaser should also consider the implications of acquiring less than the entire issued share capital of the target. If there is an errant shareholder, the purchaser may have to consider acquiring the target with that shareholder *in situ*. This can have practical implications as the purchaser will have to consider minority shareholder rights in what would otherwise have been a wholly owned subsidiary. For example, if the target were wholly owned, shareholder resolutions would normally be passed in written form signed by the sole shareholder, the purchaser. Such resolutions will now have to be signed by the purchaser and the incumbent shareholder. If the minority shareholder refuses to sign, the resolution will have to be considered at a meeting of the company held at 14 or 21 days' notice. This can be costly and inconvenient. Shareholders' agreements and articles of association of UK companies sometimes contain 'drag-along' or 'bring-along' rights which enable the purchaser to force a sale by a shareholder who refuses to sell on the same terms as those offered to and accepted by the other shareholders. This mechanism can prove particularly useful if there is a minority shareholder who refuses to sell. However, many private companies do not have formal shareholder arrangements in place and, in these cases, the purchaser should consider making the offer conditional on the acquisition of 100 per cent of the share capital of the target.

Although less common in practice, if the purchaser is buying less than 100 per cent of the target company it should be aware that shareholders' agreements and articles of association of UK companies may also contain corresponding 'tag-along' rights which enable other shareholders to take advantage of an offer made to one of their number. Therefore, the unsuspecting purchaser of a strategic interest in a UK company could find itself obliged to acquire the shareholdings of all the shareholders.

Approaching the target company

When a purchaser has decided to make an offer for the share capital of an unquoted company, it will need to communicate the terms of the offer to the shareholders of the target company. In addition to the usual caveats and conditions which may apply to the communication of the offer, the purchaser should also be aware of the provisions of the Financial Services and Markets Act 2000 or FSMA. When an offer is made by or on behalf of a potential purchaser to shareholders of a target company, this offer will constitute a 'financial promotion'. Communications made by a purchaser which constitute a financial promotion are restricted under FSMA unless the purchaser is an authorised person or an authorised person approves the content of the communication. (An authorised person includes a person who is authorised by the FSA to carry on investment business in the United Kingdom.) Therefore, before communicating the offer, the purchaser should consider whether it comes within one of the exemptions available under FSMA. If not, the communication should be approved by an authorised person and this can have consequential timing and cost implications for the purchaser.

The financial promotion restriction does not apply to certain promotions. The most significant exemption in the context of the acquisition of shares in a target company is the sale of body corporate exemption. Broadly, this exemption applies to any financial promotion communicated by or on behalf of a body corporate that relates to a transaction to acquire shares in a body corporate where the object of the transaction is the acquisition of day-to-day control of the affairs of the body corporate. Other exemptions are available for promotions to certain categories of recipient including investment professionals, certified high net-worth individuals or high net-worth companies and other unincorporated bodies. Importantly, there is no exception from promotions which are sent only to a small number of persons.

It is a criminal offence for anyone other than an authorised person to issue a financial promotion, unless an authorised person has approved it or the promotion falls within one of the exemptions discussed above. Certain agreements entered into as a result of an unlawful communication may not be enforceable and the purchaser who is in breach may be obliged to retransfer assets.[4]

Communications by the target company

It is worth noting that when the potential purchaser is approached by or on behalf of the target company, whether as the recipient of an information memorandum or other written documentation, this documentation will also constitute a financial promotion. If this communication does not fall within one of the exemptions referred to above, it must be authorised. This will generally be a matter for the vendors, being the party offering the securities of the company for sale and disseminating relevant information. However, the purchaser may be asked to certify that it comes within one of the exemptions, for example, that it is a high net-worth company. If a purchaser of a UK company is asked to certify that it comes within one of the exemptions to the financial promotion restriction, it should seek advice regarding the implications of being treated as an exempt person.

Confidentiality

At the outset of discussions between a purchaser and a target, a UK target will generally request that the purchaser enter into a written confidentiality agreement. While an unquoted company does not have the same concerns regarding market rumours, it will be concerned that the potential purchaser does not have the ability to use commercially sensitive information about the target and its business to its competitive advantage if the transaction is not consummated. The target will also be concerned that the existence of the negotiations and details of the terms do not become known to its customers, suppliers, bankers and, particularly, its employees. A confidentiality agreement will add a degree of secrecy to the proceedings and will give the target comfort that the purchaser will not disclose information relating to its business. Generally, the confidentiality agreement will contain, amongst other things, provisions to the effect that:

- all information imparted will be treated as confidential by the purchaser, will only be used by the purchaser to assess the viability of the acquisition and will not be used by the purchaser if the deal is not completed;
- the existence of the negotiations and the terms will not be disclosed to third parties;
- all information will be returned to the target company (or destroyed) if the acquisition does not proceed to completion; and
- information which is in the public domain, is already known to the purchaser or becomes known other than by breach of the confidentiality obligation will not be treated as confidential.

The signature of a confidentiality agreement at the outset has obvious benefits for the purchaser in that it will enable it to elicit more detailed information from the target, particularly relating to its suppliers and customers.

In the case of a transaction where the purchase consideration includes the issue of shares in the capital of the purchaser, the vendors may wish to carry out some level of investigation into the affairs and business of the purchaser. This will involve the disclosure by the purchaser of what may be confidential information about its business. In these circumstances it is advisable to insist on reciprocal obligations of confidentiality to cover movement of information from both parties.

Disclosure

The investigative activities of the purchaser will result in detailed disclosure being made by the vendors and the target company. Disclosure is particularly important in the context of a UK acquisition as it could have the effect of reducing/eliminating the liability of the vendors for the matter in respect of which the disclosure has been made. For that reason, much time is spent negotiating the terms on which disclosures made by the vendors will be acceptable to the purchaser. The purchaser may have relied heavily on the disclosures made at the outset for the purpose of evaluating the business as a prospective target. Therefore, it will often insist that the vendors warrant the integrity of the information disclosed as part of the purchaser's investigations and on which the purchaser relied. The vendors will then insist that all information provided to the purchaser should be treated as disclosed and that they should have no liability in respect of it. Clearly, neither position is ideal: a request that they warrant the integrity of the information supplied is often resisted by UK vendors as the information may have come from multiple sources and the vendors will have no way of determining on what information the purchaser relied. Likewise, the purchaser should not accept a broad ranging disclosure of all information supplied as it may not appreciate the full impact of each of the disclosures on the target's business.

The standard of disclosure has been the subject of consideration by the UK courts and recent authority suggests that the courts require a high standard of disclosure. Information will only be treated as having been properly disclosed if it is 'fairly' disclosed by the vendor. The purchaser should not be expected to understand the full implications of a matter which is obliquely referred to in the disclosure materials or which is disclosed out of context. Such disclosures will not be considered fair. Detailed disclosures regarding the negative aspects of the business (such as pending litigation or recent downturns in trading) may prejudice the price achieved for the target company. This means that it is not uncommon for vendors to withhold certain information until the latest possible moment for tactical reasons. The courts have recently held that fair disclosure requires a positive statement of the true position and not just an admission from which a buyer is expected to infer matters of significance.[5] Therefore, while a potential purchaser can take some comfort from the fact that UK courts require a high standard of disclosure, a valuation based on information provided at the outset, which later proves to be somewhat misleading by virtue of omissions made, may have to be revisited later on in the process.

A purchaser should also be aware that, if it has actual knowledge of matters involving the target which have not been disclosed by the target, the purchaser's right to make a claim based on non-disclosure of that matter might be prejudiced.[6]

Where a vendor makes positive disclosures which amount to a representation upon which the purchaser has relied when entering into the purchase contract, the purchaser may have recourse at common law and also under the Misrepresentation Act 1967. In a recent case a purchaser was induced to buy shares at a particular price based on a false statement that other buyers were interested. It was held by the House of Lords that the measure of damages was the difference between the contract price and the amount actually realised by the purchaser on the resale of the shares.[7]

It should also be mentioned that, in the context of a share acquisition, the directors of a purchaser or target company may be liable under Section 397 of FMSA for, *inter alia*, statements, promises or forecasts which they know to be misleading, false or deceptive in a material particular or for the reckless making of a statement, promise or forecast which is misleading, false or deceptive in a material particular. This could attract a criminal sanction and cannot be avoided as a result of a disclaimer in a document.

Therefore, a vendor seeking to rely on disclosures made out of context or unfairly will be faced with an uphill struggle. Notwithstanding this, the purchaser will want to fully understand the matters which may operate to limit the liability of the vendor. For this reason, it should seek to have the information on which it has relied warranted and, if possible, only accept those disclosures that are contained in a disclosure letter to be delivered at the time the acquisition agreement is entered into.

Heads of agreement

The purchaser and the target company will usually agree to reduce the main commercial terms of the acquisition to writing. The purpose of the heads of agreement (variously referred to as heads of terms, memorandum of understanding, term sheet or letter of intent) is to summarise the main terms of the transaction as agreed between the parties before they embark on detailed negotiations and enter into definitive legally binding documentation. The benefit of doing this at an early stage is that contentious issues can be identified and, if possible, resolved. The heads of agreement are generally an informal arrangement between the parties. While they are generally intended to deal only with the commercial aspects of the transaction and not the legal aspects, it is possible for heads of agreement to cover legal issues. This may avoid the need to abandon the negotiations at an advanced stage after the parties have expended considerable cost and effort.

As heads of agreement are becoming increasingly more sophisticated, it is recommended that both the purchaser and the vendor obtain legal input into this document. The heads of agreement tend to address issues such as non-compete covenants, warranties, limitations on liability and other matters which have legal import. In addition, the acquisition of the target may be subject to certain conditions and these should be detailed in the heads of agreement. These could include satisfactory due diligence by the purchaser and an obligation on the vendors to deliver the entire issued share capital of the target company. Heads of agreement are generally expressed to be non-legally binding and 'subject to contract' and are useful as an aide memoire when drafting the transaction documentation. However, it is often difficult for parties to move away from positions established in the heads of agreement so they should be given due consideration. This is particularly true in the case of the agreed price which may need to be adjusted to reflect matters arising in the course of further investigations carried out by the purchaser and matters disclosed by the vendor during the negotiations.

Matters to look out for

Generally, the manner in which the commercial due diligence and negotiation process is handled is indicative of the way the business is managed. There are a number of things to watch out for including the following:

- the target company creates a positive impression but when the purchaser visits its suppliers or agents or talks with its customers, they give a different account of the relationship;
- the prices charged for the target's product/service offering are substantially different from those charged to the purchaser's customers. If the target's prices are lower, then the purchaser may experience a loss of customers as it attempts to convert customers to its higher price range;
- the target has difficulty providing reliable historical data or different managers provide conflicting explanations of key business areas and strategy;
- the sale price set by the target appears to be above market price for similar companies and the vendor is unwilling to negotiate; and
- the vendor is pressuring the purchaser to move quickly. This can be a sign that the target has cash flow problems (which may not be a concern) or more importantly that it has problems that have not been fully disclosed, such as pending litigation.

All of these issues should cause alarm bells to ring and may lead to further more specific investigations by the purchaser.

Ongoing relationship or total separation?

The approach to negotiating the value of the target and the terms of the acquisition will depend on all the factors discussed above but will also depend on whether there will be an ongoing relationship between the parties. If the vendor is seeking a complete exit from the business, it will be less interested in placating the purchaser; it will want to achieve maximum value while at the same time limiting its residual liabilities to the greatest extent possible. The purchaser will be concerned to ensure that it has recourse to the vendor for any claims by being adequately protected in terms of warranties and indemnities. If the purchaser is concerned about its ability to enforce these protections, it may want to structure the transaction so as to retain part of the consideration payment for a specified period of time. Likewise, if the purchaser is concerned that the valuation placed on the business may be too high, for example, if the company has a short trading history or if the business is difficult to value due to lack of readily available market information (as was the case with many of the dotcom acquisitions), it may insist on some sort of deferred consideration structure, whereby a certain amount is paid up-front and the balance is determined by reference to the ongoing performance of the business (known as an 'earn-out').

If, on the other hand, the vendor is to remain in the business as an employee of the purchaser both parties will be more interested in preserving the goodwill between them. In the case of a non-corporate vendor, the purchaser may get some comfort from the fact that the vendor is investing some of his/her future in the business. In these cases, particularly if the valuation has been based on cash flow projections provided by the management, the purchaser may want to put in place a form of earn-out mechanism. This would involve a payment up-front with the balance to be determined by reference to the ongoing performance of the business. This has the added benefit of incentivising the management and is a common feature of share acquisitions where the incumbent management remain in place.

Conclusion

The success of any acquisition will depend on how the parties conduct themselves at the early stages. The purchaser should clearly understand its reason for carrying out the acquisition, that is, is the acquisition to be made in pursuance of an approved acquisition strategy or is it a one-off opportunity to acquire a distressed target which may be commercially compatible with its own business? In addition, the purchaser should at least attempt to understand the vendor's reason for selling, which in the case of privately owned small companies may be as much attributable to personal circumstances as it is to commercial imperatives. This understanding will enable the purchaser to identify potential risks at the outset and decide to what extent these can be absorbed. The purchaser should then be in a position to come up with a realistic and, more importantly from a negotiating perspective, justifiable valuation of the target company. This understanding will also enable the purchaser to be very focused in relation to its investigation of the target's affairs. If the information-gathering net is cast too widely, this may frustrate the vendor who, faced with a torrent of commercial, legal and accounting questions, may question the purchaser's motives and intent and become frustrated. It is important that, having identified, in so far as possible, those areas of concern to it, the purchaser appoints appropriate advisers and coordinates the whole due diligence exercise in such a manner as to avoid duplication, which is costly to both it and the target company. It should also be sensitive to the fact that many unquoted companies in the United Kingdom, particularly small private companies, will not have been involved in a transaction of this nature previously. All sides should have a clear understanding of the road map to completion of the acquisition, including the key deliverables and, if known, the obstacles, and the timetable within which this has to be achieved. Understanding motives and capabilities and a clear communication of expectations should help to smooth the negotiation process and achieve a successful acquisition.

---

[1] The Alternative Investment Market operated by The London Stock Exchange plc.

[2] Derived from reports in the *Financial Times* and *Daily Telegraph*, 19 June 2002.

[3] The contaminated land regime was set up in 2000 under Part 2(a) of the Environmental Protection Act 1990.

[4] Section 30 of the Financial Services and Markets Act 2000.

[5] Daniel Reed Limited v EM-ESS Chemists Limited [1995] BCLC 1405.

[6] Eurocopy plc v Teesdale [1992] BCLC 10-67.

[7] Smith Newcourt Securities Ltd v Scrimegour Vickers (Asset Management) Limited [1997] 1 BCLC 350.

5

Acquisition finance: the relationship between senior debt and private equity

Peter Hanratty, director and head of UK Acquisition Finance, Fortis Bank

'Price is what you pay – value is what you get'
Warren Buffett

The extraordinary growth of acquisition finance in the last decade is one of the most striking aspects of modern day banking both in the United Kingdom and more recently in continental Europe.

This growth has principally been driven by the significant increase in the supply of private equity and bank debt. This development has been so significant that in the United Kingdom, which accounts for a third of the European buy-out industry, private equity is now responsible for over 50 per cent of all takeover activity.

Transactions now include mezzanine, high yield, pay in kind (PIK), collaterised debt obligations (CDOs) and securitisation products as a matter of course – and are increasingly engineered to allow higher prices to be paid without diminishing private equity returns.

Although the growth in financial engineering, largely imported from the United States, has been an inevitable result of this rapid expansion, senior bank debt still typically accounts for 50 per cent of the capital structure and remains the essential foundation upon which private equity investments are built.

This chapter puts forward the argument that financial engineering (which at times has become excessive) has turned senior debt into a commodity and is undermining the private equity investor–senior debt banker relationship. This chapter will seek to explain why this relationship is considered vital and why it is now more relevant than ever, as the UK and European economies are once again close to recession.

Over the last decade, with the exception of the Scottish banks, the principal suppliers of senior debt have consistently changed following consolidation in the banking market.

Chemical Bank, Manufacturers Hanover, Chase and JP Morgan, who were all active play-ers in the market 10 years ago, now trade as one bank. There are now fewer senior debt providers and fewer still with a consistent track record of support through the peaks and troughs of a full economic cycle.

Furthermore, not only are there fewer debt providers, but investment conditions have now changed. Over the last decade, private equity investors have enjoyed a rela-tively attractive economic environment with a consistently strong stock market facili-tating profitable exits from their investments, via initial public offerings (IPOs) and trade sales, without necessarily needing to improve the underlying performance of the com-pany acquired.

Now, not only do private equity investors need to be considerably more proactive in improving their investment performance, they also face far more competition. In 1998, the amount raised by private equity investors in the United Kingdom alone was €7.8 billion, by 2001 the amount had increased to €18 billion.

The one positive economic development underpinning the private equity industry is the low interest rate environment that has prevailed. Indeed this is one of the principal causes of the significant expansion of the industry as pension funds, initially in the United States and more recently in the United Kingdom and continental Europe, have turned to private equity to increase their returns in a low inflationary period.

As a result, since 1998 there has been a 150 per cent increase in funds raised in the United Kingdom. Private equity investors are now relying on low cost bank debt to off-set the high prices they are being compelled to pay due to the increase in competition from other private equity investors. It is not therefore surprising that, as mentioned above, pri-vate equity now accounts for 50 per cent of UK takeovers.

This growth is clearly unsustainable. Private equity investors are now encountering more resistance in fund raising as pension funds question their ongoing support to investors who do not already have a proven and transparent track record in successful exits from their initial investments.

As the private equity market consolidates, the ultimate winners in the private equity industry will be those that demonstrate a successful track record of value creation. The pri-vate equity investor–senior debt banking relationship will therefore become crucial. The winners will be those that recognise this.

How the buy-out market has evolved

Although the origins of the market go back to the turn of the last century and developed further with 3I after World War II, it was not until 1986 that a date can be put on its real expansion when the Centre for Management Buy-out Research (CMBOR) was established

Exhibit 5.1: Average value of buy-outs/buy-ins, 1992–2001 (€ million)

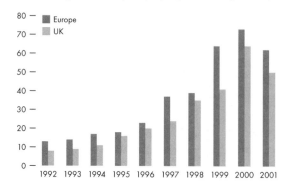

Source: CMBOR.

Exhibit 5.2: MBO/MBI as a percentage of all UK takeover activity, 1987–2002

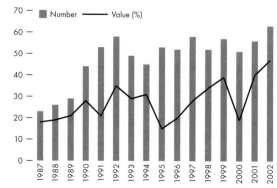

Source: CMBOR.

at Nottingham University marking management and leveraged buy-outs as a recognised financial industry in its own right.

Exhibits 5.1 and 5.2 from CMBOR demonstrate the industry's extraordinary growth both in the United Kingdom and continental Europe in the last 20 years. Exhibit 5.1 shows the increasing average value of buy-outs and buy-ins in both the United Kingdom and continental Europe between 1992 and 2001, and Exhibit 5.2 shows the increasing importance of buy-outs and buy-ins on takeover activity between 1987 and 2002.

Exhibit 5.3 demonstrates the significant increase in value between 1987 and 1989, followed by a fall in 1990 before gradually increasing to the current levels of today. The period 1987–89 is particularly relevant today since it was characterised by several high profile pioneering transactions and also some excessive lending.

Initially, 1988 saw arguably one of the most successful buy-outs ever undertaken with the MBO of Premier Brands from Cadburys led by Paul (now Sir Paul) Judge and Martin

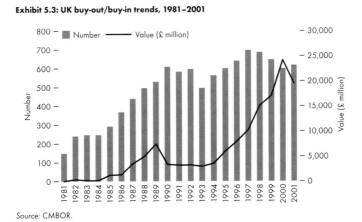

Exhibit 5.3: UK buy-out/buy-in trends, 1981–2001

Source: CMBOR.

Brailsford. This was an extraordinary transaction, as effectively the management team acquired the company through senior debt without any private equity funding. A year later, following trade creditor pressure, the balance sheet was strengthened with mezzanine. The mezzanine lenders were given a share of the operating profit but were not allocated any equity warrants. Two years after the original buy-out a trade sale provided a massive profit to management as they owned 100 per cent of the company.

At the same time, there were numerous other highly successful transactions, including the Compass buy-out from Grand Met led by Gerry Robinson and Francis Mackay, the MFI buy-out led by Derek Hunt and the Reedpack buy-out led by Peter Williams from Reed International.

The Reedpack transaction, backed by Cinven, was particularly remarkable for three reasons – all of which were to have a major effect on the industry:

i.   it was the first jumbo deal to incorporate a capital expenditure facility setting an important financial precedent allowing private equity investors access to capital intensive industries;

ii. the transaction led, after the subsequent sale to SCA, to the buy-outs of Field, Spicers and RPC. In addition, Peter Williams and John Miller (FD) left to develop David S Smith in acquiring Kaysersberg. One transaction, therefore, led to four further acquisitions significantly accelerating the consolidation of the European paper and packaging market;

iii. the transaction was the creation of the leveraged team at Chemical Bank who then left to set up Intermediate Capital Group (ICG), which along with Mezzanine Management established at the same time, pioneered mezzanine as an intermediate product between senior debt and equity. This product had a major impact on the expansion of the leveraged market.

Ironically, the establishment of these mezzanine funds – allowing higher prices to be paid – was quickly followed by a fall-off in the industry, as shown in Exhibit 5.3.

The reason for this decline was twofold. Firstly, the economic climate fell into recession with soaring interest rates. Secondly, lending excesses led to some significant losses not only for equity investors but also for the lending banks. It is perhaps pertinent to address some of the lessons from these excesses because it is still said that this will never happen again.

One example of excessive lending concerned the MBI of Lowndes Queensway, the carpets and furniture retailer. This suffered from four weak points – each one serious – but collectively fatal. Firstly, a PE of 30 was paid; secondly, the buy-in team had little knowledge of the product; thirdly, the vendor did have knowledge; and fourthly, interest rates rose by a 100 per cent in 18 months not only affecting leverage but also following the government's policy of curbing consumer expenditure. Although valiant efforts were made to salvage the situation, there were too many problems conspiring against it. The key point to note however was that the transaction was actually well capitalised but still could not sustain the debt.

Another famous example was Isosceles. This was the result of a hostile takeover of Gateway, the supermarket chain. The race was intense, and to win the transaction the final offer drew on part of the working capital facility. This resulted in a reduction in 'headroom' when the acquisition was finally made. However the key issue was reliance on asset sales. Crucially the sale of a US subsidiary was delayed and by the time it was sold, cash flow had become tight and creditors nervous.

In both instances – involving retail with high existing operating leverage and therefore little margin for error – these high profile situations were played out in the national newspapers. Delicate creditor and bank syndicate management therefore became quite impossible. It seems it may well happen again.

The current situation

The past five years have been characterised by a surge in financially engineered deals, principally driven by US investment banks, which quickly recognised the importance of acquisition finance not only in obtaining new relationships but also in preserving the relationships they already had. In contrast, European banks traditionally continued to perceive most private equity investors with, at best, suspicion.

This 'Americanisation', which has undoubtedly been innovative and at times ingenious in its financial engineering, has similarly moved into the realms of excess, akin to the traditional lending excesses seen 10 years ago.

Specifically, we have seen the introduction of high yield replacing mezzanine in jumbo transactions, especially in the rapid development of the telecoms industry. High yield has been a most effective product for the US investment banks playing to their distribution strengths in both the United States and more recently continental Europe. High yield is perceived as cheaper than mezzanine provided the investment is held for more than four years. However, in view of the transient (and at times predatory) nature of the bondholders, if there is a need to restructure, negotiations can become considerably more onerous.

A further development has been the introduction of pay in kind (PIK), which sits above equity but below mezzanine and high yield in the capital structure. This is an additional product to allow higher prices to be paid while preserving equity returns.

Finally, the most recent innovation, again from the United States, is a senior debt product delivered through leveraging a layer of equity with a succession of lower yielding instruments resulting in a stand-alone senior debt fund investing in small tranches of long-term leveraged senior debt. These funds are known as collaterised debt obligations (CDOs).

The result of these innovations is that equity investors now have a multitude of financial products at their disposal. However, this choice is leading to an over-complication of financial structures, all apparently designed to increase private equity returns. Attention is focused on attracting ever new layers of financial support while senior debt is simply taken for granted. The fact remains that senior debt continues to make up the lion's share of the financial structure and continues to be the main source of liquidity after the transaction has been completed.

It is ironic that this increasing sophistication in financial engineering – designed to enhance equity returns – is now undermining these returns. Private equity investors increasingly now need to buy-and-build in order to create value. This requires a flexible funding structure. However, the advantage of these financial products in allowing equity investors to pay a higher price is now being eroded by the financial inflexibility that these same products impose.

To illustrate this point, one of the earlier buy-outs to use high-yield bonds as part of the original acquisition embarked on a buy and build strategy before encountering liquidity problems. The equity investor was compelled to inject new funding, while some of the senior debt banks had to increase their exposure to take out those banks that no longer wished to provide support. The high-yield facility remained unchanged throughout. The high-yield investors continued to receive interest in cash even though they were subordinate to the senior debt banks. Although the transaction subsequently recovered and the private equity investor made a considerable return, the private equity investor–senior debt banking relationship was pivotal in turning this situation round.

This relationship is also vital since covenant breaches and financial amendments are triggered first at the senior debt level. Furthermore, as the above example demonstrates, senior debt banks, in contrast with the majority of the other fund suppliers, are able to inject new funding if required and sanctioned by credit committee.

However, credit committees across Europe are becoming increasingly concerned that creditors who are supposed to be structurally and contractually junior to senior debt banks are effectively holding a senior position. There are three obvious ways subordinated investors can effectively become senior:

i.   by insisting on their interest being paid in cash despite a downturn;
ii. by insisting on excessive equity in a downturn; and
iii. by insisting on repayment at par after acquiring the bond at a discount; threatening insolvency.

In each of these instances, the junior holders could trigger a collapse in the financial structure, possibly causing a loss at senior level in spite of the fact that the bond was itself acquired at a massive discount.

Equity investors therefore need to balance the advantages of financial engineering with the dependency they could have on financiers who do not necessarily share their same strategic objectives and indeed may not even know when the acquisition was originally made. This is particularly important in conditions of a stock market downturn.

Effectively, the natural result of excessive financial engineering will be the breakdown of the investor–bank relationship. Senior debt banks playing the same game will either underwrite for league table/fee purposes but sell down to a minimal level or not underwrite and simply acquire the asset at a discount in the secondary market reflecting exactly the same approach of the predatory bondholder.

Neither of these two approaches is particularly conducive to transaction stability. If the transaction runs into problems (increasingly likely if a high price has been paid in an uncertain market) then a perfectly good business could be undermined. Furthermore, the acquisition finance market itself will become discredited in the eyes of international credit committees whom, it should be remembered, are the oxygen for future transactions. There is little point in being a relationship bank if noone else believes in relationships.

If this practice continues private investors may well start to experience the harsher side of Warren Buffett's observation that: 'price is what you pay and value is what you get.'

Outlook

Although there will always be excesses, there is however no doubt that the private equity investor has truly arrived on the financial landscape. In line with the thinking of the US investment banks, European banks have now also realised the enormous potential of this asset class either directly through their own investments or indirectly by recognising their potential in both deal and relationship origination.

The fact remains that corporate events in realising shareholder value will always exercise the mind of the principal industrial decisionmakers. The banks that play a role in these events know that they will take the lion's share of the ongoing lending and advisory business. Conversely the banks that do not, won't.

One of the key challenges, however, facing banks and investors alike is the requirement to move quickly if an acquisition is to be successfully realised. Inevitably, this will mean that, as stated above, the success will largely be determined by the trust that exists between banker and investor based on previous experience with a mutual recognition of the key issues that each one faces.

The principal challenge facing both is how to deal with due diligence, covered elsewhere in detail in this book. Ironically, at a time when the perfect conditions are now in place for significant private equity expansion, senior debt banks are becoming increasingly concerned with the methodology of due diligence. Interest rates are low and so is the stock market, thereby creating the supply and demand for a massive surge in public-to-private transactions. However, accounting irregularities both in the United States and Europe have now resulted in far more caution being exercised. This is a further example of how important the private equity–bank relationship is becoming since investors and banks vary considerably in their approach as to which issues they regard as deal-breakers.

However, as the market for private equity continues to consolidate and as the supply of senior debt is further reduced to those banks that have avoided some of the recent excesses, a more sensible approach will be adopted towards due diligence. The current European practice of expecting bank commitments to be binding, often after only three weeks' due diligence, is not sustainable particularly as the majority of targets do not adopt US GAAP resulting in significant differences in major areas of accounting covering, for example, the treatment of pensions and provisions.

In smaller transactions (below €100 million) this issue can be overcome with local relationship banks content to support the acquisition. However, if the transaction requires international support, there needs to be more transparency and therefore more time.

Specifically, more time needs to be given to the senior debt lender who in turn needs to demonstrate a thorough understanding of the industry. Unfortunately, the ease of electronic transmission has now created an excessive volume of material provided by legal, financial and technical advisers to whom the lending banks have effectively out-sourced judgement. These advisers have no stake in the business and minimal liability. This judgement out-sourcing has, in some cases, effectively changed the nature of the lending banker from being a thinker to being a processor, which has resulted in senior debt being treated as a mere commodity. It is hardly surprising that the more creative bankers have left banking for private equity and mezzanine fund management.

Exhibit 5.4: Exits of UK buy-outs/buy-ins, 1992–2002*

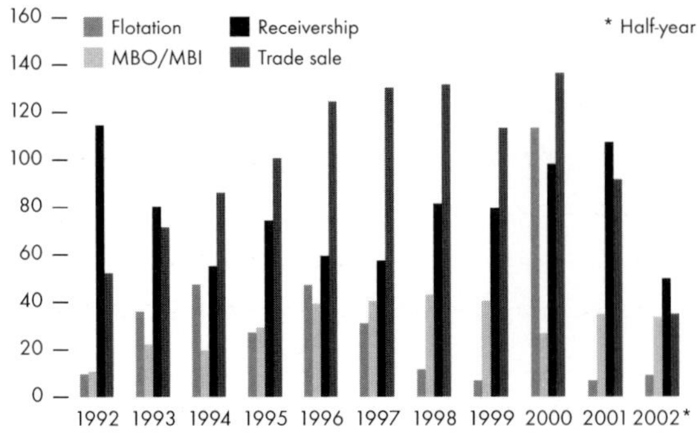

Source: CMBOR.

However, the judgement of the banker remains crucial particularly as 30 per cent of exits are through receivership (see Exhibit 5.4). This is, therefore, a clear warning for the private equity investor and senior debt lender to work closely together from the start. Exhibit 5.4 also shows the importance of lender and investor continuing to meet regularly after the transaction has been completed and not simply when there is a request for more funding.

However, if the lender is to be taken seriously and not merely treated as a commodity, the lender needs to demonstrate a proactive understanding of the industry as well as the investments in related industries made by the equity investor. In practice, this means that lending banks should actually employ industrialists with in-depth sector experience. This approach not only adds value to the investor but equally important adds internal value in improving the quality of analysis when presenting to credit committee. This will help improve the quality of due diligence, ensure the financial structure is appropriate and most important of all (for the investor) identify from the start the most likely source of exit.

In addition to improving the quality of the equity–bank relationship, there also needs to be more stability. Currently, as previously mentioned, senior lenders are being encouraged to take the fees and sell down, thereby promoting a short-term trading culture instead of a long-term lending approach. This is undermining stability and syndicate management. This could be avoided if private equity investors paid a small fee, circa 50 basis points, which would only be payable after two years to those banks that have not sold below their agreed final take at the start of the transaction. This would promote syndicate stability and bank loyalty in a climate of increasing economic uncertainty.

This theme of emphasising the private equity–senior debt banker relationship is particularly important since the attitude of European banks to private equity has changed in the last 10 years. Originally suspicious, they then began to recognise the extraordinary profitability of private equity as an asset class in its own right. As a result they established their own private equity operations, invested heavily, lost money as the market declined before ultimately divesting control to their own management teams.

Although their experience in private equity investment has been mixed, European banks have nevertheless come to recognise the role private equity can play not only in winning new business for the lending bank but also in preserving long-cherished relationships when corporate ownership changes.

Therefore, while European banks may have lost their enthusiasm for direct private equity ownership, private equity investors are now regarded as priority target clients for both US and European banks.

However, while private equity has clearly won recognition, it has also now reached a crossroads. Just as the excesses of the market 10 years ago were fatally affected by high interest rates, the current challenge facing the market has ironically been caused by low interest rates. This has created a wall of money looking for yield with some transactions being structured to meet the aspirations of the investor instead of what is appropriate for the transaction itself.

As some of these investments have quickly unravelled, it has become apparent that the senior position of lending banks can prove to be anything but senior, with junior bond-holders undermining not only the financial structure but the ability of the company to trade as a going concern.

It is hardly surprising that this activity has also successfully undermined credit committee confidence in these over-structured deals, affecting not only the banks directly concerned but more seriously the appetite for this form of lending from a much wider audience.

The challenge going forward is to recognise these excesses and for private equity investors to resist the temptation of taking the wrong turning with their transactions being over-engineered by over-zealous corporate financiers and advisers with no future stake in the transaction. While it is recognised that private equity investors need to safeguard their returns, it should not be at the risk of the transaction itself.

Quite simply, if this wrong turning is taken, senior bank debt will become increasingly scarce as credit committees question the risk/reward of lending into highly leveraged situations where they have no effective control and where the majority of debt providers are not lenders but traders. This trading culture will not only undermine the senior debt–private equity relationship but more importantly the growth of the entire buy-out market as private equity investors will no longer have a stable source of financing upon which they can rely.

The right turning is to ensure that those with a stake in the transaction are the architects of it. The market therefore needs to see a strengthening of the senior debt–private equity investor relationship. This will require a change in approach from both sides. Private equity investors need to recognise that senior debt should not be treated as a mere commodity while senior debt providers need to demonstrate relevant industrial knowledge to add more value. This will result in a healthy disintermediation of the middle-man, with lenders and investors forging their own relationship with a mutual focus on specific industry sectors.

In this way, credit committees will remain open for business, the market will continue to expand and the private equity investor can confidently tell Warren Buffett: 'This is the price I paid – and this is the value I received.'

6

Financial structuring of corporate acquisitions

Chris Harrison, partner and Phillip Slater, associate, Weil, Gotshal & Manges, London

Introduction

Once the potential target company or business (the 'Target') has been identified and the determination has been made that acquisition of the Target provides an attractive investment opportunity (in the case of an MBO, MBI or IBO[1]) or presents an opportunity to collect together business synergies that will enhance or complement existing operations and business aims (in the case of a trade purchase), the next major step will be to look at the way the acquisition will be funded.

Depending upon the size of the transaction, strength of the credit and the prevailing market conditions, funding for a corporate acquisition may be structured utilising a variety of financial products either individually or, more commonly, in differing combinations. This chapter sets out an overview of the principal issues and considerations relating to, and impacting on, the financial structuring of corporate acquisitions, with a particular emphasis on debt funding. The key areas that will be addressed are:

- categories of corporate acquisition;
- basic transaction structures;
- the Target and financing issues; and
- financing structure and pricing.

To provide a consistent frame of reference the basis used for this discussion and analysis is the typical funding structure that would be employed in a medium-sized acquisition of a UK Target. Where appropriate, additional issues that may need to be considered are highlighted and addressed in the context of larger and more financially engineered leveraged acquisition deals as well as transactions with cross-border elements.

Categories of corporate acquisition

In order to put the financial structuring issues into context, it is worth setting out a brief overview of the various categories of corporate acquisition that are most commonly encountered.

At the broadest level, acquisitions can be broken down into two generic categories, set out below.

Asset purchase

The acquisition of certain identified Target assets or businesses rather than the purchase of the whole of the issued share capital of a Target company.

This may be favoured over a share purchase by both a purchaser and a vendor, although for very different reasons. For the purchaser it will allow cherry-picking of assets and business lines that are most favourable to its investment programme (or in the case of an MBO, MBI or IBO, the investment profile of the private equity houses and, where appropriate, the business plan of the management team), and will allow the purchaser to pick up assets without necessarily taking on significant existing liabilities of a Target company or group of companies.

For the Target, and particularly where the individual business lines of the Target have not been hived down into separate corporate entities within the Target group, this may allow the divestment of certain business lines which have become non-core or otherwise are no longer part of the Target's long-term business planning, whilst facilitating the retention and ongoing operations of its core businesses and assets.

Share purchase

The acquisition of the whole of the issued share capital in the Target company by the purchaser, effectively bringing the Target, and the companies that are members of the Target group, as subsidiaries of the purchasing vehicle.

In contrast to the cherry-picking approach discussed above, this will bring with it all assets and liabilities of the Target. However, in certain circumstances the acquisition of liabilities may bring about positive effects for, in particular, a trade purchaser. For example, a Target may have significant tax losses that a trade purchaser may be able to utilise and which will have an overall perceived tax benefit to the purchaser.

For the purposes of this chapter, we have concentrated on share purchase as the primary method of corporate acquisition.

Below these generic categories, acquisitions can be further subdivided into the following types.

Management buy-out (MBO)

The existing management of the Target acquire the Target from the existing shareholders. This would generally arise where current management feel that they are not necessarily receiving sufficient support or the investment they require in order to best fulfil their business aims, but are confident that, with such support, the Target will thrive.

An MBO would ordinarily involve management having the backing of one or more private equity houses or investment banks that are supportive of the management team's business plan and are willing to inject equity and shareholder loan capital to assist with the financing of the acquisition.

Management buy-in (MBI)

A Target is identified as having unfulfilled potential due to existing poor management or lack of entrepreneurial flair. For the purposes of making the acquisition, the private equity funders and intermediaries will identify and assemble a management team with the combined skill set that will hopefully facilitate a turnaround of the fortunes of Target.

Again, an MBI would ordinarily involve the assembled management team having the backing of one or more private equity houses or investment banks that are supportive of their plans and are willing to inject equity and shareholder loan capital to assist with the financing of the acquisition.

Buy-in/management buy-out (BIMBO)

This is a hybrid of the MBO and the MBI. All or some of the existing management team link up with an opportunistic external team with a view to combining their complementary skill sets in order to realise undeveloped business potential in the Target.

Institutional buy-out (IBO)

IBOs tend to focus more on the larger acquisition deals and contemplate the acquisition by one or more private equity houses or investment banks of a whole group of companies or subdivision of a large conglomerate with a view to streamlining the Target business and/or pursuing buy-and-build strategies (where further business in the same sector as the Target are acquired in future to achieve economies of scale) to enhance profitability and value.

Trade purchase

This is the acquisition by one existing and established corporate of another corporate or business.

Each of the above types of corporate acquisition may involve the acquisition of either private companies or a public company with usually private company subsidiaries. For the sake of completeness the following generic terminology, describing any combination of the above categories, may also be used.

Leveraged buy-out (LBO)

The acquisition by the purchasing company of the Target company/business in circumstances where the purchaser relies on a high proportion of debt finance to fund the purchase price with a minimal amount of equity investment being made in the purchasing vehicle.

Public-to-private

The acquisition of a Target company that is publicly quoted on the London Stock Exchange by way of public offer in accordance with the provisions of the City Code on Takeovers and Mergers. Post-acquisition, the Target will be de-listed and return to the status of a private limited company.

Basic transaction structures

Set out below is a summary of the basic transaction structures that may be employed in making acquisitions.

Exhibit 6.1 reflects a basic transaction structure that may be employed in connection with an MBO, MBI or IBO. The acquisition vehicle would typically be a new private limited company (Newco) formed by the private equity investors and the management in which each will take an equity stake. The nature of the equity stake taken by each investor and the rights attaching to the shares offered to each investor will vary from transaction to transaction and will be fully documented in an investment agreement between the investors and Newco and the articles of association of Newco.

Funding of the acquisition purchase price and acquisition costs is met by a combination of investment by way of equity and/or shareholder debt from the private equity houses (and to a limited extent by management) and bank debt. The transactions are typically relatively highly leveraged with typically around 60 per cent or more of the funding costs for the acquisition being raised by way of bank debt. Ultimately, the level of debt funding will be a function of the size of the acquisition, the perceived credit profile of the proposed Target, the results of the financial modelling, and the prevailing market conditions and appetite among the lending community. Third-party debt funding options available to Newco are discussed in greater detail in the section of this chapter headed 'Financing structure and pricing'.

Exhibit 6.2 reflects a basic transaction structure that may be employed by a purchaser in connection with a trade purchase. It should be noted that this contemplates that the

Exhibit 6.1: MBO/MBI/IBO basic transaction structure

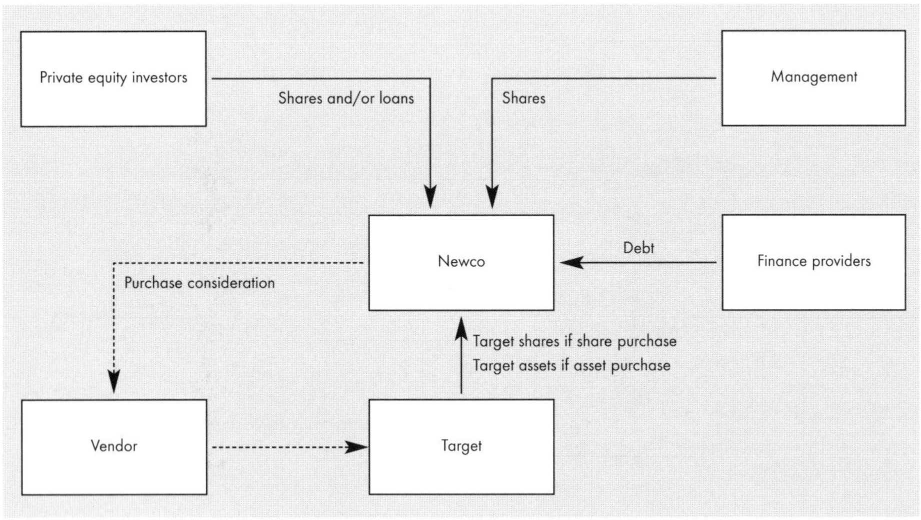

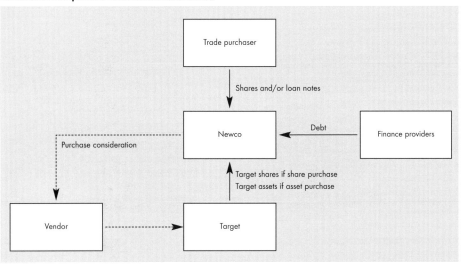

Exhibit 6.2: Trade purchase basic transaction structure

purchaser will establish a new special purpose company (Newco) specifically for the purpose of making the acquisition. This may not always be the case. For example, the purchaser may be a group of companies that has an established corporate structure including companies that act as holding companies for operating subsidiaries. In this case, it may be more appropriate for the existing holding company to be the purchasing company thereby avoiding the need to establish Newco. The identification of the purchasing vehicle in a trade purchase will depend upon many factors including, considerations as to desired group

Exhibit 6.3: Cross-border acquisition basic transaction structure

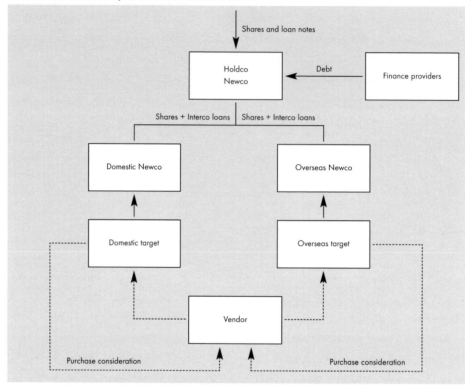

corporate structure, tax issues and accounting factors, such factors being a matter for consideration by the purchaser from a business perspective.

It will also be necessary for the purchaser to consider the most appropriate transaction structure in the context of the proposed financing for the acquisition. The relevant acquisition may be:

(i) balance-sheet financed within the purchaser group without the need to have recourse to third-party debt funding;

(ii) financed by utilising existing credit lines available to the purchasing group, provided that such an acquisition and use of proceeds is permitted pursuant to the terms and conditions of the existing credit lines;

(iii) financed by new third-party debt raised by the existing holding company (or principal operating company) within the group; or

(iv) financed by third-party debt established by a Newco.

Depending upon the level within the purchaser group at which the funding for the acquisition is raised, the money will need to flow down through the group by way of equity subscription and/or intercompany loan (the precise split between the two funding methods being usually determined by such considerations as favourable tax treatment of repayments or distributions and minimum capitalisation requirements) in order to ensure that the money ultimately sits in the vehicle that will be used to make the acquisition.

The use of a new special purpose vehicle may be attractive in circumstances where the purchaser wants to ring-fence the acquired company/business and the associated funding for such acquisition from the rest of the purchasing group.

The structure set out in Exhibit 6.3 reflects a typical basic structure that may be adopted in circumstances where the proposed acquisition involves a Target with a cross-border element.

The Target and financing issues

Once a Target has been identified it will be necessary to focus on assessing the issues that will impact upon the desire of the equity investors or the trade purchaser to make the acquisition, the price that should be payable and the considerations that may affect the ability of the purchaser to raise debt finance for the purposes of funding the purchase price and the associated acquisition costs.

Whilst it is not possible within the scope of this chapter to cover all matters that will need to be considered in respect of each type of transaction, there are certain key issues that impact on corporate acquisition transactions utilising a Newco as the acquiring vehicle:

(a) due diligence on the Target;

(b) requirements of the debt providers;

(c) specific issues in the context of public-to-private acquisitions; and

(d) funding requirements of Newco.

Due diligence on the Target

One of the key elements in any acquisition for both the equity investors in the purchasing vehicle and the financial institutions providing debt finance to fund the acquisition is the conduct of due diligence on the Target.

The aim of the pre-acquisition due diligence exercise is to uncover as much detail as possible about the Target, its business and its assets and liabilities so as to determine both the merits of proceeding with the acquisition and to further avoid any unexpected surprises once the acquisition has been completed.

Whilst it is usual for the share purchase agreement or asset purchase agreement to contain warranties given by the vendor in relation to the status, operations, financial and tax position, business and assets of the Target, it is clearly preferable to obtain knowledge of potential problems prior to execution of the share purchase or asset purchase agreement. This allows such issues to be effectively addressed up front in the context of the negotiations rather than leaving the purchaser to rely on recourse to the vendor by way of contractual claim for breach of warranty post-completion. This issue may be exacerbated in an MBO since the vendor may be willing only to provide limited warranties to Newco on the basis that the management team that are making the acquisition will already have a good working knowledge of the Target, its business and its assets and liabilities.

The debt providers to Newco will be interested in the results of the pre-acquisition due diligence since, in most cases, they will be looking to both the cash flows and financial standing of the Target as their principal source of repayment and to the assets of Target as security for the repayment of their debt. This is principally because Newco will typically have no assets other than those assets it acquires pursuant to the acquisition.

Consequently, the equity investors and the debt providers will be looking to ensure that all major risks have been highlighted and factored into the purchase price for Target (possibly by means of purchase price retentions or staged payments) or otherwise adequately allocated between Newco and the vendor in the legal documentation (through vendor warranties and indemnities). In addition, where necessary, such matters can be factored into the financial modelling that will underpin the debt providers' assessment as to the ongoing financial viability of Newco and Target post-acquisition and their ability to service and ultimately repay the debt.

Due diligence is usually split into three areas – legal, financial and commercial. The following principal areas will typically be covered in a due diligence exercise.

Legal due diligence

- a review of the constitutional documents of Target, each member of the Target group and of the vendor;
- an analysis of the real property owned by Target and the members of the Target group or otherwise utilised (under a lease or a licence) by Target and the members of the Target group;
- an analysis of the assets owned by Target and the members of the Target group that are used by or are otherwise instrumental to the ongoing operations and business of Target or the members of the Target group;
- a review of all contracts that have been executed by Target and the members of the Target group that are material to the ongoing business and operations of Target and the members of the Target group. This may take on a particular importance where the acquisition is to be an acquisition of the share capital of Target since certain contracts

may, amongst other things, stipulate that a change of control may entitle a counterparty to terminate the contract. In this case, further negotiations may be required with counterparties to contracts that are material to the business of Target and the Target group to ensure that, for example, revenue streams from large customers are not lost, vital contracts with suppliers are not jeopardised or leverage is not afforded to key suppliers resulting in the potential for them to increase prices;

- a review of all current indebtedness of Target and the members of the Target group together with an analysis of any security interests that may subsist over the assets of Target and the Target group. This will be of particular importance to the debt providers and is discussed in more detail below;
- a review of the employment issues affecting and the current employees of Target and the members of the Target group, details on pension funding (where applicable) and an analysis of the current insurance position of the Target and the members of the Target group;
- a review of all information regarding existing, pending or threatened litigation or arbitration proceedings against Target or any member of the Target group; and
- a review of the intellectual property owned by or otherwise licensed by the Target and the members of the Target group.

Financial due diligence

- an analysis of the structure of the business of the Target group;
- a synopsis of the history and the business of the Target and the members of the Target group;
- a review of the current position as to the assets and liabilities that are proposed to be acquired by the purchaser;
- a summary of the tax position of the Target and the members of the Target group; and
- an overview of the current trading position of the Target and the members of the Target group.

Commercial due diligence

The scope of the additional commercial due diligence that may be required will be dependent upon the size of the acquisition and the nature of the business to be acquired. By way of example, the following additional diligence may be required:

- a review by a market consultant of the market in which the Target and the members of the Target group operate, together with an analysis of the key competitors within that market and the ongoing viability of the Target and the members of the Target group to compete in such market;

– a detailed review of environmental issues affecting the Target and the members of the Target group in circumstances where the Target group is involved in certain environmentally sensitive activities such as engineering and/or petrochemical activities.

Requirements of the debt providers

As highlighted above, the debt providers will require the legal due diligence on the Target to cover a detailed analysis of the existing indebtedness of the Target and the members of the Target group and an appraisal of the existing security interests that subsist over their property and assets. The results of this analysis will be material to the debt providers since they will be reliant upon recourse to those assets to protect their debt investment.

As already discussed, in the majority of acquisitions the debt funding will be provided to a Newco in order to facilitate the payment by Newco of the purchase price for Target. However, since Newco will be a special purpose company formed for the specific intention of making the acquisition it will not itself have any assets (other than, post-acquisition, its shares in Target, in the case of a share purchase, or the Target business and assets, in the case of an asset purchase). Consequently, the debt providers need to be sure that the acquired assets are available to be charged in their favour as security for the obligations of Newco to service and repay the debt.

Asset purchase

In the case of an asset purchase by Newco, this will involve ensuring (pursuant to the due diligence process) that the assets to be purchased are capable of being provided to the debt providers as first ranking collateral. This will typically mean that all current security interests in favour of third parties that may exist at the time of the acquisition are discharged and new security interests over such assets are provided by Newco to the debt providers contemporaneously with the acquisition.

The discharge of pre-existing encumbrances on the acquired assets will undoubtedly be a condition of the asset purchase agreement and first ranking security over such assets will most certainly be required by the debt providers to Newco. Such security will usually take the form of a debenture granted by Newco in favour of the debt providers or their agent and trustee which will create fixed and floating charges over all the business and assets of Newco, including the assets acquired pursuant to the acquisition of the Target business and any other future acquired assets.

Share purchase

In the case of a share purchase by Newco it will be necessary for each of Newco, the Target and each member of the Target group to provide security in favour of the debt providers over all, or substantially all, of their business assets and undertaking. Again, given that the debt providers to Newco will be looking to secure first ranking security interests, this will likely require that all existing security interests in favour of third parties that may exist at the time of the acquisition are discharged simultaneously with the acquisition.

It may be that any pre-existing indebtedness of the Target or any other member of the Target group that has the benefit of security over the assets of Target or such member of the Target group will need to be discharged in full at the time of the acquisition in order that all assets can be acquired by Newco 'free and clear'. In this regard, see the observations made in the section entitled 'Funding requirements of Newco' below.

Typically, the debt providers will look to receive debentures from Newco, Target and each member of the Target group, which will create fixed and floating charges over all, or substantially all, the business and assets of each of those companies. Whilst it is possible to take such security from Target and the members of the Target group as collateral support for the debt obligation of Newco to the debt providers, it would usually be the case that each of Target and the members of the Target group would also provide guarantees to the debt providers for the due and punctual performance of the obligations of Newco to service and repay the debt under the debt documentation. The security provided by Target and the members of the Target group would then secure the obligations of those companies under the guarantees.

Exhibit 6.4: Typical security structure in a share purchase

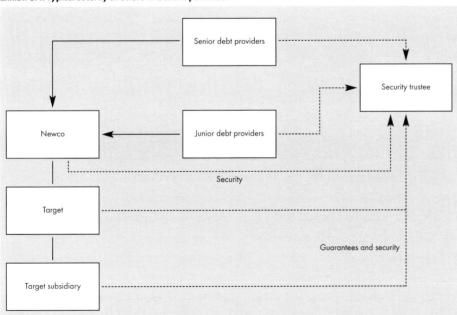

The guarantees may be put in place by means of independent guarantee documentation but will, most likely, be achieved by the accession of Target and the members of the Target group to the guarantee provisions that are included in the loan documentation governing the terms of the loan to Newco.

Exhibit 6.4 sets out the typical security structure in a share purchase.

Financial assistance

One issue that arises in relation to the creation of security in the case of a share purchase, and which must be considered, is the concept of financial assistance under English law.

The provisions of Sections 151 to 158 of the Companies Act 1985 set out restrictions which prevent a company from giving financial assistance for the purchase of its own shares. The scope of the prohibition is drafted widely and will include any assistance given by way of:

(i) gift;
(ii) guarantee, security or indemnity;
(iii) a loan or other agreement under which obligations of the person giving the assistance are to be fulfilled at a time when in accordance with the agreement any obligation of another party to the agreement remains unfulfilled or by way of novation or assignment of rights under a loan or such other agreement; or
(iv) any other financial assistance given by a company, the net assets of which are thereby reduced to a material extent or which has no net assets.

Financial assistance is prohibited in two situations:

(i) where it is given for the purpose of the acquisition before or at the same time as shares are acquired; and
(ii) where it is given after the acquisition for the purpose of reducing or discharging a liability incurred for the purposes of the acquisition.

Consequently, unless an exemption from the provisions of the Companies Act 1985 can be successfully invoked, Target or any member of the Target group may not lend money to Newco nor may Target or any member of the Target group provide any security or guarantee in favour of the debt providers as collateral support for the servicing and repayment of the debt funding provided to Newco for the purpose of acquiring the shares in Target.

The financial assistance provisions are intended to help maintain a company's share capital for the benefit of shareholders and creditors, and contravention of the provisions is an offence for which the company may be liable to a fine and its officers may be liable to imprisonment and/or a fine pursuant to the terms of the Companies Act 1985.

One important exemption from the prohibition on financial assistance is that private limited companies in the United Kingdom (but not public companies) are permitted to grant financial assistance for the acquisition of their shares provided that:

(i) the company providing the financial assistance has net assets that are not thereby reduced or, to the extent that they are reduced, the assistance is provided out of distributable profits; and

(ii) the conditions prescribed in Sections 155 to 158 of the Companies Act 1985 are complied with (commonly known as the 'whitewash' procedure).

Given what has been said in the context of the security and guarantees that the debt providers to Newco will require in the context of a share purchase of Target, it is clear that issues as to financial assistance are paramount and must be addressed. Where Target and its subsidiaries are private limited companies, it would be commonplace to ensure that the whitewash procedure is followed. The financial assistance issues that are raised in the context of a public-to-private transaction are discussed in the next section of this chapter headed 'Specific issues in the context of a public-to-private acquisition'.

By way of overview, the whitewash procedure requires the following steps to be taken:

(i) a statutory declaration must be sworn by all of the directors of the company proposing to give the financial assistance. This declaration includes a statement that, in the opinion of the declaring directors, the company giving the assistance will be able to pay its debts as they fall due during the 12 months immediately following the financial assistance being given;

(ii) the statutory declaration described in paragraph (i) above must have annexed to it a report from the company's auditors stating that the auditors have enquired into the state of affairs of the company and are not aware of anything to indicate that the opinion of the directors expressed in the declaration is unreasonable;

(iii) unless the company in question is wholly-owned, a special resolution must be passed by the company's shareholders approving the giving of the financial assistance. This special resolution must be passed within one week of the directors' statutory declaration being sworn; and

(iv) the directors' statutory declaration, the auditors' report and, where appropriate, the text of the special resolution must be filed with Companies House in the United Kingdom.

Once the whitewash procedure is complete, the provision of financial assistance is no longer prohibited.

Where a proposed acquisition involves both a domestic and a foreign Target (see Exhibit 6.3), it will be necessary to take legal advice in the applicable foreign jurisdiction to ensure that any provisions equivalent to the UK financial assistance rules are noted and any available exemptions complied with.

Specific issues in the context of a public-to-private acquisition

Certain specific financing issues are raised in the context of acquisitions that involve the acquisition of a Target company that is publicly quoted on the London Stock Exchange. Such issues are fundamental to the efficacy of a public company acquisition and it is important that all parties to such a transaction have a full understanding of their impact on any proposed debt financing for the purposes of such a transaction.

Committed funding, lending into default and the certain funds period

General Principle 3 of the City Code on Takeovers and Mergers (the 'Code') specifies that:

'An offeror should only announce an offer after the most careful and responsible consideration. Such an announcement should be made only where the offeror has every reason to believe that it can and will continue to be able to implement the offer: responsibility in this connection also rests on the financial adviser to the offeror.'

In addition, the Takeover Panel have issued the following guidance:

'The Executive's view is that, when a financial adviser is acting for a newly created offeror ... the standard of care required under General Principle 3 clearly has an additional dimension. In short, the only way in which an offeror and its financial adviser can be sure that the funds will be available is to have an irrevocable commitment from a party upon whom reliance can reasonably be placed, for example a bank, at the time of the announcement of the offer'. (Takeover Panel announcement No. 0557n).

Rule 24.7 of the Code places the financial advisers to Newco under an obligation to confirm in the offer document that Newco has the funds available to finance in full the cash element of the bid. Accordingly, the advisers will need to be satisfied at the point the offer is announced that the acquisition finance to be provided by the debt providers will be available at all times when, after the offer has become unconditional in all respects, Newco is required to pay shareholders who accept the offer.

Debt providers in these circumstances must therefore be prepared to commit to lend on the date Newco announces its offer and then to lend to Newco even though there is a default (except for specified major events of default, discussed below) so that Newco can pay accepting shareholders. This, of course, contrasts sharply with an acquisition of a non-public company, where the debt provider will be entitled to withdraw its finance if there are breaches of representations and warranties, or of the financial covenants or other events of default enumerated in the debt documentation.

This concept of the enduring availability of the acquisition funding is frequently referred to as the certain funds period. In the debt documentation, the certain funds period will typically be defined as the period between the release of the press announcement, which confirms the intention of Newco to make an offer, and the date 14 days after the offer closes (because under the Code, the offerer has to pay the consideration to accepting shareholders within 14 days after the shareholder has accepted the offer and the offer has become unconditional in all respects) or, if earlier, the date when the compulsory acquisition procedure set out in s.429 Companies Act 1985 has been completed (squeeze-out of minority shareholders where the offerer has received acceptances in respect of 90 per cent of the shares of each class of the share capital of the Target).

During the certain funds period, the only events of default which may exempt the debt providers from their obligation to lend are typically restricted to:

(a) Events of material insolvency, for example:

    (i)   the winding-up or dissolution of Newco;

    (ii) the appointment of a liquidator, receiver or similar officer in relation to Newco;

    (iii) the presentation of a petition for an administration order in relation to Newco;

    (iv) Newco becoming insolvent for the purposes of s.123 Insolvency Act 1986; or

    (v)   Newco entering into a voluntary arrangement with its creditors under Part I Insolvency Act 1986.

Given that Newco is a new company incorporated for the purposes of making the offer, the only liabilities it will have incurred during the certain funds period will be in connection with the offer, the funding of the offer and associated fees and so it is difficult to envisage this category of default being significant from a practical point of view.

(b) Events of default relating to the offer to the extent they are within the control of the offerer; for example, breaches of the following covenants:

    (i)   to issue the press release within an agreed period after the debt documentation is executed;

    (ii) to despatch the offer document within an agreed period after the date of issue of the press release;

(iii) to ensure that the terms and conditions of the press release and the offer document comply with the Code and all applicable laws;

(iv) to comply with the Code in connection with the conduct of the offer; or

(v) not to make purchases of shares in Target which will trigger a Rule 9 bid (a Rule 9 bid only has an acceptance condition of 50.1 per cent of the shares of each class of Target's share capital, which would be potentially disastrous for the debt provider) (see the discussion under paragraph (b) below).

In view of the fact that the debt providers will be irrevocably committed from the date of issue of the press release announcing the offer, the debt providers will be concerned to ensure that the press release is not issued until they are satisfied with the results of the commercial and legal due diligence.

Delay in obtaining security over the assets of the Target

Lending into default is one the idiosyncratic features of the debt funding of public-to-private takeovers. It runs contrary to the normal principals of bank lending, but the credit committees of lenders have become comfortable with the concept. A more concerning feature of public-to-private takeovers for debt providers is the inevitable delay there will be in obtaining security over the assets of Target and its subsidiaries, or, in the worst-case scenario, the possibility that they may end up with no security at all.

This delay arises because the guarantees and security from Target and its subsidiaries cannot be provided until Target and its subsidiaries have been through the financial assistance whitewash procedure. But before Target can do this, it needs to be re-registered as a private company. This is because public companies cannot avail themselves of the financial assistance whitewash procedure. In addition, the subsidiaries of Target cannot give financial assistance while their parent is still a public company.

The re-registration of Target as a private company requires a special resolution of shareholders in the Target company. The subsequent requirement for Target to provide security will also require a special resolution of the shareholders in accordance with the requirements for whitewash as discussed above. Consequently, the debt providers will be keen to ensure that the offer cannot be capable of being declared unconditional as to acceptances unless and until they are sure that these special resolutions can be passed. A special resolution requires the assent of shareholders holding not less than 75 per cent of the issued share capital of Target.

In view of the foregoing, it will be common to see a covenant in the debt documentation that will restrict Newco from declaring the offer unconditional as to acceptances unless the level of acceptances to the offer (when combined with the number of shares in Target already held by Newco) represents not less than 90 per cent of each class of share capital of the Target or, in some circumstances, not less than 75 per cent of the issued share capital of the Target. In the former case, the debt providers can take comfort from the fact that once the 90 per cent threshold is reached, Newco can invoke the compulsory acquisition provisions in the Companies Act 1985 and acquire the remaining shares; consequently, they will be certain that the necessary resolutions will be obtained.

In the latter case, the position is slightly more problematic. Control of 75 per cent of the issued share capital of Target would be sufficient to pass the necessary special resolutions. However, there are two further issues to consider:

(i) *Section 54, Companies Act 1985* – shareholders representing not less than 5 per cent of the issued share capital of the Target, or being not less than 50 in number, can apply to the court for the cancellation of the resolution re-registering the Target as a private limited company (provided that those shareholders did not vote in favour of the special resolution); and

(ii) *Section 157, Companies Act 1985* – shareholders representing not less than 10 per cent of the issued share capital of Target can apply to the court for cancellation of the resolution of Target required in connection with the whitewash procedure (provided that those shareholders did not vote in favour of the special resolution).

Debt providers will look to build certain protections into the debt documentation addressing each of these potential issues which may take one of a number of forms:

(i) a covenant that Newco will not declare the offer wholly unconditional at the 75 per cent acceptances level unless the debt providers are satisfied that there is no reasonable likelihood of a shareholder or group of shareholders looking to have the required resolutions cancelled;

(ii) providing for an event of default in circumstances where the security to be given by the Target after the whitewash has been completed is not supplied by a certain date. This would trigger a potential acceleration of the debt and the obligation of Newco to repay the whole of the funding; or

(iii) providing for the interest rate applicable to the debt to increase in the event that the security to be given by Target is not supplied by a certain date. Such an increase in interest would, *inter alia*, be sized to reflect the increased risk to the perceived debt providers.

Funding requirements of Newco

In considering the financing that will be required by Newco in the context of the acquisition, it will also be necessary to consider the types of financing that may be required.

Typically, Newco will need to consider certain factors, listed below.

Term financing to fund the purchase price and the acquisition costs

In the context of a share purchase, this may need to be sufficient to cover sums required to repay any existing indebtedness of Target or the members of the Target group such that Target can be taken debt free.

Debt providers for the acquisition will likely insist that Target is, where possible, taken debt free since they will wish to avoid having to spend time and money negotiating potentially complex intercreditor arrangements with the existing creditors of Target. In addition, they will want to ensure that Target assets are free from encumbrances which may have been given in favour of such existing creditors in order that the acquisition debt takes the benefit of a full package of first ranking security over the assets of Target.

In circumstances where the proposed acquisition comprises a cross-border element, thought needs to be given to the currencies in which the purchase price is payable. The purchase price for the overseas assets may be payable in local currency which may give rise to the need for a multicurrency debt facility.

Working capital facilities

Following the completion of acquisition it is likely that Target and the operating subsidiaries within the Target group will need working capital to facilitate their ongoing business operations. Thought needs to be given as to the currencies in which working capital may be needed and the potential requirement for Target and/or one or more of the operating subsidiaries within the Target group to accede to the debt documentation as borrowers in order to be able to directly draw on any working capital provision.

Other ancillary facilities

Depending upon the specific nature of Target's business and the business operations of the members of the Target group, other types of facility may be required. These may comprise overdraft facilities, guarantee facilities or letter of credit facilities. The determination as to any ancillary facilities that may be required will, of necessity, need to be made on a deal-by-deal basis.

Financing structure and pricing

This section looks at how the debt financing, in the context of an acquisition, may be structured. First, it looks at the most typical and basic financing structure in the context of a medium-sized UK acquisition; then it discusses some possible alternatives to that basic structure.

Basic financing structure

Senior debt

This will most likely be the principal form of debt finance in any acquisition transaction. Such debt is typically made available to Newco by one or more banks and is termed senior since it will rank in right of repayment prior to other forms of debt made available to Newco in connection with the acquisition (eg, mezzanine debt and shareholder loans). The senior banks will also take the benefit of first ranking security over the assets of Newco and the assets of the Target group once all whitewash procedures are completed.

Typical features of the senior debt are:

– at least two tranches of debt will be provided – a term loan facility providing the funding to meet the purchase price and acquisition costs, and a revolving credit facility to be used by Newco and Target for working capital purposes in connection with their ongoing business operations. In some cases, the term loan facility may be split into more than one tranche with each tranche attracting different terms and conditions principally as to repayment term and interest rate;

– where ancillary facilities are to be provided (eg, letter of credit facilities, guarantee facilities or overdraft facilities) these will most likely be catered for by way of a separate ancillary facilities letter and made available on an on-demand basis on standard banking terms. Consequently, they do not need to avail themselves of the specific event of default triggers that would be set out in the senior debt documentation, although a prudent borrower may seek to restrict the on-demand nature (by tying the facilities to the defaults in the senior debt documentation) to provide greater certainty of facilities;

– Newco will be the principal borrower under the senior debt documentation since it is Newco that needs the proceeds of the debt to fund the acquisition. There will likely be provision for Target (and possibly one or more key operating companies in the Target group) to accede to the senior debt documentation as borrowers post-acquisition in order to avail themselves of the working capital facility;

– Target and each member of the Target group, post-acquisition and once the whitewash procedure has been completed, will execute guarantees in favour of the debt providers guaranteeing the obligations of the borrowers under the debt documentation as referred to earlier;

– Newco and, post-acquisition once the necessary whitewash procedures have been completed, Target and the members of the Target group will execute security documents pursuant to which they will grant first ranking fixed and floating charges over all their assets and undertaking as security for their obligations under the senior debt documentation. Such security would typically be granted in favour of a financial institution appointed by the debt providers to act as agent and trustee for all the debt providers.

Mezzanine debt

Mezzanine finance is a secondary source of finance for Newco in the context of an acquisition. The advent of mezzanine originally came about to provide purchasers with a source of finance that would bridge the gap between (i) the purchase price, and (ii) the amount of equity funding that the investors are prepared to put in and the amount of senior debt that can be raised in the market.

Mezzanine as a source of funding affords Newco the opportunity to achieve greater leverage in circumstances where debt multiples required to make the acquisition are multiples of the EBITDA (earnings before interest, taxes, depreciation, and amortisation) of the Target group (say 4+) that will not be funded fully by the senior secured debt providers.

Typical features of mezzanine debt are:

– mezzanine debt will comprise only a term loan to be utilised in conjunction with the senior term loan to meet the purchase price and acquisition costs. Working capital facilities and ancillary facilities would not be provided on a mezzanine basis. The terms and conditions of the mezzanine debt will generally mirror the terms of the senior debt with some small differences to reflect the nature of the mezzanine debt as junior finance. The scope of this chapter does not allow these matters to be examined in great detail but the main issues are set out below;

– mezzanine debt will be junior to the senior debt. In other words, it will rank in right of repayment at all times behind the senior debt and will take the benefit of a second ranking interest in the security package taken by the senior debt providers. In addition, the principal amount of the mezzanine debt will typically be repayable in one lump sum (so-called bullet repayment) at the end of the term of the debt, such term of the mezzanine debt being typically six months or a year longer than that of the senior debt;

– mezzanine debt will frequently contain pre-payment penalties in the early years of the loan restricting and disincentivising Newco from repaying the debt prior to its contractual term;

– due to the junior nature of mezzanine debt and consequently the greater risk to the mezzanine debt providers of ensuring repayment in full, mezzanine debt typically commands a higher rate of return than senior debt. This higher rate of return is generally made up of two components:

(i) a higher interest rate on the debt which will usually be split into a rate of cash pay interest (interest that must be paid on a quarterly or six-monthly basis by Newco) and non-cash pay interest (interest that is calculated on the outstanding debt on a quarterly or six-monthly basis but is rolled up and only payable at the end of the term when the principal is repaid). This is referred to as payment in kind (PIK); and

(ii) an equity kicker. This refers to the issue of warrants by Newco to the mezzanine debt providers which will allow them to subscribe for shares in Newco at the time, for example, of a sale or listing of Newco. These warrants are aimed at providing (hopefully) an enhanced performance-related return for the mezzanine providers over and above the cash pay interest and the PIK.

The equity kicker has been seen by private equity houses as a necessary evil of mezzanine finance and has been a requirement of mezzanine finance providers to ensure that they have achieved the necessary internal rates of return that they have required on their investment. Of course, the reason the private equity houses are generally opposed to the equity kicker is because it has the effect of diluting the share capital owned by the private equity houses at the time of the sale or listing of Newco and ultimately reduces their rate of return on their equity investment. This view is not however universal as there can be tangible relationship and other benefits by ensuring that the mezzanine provider has an equity interest in the business.

Recently, the market has seen a growing trend in warrantless mezzanine with the mezzanine providers receiving only cash pay interest and PIK. This has been positive for private equity houses since it avoids the dilution issue and, whilst not necessarily welcomed by the traditional mezzanine houses, the certainty of return on warrantless mezzanine has appealed as an investment to the increasingly prevalent CDO (collateralised debt obligation) and CLO (collateralised loan obligation) funds.

Investor debt

The tertiary source of funding in the basic financing structure is investor debt – that debt which is provided by the equity investors to Newco by way of shareholder loan in addition to the equity contributions that they have made. Investor debt will be unsecured and the investors will usually be prevented from receiving any payments (whether attributable to interest, principal or otherwise) until such time as the senior debt and the mezzanine debt has been repaid in full. In addition, the rights of the investors under the investor debt documentation will typically be assigned by way of security as part of the overall security package granted in favour of the senior debt and mezzanine debt providers.

Intercreditor issues

With three different levels of debt being provided to Newco on different risk/rate of return profiles, one of the key things that must be regulated are the respective rights and rankings of each type of creditor throughout the term of the financing. These matters are dealt with in an intercreditor agreement which will be signed by Newco and all debt (senior, mezzanine and investor) providers.

Intercreditor agreements by their very nature are heavily scrutinised by each set of debt providers and will often be heavily negotiated. The scope of this chapter does not afford the opportunity to explore in great detail the issues that arise in the context of intercreditor agreements, however, a brief summary of the key matters that will be covered in an intercreditor agreement is set out below:

– The rights of the investors in respect of the investor debt will be deeply subordinated to the rights of the senior and mezzanine debt providers. This essentially means they will not be entitled to receive any payments until both the senior and mezzanine debt are repaid in full.

– Mezzanine debt providers will be subject to certain payment restrictions. The previous section of this chapter explained that the terms of the mezzanine debt will usually have the debt principal repayable in one bullet repayment scheduled to occur either six or 12 months following the contractual term of the senior debt. On top of that, the servicing by Newco of periodic cash pay interest obligations on the mezzanine debt will generally be subject to restrictions should an event of default in respect of the senior debt occur. Such payment blockage would typically remain in place until the senior event of default is cured.

– Provisions will be included as to how monies are to be applied in the event that Newco is unable to service its debt and the security package is enforced. In keeping with the intended priorities of senior and mezzanine debt, once all costs of enforcement have been met, the remainder of the proceeds of enforcement will first be applied to meet outstanding obligations in respect of the senior debt and, second, to meet outstanding obligations in respect of the mezzanine debt.

– Certain restrictions will be placed on the ability of the mezzanine lenders to take any of the following actions in circumstances where Newco is in default under the terms of the mezzanine debt:
   (i)   exercising any right to enforce any security;
   (ii) suing or instituting any other creditors' process against Newco;
   (iii) petitioning for or taking any steps to initiate any insolvency, liquidation or dissolution proceedings against Newco; or
   (iv) accelerating and calling for immediate repayment of any of the mezzanine debt or otherwise putting the mezzanine debt due and payable on demand.

These restrictions are generally designed to ensure that the senior debt providers retain as much control over the destiny of Newco in a default scenario as possible since they would typically have the most to lose. Rather than being a strict prohibition, these restrictions are usually coupled with a concept of standstill. Standstill puts a maximum time limit on the inability of the mezzanine debt providers to take action following an event of default by Newco (usually between 90 and 180 days).

This standstill period affords the senior debt providers a period of time in which to work out a strategy to deal with the Newco default but gives the mezzanine lenders comfort that they can ultimately take action at the expiry of the standstill period if a suitable strategy for maintaining the loans or otherwise has not been agreed.

Pricing

The pricing that will attach to the senior and mezzanine debt tranches is very much dependent upon the amount of debt that is being provided, the financial strength of the Target and the Target group, the appetite among the senior and mezzanine bank markets to invest in the particular transaction and the prevailing market and sectoral conditions.

Typically, pricing will be expressed as a certain margin over Libor (in the case of debt denominated in sterling) and Euribor (in the case of debt denominated in euros). These rates reflect the cost to the debt providers of obtaining the necessary funding in the London Interbank Market or, as the case may be, the European Interbank Market in order to make the required finance available to Newco. In addition, the debt providers will look to pass through to Newco the cost of their compliance with the reserve asset requirements imposed upon them by the Financial Services Authority and, where appropriate, the European Central Bank.

As a rough guideline, Newco can probably expect debt providers to require a margin of 2.00 to 3.50 per cent over cost of funds, in the case of senior debt, and a margin of 10.00 to 12.00 per cent over cost of funds in the case of mezzanine debt. These figures are necessarily only a guide and the actual margins that may be negotiated in the context of a particular deal will be dependent upon many factors, including those specified above and the structuring of the particular deal.

Alternative financing structures

In the context of the larger acquisition finance deals that were completed in the late 1990s, there was an increasing trend for funding to be drawn from a combination of senior debt finance and high-yield debt with the high-yield debt being utilised in favour of mezzanine debt. This alternative is only really worth considering in the larger deals since, in general terms, the minimum size of offering worth pursuing in the high-yield bond market is about €150 million.

However, in such larger deals, the utilisation by Newco of the capital markets to raise capital by issuing medium to long-term debt instruments presents an attractive source of financing for the following reasons:

- the term of high-yield bonds usually runs to between eight and 12 years which is substantially longer than the term usually seen in mezzanine finance agreements;
- high-yield bonds generally attract a lower rate of return than mezzanine finance. Whilst the interest payable on high-yield bonds will all be cash pay (ie, no deferred PIK), high-yield bondholders do not require the provision of warrants;
- high-yield bonds typically do not benefit from security over the assets of Target or the members of the Target group; and
- in transactions that utilise a combination of senior debt and high-yield debt it has generally been possible to achieve higher leverage ratios. In other words, Newco has been able to raise higher levels of debt thereby increasing the debt-to-equity ratio required in connection with the acquisition and consequently facilitating higher rates of return for the private equity investors.

Recently, given the downturn experienced in investor confidence in the capital markets, the use of high-yield bonds has been more muted. However, the market will no doubt return and this type of finance will once again feature heavily in acquisition finance structuring.

One of the key problems with using high-yield debt funding in the context of an acquisition is the logistical issue of ensuring that Newco has access to sufficient funding on the day that the acquisition is due to close in accordance with the terms of the sale and purchase agreement (and, in the case of a public-to-private, the requirements as to certain funding, discussed above, are satisfied). Given the nature of raising finance in the capital markets it is unlikely that this certainty will be afforded, consequently bridge financing techniques may be employed.

Bridge debt

Depending upon the confidence of the equity investors in Newco as to their ability to raise funding by way of a high-yield debt offering, the financing structure for an acquisition may take one of two forms:

(i) senior debt funding coupled with mezzanine bridge funding (to be refinanced by way of a high-yield take-out offering); or
(ii) senior bridge funding to be refinanced by way of a high-yield take-out offering.

The use of bridge funding ensures that Newco has total committed bank facilities in an amount sufficient to pay the purchase price for Target and meet all acquisition costs on the date on which it is obliged to do so. However, due to the perceived benefits and the cheaper cost of high-yield debt, the full intention of Newco and its equity backers is to have the bridge funding refinanced very quickly following the completion of the acquisition with high-yield debt.

Given the nature of bridge lending, there are two particular features of this type of finance that should be noted:

(i) Interest rates are typically subject to a ratchet. Essentially, the longer it takes before the high-yield take-out offering is completed and the bridge debt repaid, the higher the rate of interest on the bridge debt becomes. The frequency of the ratchet and the amount of each increase in interest rate will be negotiated on a deal-by-deal basis but they are intended to be painful since the underlying rationale is to incentivise Newco to refinance the bridge debt as soon as possible.

(ii) Cramdown. This term refers to a situation where, if the proposed high-yield take-out has not occurred within a specified period of time, then the bridge lenders can arrange a high-yield offering for Newco on the terms that they feel are required in order to ensure that such offering is successful and require that Newco accept such terms and proceed with such offering.

Structural subordination

One further financial structuring issue that needs to be borne in mind in the context of a transaction where there is a proposed high-yield element is the potential requirement to factor in structural subordination.

In the discussion as to the regulation of priorities between senior debt, mezzanine debt and investor debt it was noted that the relative priorities and rankings of these types of debt were policed and regulated by the terms of an intercreditor agreement between the financing parties and Newco. In other words, they were policed by contract.

Senior lenders are often more tolerant of such contractual subordination arrangements in mezzanine deals since the mezzanine market has historically comprised fewer participants and these are well known to the senior lenders in the United Kingdom and Europe (and whose behaviour in the context of an insolvency situation may be predicted), whereas the high-yield market comprises a diverse, global, anonymous community of bondholders that changes frequently and, to date, has a limited track record with senior lenders in European insolvencies.

Consequently, senior lenders may require any high-yield bond debt to be structurally subordinated to the senior debt funding. Achieving such structural subordination would typically involve:

– interposing a Topco above Newco in each of the structures shown in Exhibits 6.1, 6.2 and 6.3;
– having the senior debt funding and the bridge funding going into Newco;
– having the high-yield note issuance completed by Topco with Topco on lending the proceeds of issuance to Newco (by way of intercompany loan) for Newco to repay the bridge debt; and
– restricting payments under the intercompany loan by way of the intercreditor agreement but making contractual provision for Newco to upstream monies to Topco in the amounts and at the times required to enable Topco to service the debt on the bonds (subject to blockage of such payments following the occurrence of an event of default in respect of the senior debt).

---

[1] Management buy-out (MBO); management buy-in (MBI) and institutional buy-out (IBO).

7

Negotiation tactics and strategy

Rosemary Jackson, partner, Denton Wilde Sapte

Introduction

There are a number of different types of M&A transactions in the United Kingdom and each is likely to require a different type of documentation. The tactics and strategy by which an acquisition can be achieved can also differ significantly. This chapter deals with the variety of types as follows:

– acquisition of privately owned companies (other than by auction);
– acquisition of private companies by auction;
– a business sale;
– acquisition of publicly listed and non-listed companies (including recommended, hostile and contested offers) and substantial holdings of shares in publicly listed companies; and
– privatisations and public/private partnerships.

In the United Kingdom, a 'merger' will invariably be an acquisition by a company of another company or of a business, even though because of the similar sizes of the companies/businesses involved the transaction may be presented as a merger. There is no UK transaction which involves a true combination of the shares of two companies

General

In any sale process, it is important for the seller to be well prepared and in particular to:

– consider the appropriate structure of a sale; ie, is the company or business to be sold;

- what drives the decision (tax is probably the most common) and is there likely to be a disadvantage of either route, both for the seller and a potential buyer?
- consider the appropriate timing for a transaction. This may be impacted by the business and/or accounting cycle of the target; for example, is the sale likely to require the preparation of accounts to determine the consideration? If so, a sale at the financial year end is likely to be most efficient;
- ensure that all material information is available and provided at an early stage. Holding back (whether knowingly or otherwise) material information reduces the credibility of a seller and can create a lack of trust, unless the information is sensitive in the context of the transaction and later delivery is agreed with the potential purchaser (see below).

Good preparation helps a timely sale and avoids wasted costs for both parties.

In contemplating an acquisition, it is important for the purchaser to:

- make its advisers aware of the key reasons for the acquisition, explain any tax considerations and how the transaction will be financed; this will help ensure that financial and legal advisers concentrate, in relation to due diligence and negotiation of the purchase agreement, on the issues which matter to the purchaser and enable them to consider in advance whether any tax clearances and the funding documentation will have an impact on the timing of the transaction;
- understand whether the existing management are incentivised in relation to the transaction; and
- have a well thought-out integration or operational plan for the acquisition post completion.

Acquisition of privately owned companies (other than by auction)

Acquisition process

An acquisition of a privately owned company will normally proceed along the following lines:

Initial negotiations

The parties will enter into negotiations (the seller may be in discussions with one or more potential purchasers at the same time) for the sale and purchase of a company. This process will invariably involve a flow of information and ideally the potential purchaser should have familiarised himself with the key drivers of the target's business and the existing management structure. A general consensus on the key terms, principally the price (or the means by which the price will be calculated) and any conditions precedent to completion (eg, any required shareholder approval) will be reached. At this stage the parties may document the principal terms in a heads of agreement or in an exchange of letters.

Heads of agreement

Heads of agreement or an exchange of letters would not normally be legally binding. However, they can include binding provisions relating to exclusivity and confidentiality (see below). Heads of agreement can be a double-edged sword. They can be useful as a means of providing instructions to lawyers preparing and reviewing the share purchase agreement. On the other hand, they can be an irritant if the lawyers respectively treat them as an initial battle ground. It is therefore important not to start detailed negotiating, for example, *de minimis* thresholds for the warranties, at heads of agreement stage.

Other agreements

If heads of agreement are not signed, the parties may enter into separate independent documents relating to exclusivity and confidentiality.

Exclusivity

The purchaser will be involved in considerable expense in undertaking the due diligence and negotiating process necessary to complete a private sale, including engaging accountants and lawyers. It is common, therefore, to require the seller to grant a period of exclusivity (three months would be a common timescale) during which the seller cannot simultaneously negotiate with and provide information to any other potential purchaser. The sanction for a breach of an exclusivity commitment would be the payment of the purchaser's fees incurred to the date of breach in undertaking the due diligence and other matters preparatory to the proposed purchase. From a seller's point of view, it is reasonable to agree to a period of exclusivity, but it is important to ensure that the time allowed is sufficiently short to keep the pressure on the purchaser and (if possible) to maintain any other competitive interest. It is also reasonable, subject to resources for the seller, to agree to pay a break fee on any breach of the exclusivity obligation but to negotiate a financial cap on liability for breach. There are legal issues to be addressed in relation to break fees payable by a UK company (see below) which are less likely to be a concern in other jurisdictions.

Confidentiality

The sellers will require the purchaser to enter into a non-disclosure agreement under which the purchaser, as the recipient of information about the target, agrees not to disclose or use the information other than for the purposes of the sale process. This non-disclosure agreement should not be controversial, but the seller should ensure that it covers information provided by the seller, the target company and their respective advisers to the purchaser and its advisers, whenever given, including prior to signature of the non-disclosure agreement. It is also important, where the purchaser is a competitor of the target, to consider whether certain information/documentation is so sensitive that it needs to be held back until later in the negotiation process (but there are obviously difficulties with this approach) or needs to have a more restricted circulation.

Due diligence

The parties will then enter into a period of due diligence. This will normally commence with a list of required information about the target produced by the potential purchaser. This information will be provided by the vendor. The vendor may at the same time proffer further information about the target so that the due diligence process and the disclosure exercise (see (a) below) are largely contemporaneous. At the same time the parties' lawyers will negotiate a share sale agreement and a deed of tax covenant which would contain warranties about the target's business and the shares to be acquired and a tax indemnity specific to the transaction. These agreements will normally be drafted by the purchaser's solicitors as the purchaser will want to include substantial protection. The vendor's solicitors will seek to limit the liability of the vendor under the warranties including:

Disclosure of information

By disclosure of documentation/information (including that delivered as part of the due diligence process) which is inconsistent with the agreed warranties (given in the form of a 'disclosure letter').

Financial limits

Financially, usually by agreeing:

- a *de minimis* (ie, a non-material amount) threshold below which a claim will be ignored for all purposes;
- an aggregate *de minimis* threshold before the vendor will have liability for any claims (probably somewhere between 0.5–5 per cent of the consideration); the parties need to agree whether if the aggregate threshold is reached, the vendor pays the total amount of the claims or simply the excess over the aggregate threshold; and
- a maximum liability which is usually the maximum consideration.

Time limits

As to time; notice in relation to normal business warranties must be given on or before, say, two years from completion; as an alternative the cut-off time could be calculated by reference to the production of audited accounts of the target; the notice cut-off date for tax warranties is traditionally six to seven years.

Deed of tax covenant

In a UK private company acquisition, it would be normal for the parties to enter into a deed of tax covenant (essentially an indemnity in respect of tax liabilities of the company being acquired), although there may be circumstances where a separate document would not be sought by the purchaser (for example, in a very small transaction and/or (perhaps) where all tax returns had been agreed with the Revenue). In such a case, the purchaser may feel comfortable to rely on the tax warranties or a short form indemnity contained in the share purchase agreement.

Over the last few years, it has become normal to agree that the principal limitations which apply to the warranties in the share purchase agreement should also apply to the deed of tax covenant (although as a matter of structure, they tend to be repeated in the deed of tax covenant rather than be incorporated by reference from the principal agreement). However, the one exception is disclosure. Disclosure would negate the deed of tax covenant and so should not generally be accepted.

A more consensual approach to negotiation of the warranties and the deed of tax covenant has arisen over the last five to 10 years and it would be normal for the lawyers representing the parties to reach agreement on the bulk of the documents without constant reference to clients and without lengthy meetings at which tedious legal arguments are put forward by each side. This approach is strongly recommended as the parties will then be able to meet to reach agreement on points which are outside the lawyers normal authority to agree.

Financial investors, for example, a venture capital house or similar, would not normally give warranties other than in relation to title to the shares the subject of the sale.

In the event that the sale is to an existing management team which is not seeking outside finance, it would be usual for the vendors to resist the business warranties that would otherwise be expected. However, this position is rare because a management team will generally require third-party finance, and therefore warranties, although sometimes slightly less onerous, will normally be required if the acquisition is to proceed.

Conditional agreements

In a private sale, it may be necessary for completion of an acquisition to be dependent on the satisfaction of certain conditions, for example, shareholder approval if the purchaser is listed or the target is a substantial subsidiary of a listed company; competition clearance; satisfaction of pre-conditions to the financing.

The issue for the parties to negotiate is who takes the risk during the interim period. In practice, this is usually (but not always) the party who is required to satisfy the condition. In the event this is the seller, the seller is likely to be required to repeat the warranties both at exchange of agreements and again at completion, with no ability to limit liability by further disclosure. A half-way house is for the seller to agree that the warranties should be repeated, but with any appropriate disclosure, leaving it up to the purchaser to decide whether he wishes to accept the disclosures and proceed with the transaction as envisaged, to withdraw or to renegotiate the terms as a result of the disclosures.

The position may be complicated where the party is listed and requires both shareholder approval to proceed with the transaction, but is also seeking debt or equity financing to fund the acquisition. The purchaser may argue that the terms of the financing require the vendor to take the risk between exchange and completion and it may be difficult for the vendor to resist this. The half-way house approach may work in this situation.

Acquisition of a private company by an auction transaction

Auction transactions are typically organised by a corporate finance house or investment bank and generally, given the costs involved, are unlikely to be appropriate except in medium and larger transactions and where there is likely to be competition for the target. That said, this is a significant proportion of all acquisitions and auction sales are increasingly common. An auction process is likely to involve potential purchasers in considerable costs and this needs to be weighed up by the vendor. The vendor may lose potential purchasers as a result of the time pressure and costs incurred in an auction process. As a purchaser, it is important to assess the management time involved in participating and the chances of success at the likely price. If a decision to participate is made, then efforts to conduct the process in a timely and organised fashion will be rewarded, but ultimately, unless the vendor has a particular requirement (whether or not made known), it is the price payable at completion which is likely to be the governing factor.

An auction will normally start with the advisers producing an initial information memorandum to gauge interest. This will be followed by the collation of the material documentation relating to the company. The documentation will be indexed and made available to potential purchasers in what is known as a data room. It is very important to the success of the auction that the information included in the data room is comprehensive and that any questions arising from potential purchasers relating to the information are answered promptly.

In addition, the vendor (as opposed to the purchaser in the above situation) will usually prepare a draft share purchase agreement which will be circulated to interested parties.

Interested parties will normally be given a particular period of time in which to undertake their due diligence in the data room following which bids will be submitted together with a mark-up of the purchase agreement. It is important for the adviser operating the data room to ensure that potential bidders are kept apart and are unknown to each other, although in practice rumours are common. However, the ability of a potential bidder to assess the price a competing bidder may be prepared to, or may be able to, pay could affect the price offered (both up and (but more often) down).

The bidding can comprise one or more rounds – depending on the numbers of interested parties. With multiple rounds, the first round, for example, can seek indicative offers, subject to due diligence and the weakest and/or lowest purchasers can be weeded out. The offers can be firmed up at a subsequent round. The precise number of rounds will depend on the individual circumstances of any auction.

When acting for the vendor it is important to ensure a momentum to the auction process. When acting for a potential purchaser it is equally important to comply with the time constraints imposed by the advisers to the seller. If the timescale is not tightly controlled and latitude is allowed, this can suggest to a potential purchaser a lack of competitive bidders.

As the vendor provides the draft sale and purchase agreement, the scope of warranties and other protection offered will be more restricted than if prepared by the purchaser's advisers. However, given the competitive nature of the auction process, when acting for the purchaser it is wise to restrict changes proposed to those which are sensible and meaningful and to resist changes which may improve drafting but bring no commercial benefit to the purchaser.

The vendor may at an agreed stage enter into exclusive negotiations with a preferred purchaser or competing bids may be negotiated until one party is ready to sign. Where a preferred purchaser is appointed, the power tends to swing away from the vendor, particularly if the other candidates are told they have been unsuccessful. Exclusivity is therefore a much more important feature of a sale handled by competitive auction because it gives one bidder a tactical advantage. In the case of a sale which proceeds without an auction, exclusivity gives an element of security, but is rarely so tactically important.

Business sales

In certain cases, it may be appropriate for an acquisition to proceed by way of a business sale, that is, the sale of the underlying business and assets of the company, but not the shares themselves. This is likely to be for tax reasons (usually driven by the seller's tax position) or because the business to be acquired is a division of a company. However, one key advantage over a company sale (and another potential reason for such a structure) is that certain liabilities can be retained by the sellers. This might be important in the event the company has significant contingent liabilities, for example, litigation.

The process will be similar to the acquisition of a private company (in some cases involving the auction process), although the documentation, including the warranties will need to reflect the different nature of the transaction. The following are likely to be the key differences:

- only those assets and liabilities set out in the business sale agreement will be acquired (with the exception of employees (see 'TUPE' below) and environmental liabilities); it is therefore important to ensure that key assets are clearly identified and that any non-transferring liabilities are also specifically excluded;

- in theory, the burden of contracts cannot be transferred without the consent of the other contracting party (technically a 'novation' signed by both parties to the original contract and the purchaser); in practice, it is relatively uncommon to execute a novation to routine contracts (other than those relating to real property), but if a contract is crucial to the business, then a novation should be a pre-condition to completion; if the business has leasehold property which is to be acquired this will invariably require the consent of the landlord and this can have a significant impact on the timing of a transaction; it is important therefore for both parties to seek landlord's consent as soon as possible. The landlord may, for example, seek detailed information about the financial strength of the purchaser and require a rent deposit or bank guarantee from the new tenant; and

- the Transfer of Undertakings (Protection of Employment) Regulations 1981 (TUPE) will apply in relation to the transfer of a business – the result is that the employment of the employees of the business will automatically transfer to the purchaser. If any employees' employment is to be terminated substantially contemporaneously with the sale, such terminations will automatically be unfair unless they can be shown to be for technical, economic or organisational reasons; this is a complex area of law which is outside the scope of this book but can have a considerable impact on the procedure, the terms and the timing of the transaction.

Listed and other public company takeover offers

There are a significant number of small- to medium-sized companies listed on the UK stockmarkets and it is relatively easy to acquire a UK listed company. Listed company takeovers are therefore a real feature of the life of a UK corporate finance or legal practitioner (although in decline over the last couple of years given the market conditions). This is in stark contrast to the position in many other jurisdictions.

The acquisition of such companies is governed by the City Code on Takeovers and Mergers ('the Takeover Code') which is a non-statutory code regulated by the Panel on Takeovers and Mergers ('the Takeover Panel'). The Takeover Panel will consist at any time of professionals with the requisite experience drawn from investment banks, corporate finance houses, accountants and lawyers.

Such an active takeover regime is rare outside the United Kingdom although this may change. There are moves to harmonise the regimes within the European Union (and it is anticipated that the UK position will be used as a model for at least part of any such harmonisation), but as at March 2003, the passing of the European Takeover Directive and its implementation into local law was still some time away.

It is worth noting that the Takeover Code applies not just to the acquisition of UK resident listed companies. With certain limited exceptions, it applies to the acquisition of any UK resident public limited company, whether or not it is listed and to any UK resident private company whose shares were, in the preceding 10 years, listed or otherwise generally made available to the public (it is possible under English company law for a public limited company to be re-registered as a private company and vice versa).

An acquisition of a company to which the Takeover Code applies may be:

–   recommended (ie, recommended by the board of the target company to its shareholders);
–   hostile (ie, not recommended by the board of the target company to its shareholders); or
–   contested, (ie, there are competing offers, one can be recommended or both can be hostile).

The decision of the board on whether or not to recommend an offer is likely to depend on the price the third party is prepared to offer, but any offer price will almost invariably be at a premium to the then market price.

The process of such a transaction will be largely driven by the Takeover Code which requires any offer (which is technically made to the shareholders of the target) to be notified to the board of the target. The board of the target is required to make the terms of the offer (and their advice on the offer) known to their shareholders. All shareholders must be treated equally.

There is limited scope for a potential bidder to undertake due diligence on the target and negotiate a deal even in a recommended offer. This is because the board will be reluctant to provide confidential information to one bidder in case a further bidder emerges to whom they will then be required to provide the same information. It is more likely that the offer will be made on the basis of documentation which is publicly available. There will be no due diligence material provided in a hostile offer. In addition, because there will be a large number of shareholders who have no day-to-day involvement with the business of the company, the transaction does not proceed by way of a share sale agreement with warranties.

The terms of the offer will be little more than the price for the shares. Whilst the bidder may include conditions in the offer, these are subject to the approval of the Takeover Panel who permit relatively little latitude. The following are the most common permitted conditions attaching to a public offer:

- acceptances being received in respect of (usually) 90 per cent or more of the shares in the target (90 per cent is the threshold required to permit the purchaser to operate the compulsory purchase provisions of company legislation necessary to ultimately purchase 100 per cent); however, a level above 50 per cent is generally permitted;
- there being no referral to the competition authorities;
- there being no material adverse change in the business or financial position of the target; and
- if necessary, the approval of the shareholders of the bidder.

The limited ability of an offeror to utilise the material adverse change condition as a reason to revoke an offer was highlighted following the contested offer made in 2001 by WPP Group plc for Tempus Group plc. A lower offer from the French company Havas was trumped by WPP. Following the terrorist attacks on September 11, WPP itself made a purchase in the market and, together with acceptances, the offer became unconditional as to acceptances (ie, the acceptance condition referred to above was satisfied). However, after further consideration of the financial position of Tempus, WPP sought to revoke their offer on the material adverse change ground, citing in particular the impact of the terrorist attacks in the United States; the proposed revocation was rejected, on appeal, to the full Takeover Panel.

A key strategic decision for an offeror is whether to purchase shares in the target before making the offer (the dawn raid) or at any time afterwards. This has become less common over the past decade. The purchase of shares in the target may affect the terms of any offer which would be permitted under the Takeover Code (eg, price and whether the offer must include a cash alternative). In addition, the prohibitions on insider dealing (Criminal Justice Act 1993) and market abuse (Financial and Markets Act 2000) and requirement for disclosure need to be taken into account.

Another key decision for the offeror will be what, if any, irrevocable commitments to accept the offer can be obtained from shareholders of the target company prior to making the offer.

An adviser to the board of an offeree company on a contested bid will need to judge the timing of any announcements carefully and to understand the scope of any permitted defensive action. This is relatively restricted under the Takeover Code and English company law. For example, any issue of shares or grant of options over shares or disposal of assets of the offeree (other than in the normal course of business), other than pursuant to a pre-existing contract, during an offer period or when an offer is expected, will require shareholder approval and/or the consent of the Takeover Panel.

The payment of an interim dividend (other than in the normal dividend cycle of the company) and the amendment of directors service agreements (particularly the inclusion of a poison pill payment) are also likely to be regarded as prohibited frustrating action.

Public to private

A public-to-private transaction is the acquisition of a listed company, usually by a management team funded by a private equity house with the result that the company ceases to be listed (and becomes a subsidiary of a private limited company). These transactions have been relatively common over the last few years as a result of the poor stock market conditions and the growth of the UK private equity market. The procedure will be substantially the same as set out above and the Takeover Code will apply to the transaction. However, the institutional investors in the target company will want to be satisfied that the price being offered properly reflects the value of the company as the management, being the offeror, will have a vested interest in maintaining an offer price which is as low as possible. The result is that such an offer is unlikely to proceed without substantial testing of the water with key institutional shareholders. In practice, the directors of the target company who will form the MBO team will not take part in the discussions on whether or not the board should recommend the offer to shareholders. This advice will be dealt with by the independent directors who will, in practice, represent the target company and the interests of its shareholders.

Break fees in a takeover offer

It became reasonably common practice in the large recommended takeovers involving a listed US company, particularly in the heady days of 1998–99 and early 2000 for the offeror to negotiate a break fee to cover their costs in the event that, notwithstanding the recommendation, the target was the subject of a higher offer which was accepted. These are now more common to UK transactions, although there are several legal issues involved, including whether such a payment could be approved by the directors (ie, is it in the best interests of the company), financial assistance where the payment is by the target company and the requirements of the Takeover Code (which permits break fees up to 1 per cent of the purchase price). Further consideration of break fees are outside the scope of this chapter.

Acquisition of significant stakes in publicly listed companies

A tranche of shares in a publicly listed company may be acquired from one or more shareholders, in addition to in the market. It is not uncommon for large sales to be placed by institutions and in such a case a detailed share sale agreement is unlikely to be entered into. No warranties, except as to title, would be expected to be given by the vendor.

The Takeover Code contains certain restrictions where the person is buying shares or rights over shares representing 10 per cent or more of the voting rights which when aggregated with any shares or rights over the shares already held would carry 15 per cent or more but less than 30 per cent of the voting rights of a publicly listed company.

The Takeover Code considers the acquisition of 30 per cent or more of a listed company as giving *de facto* control. Accordingly, when a person (or series of connected persons) acquires more than 30 per cent of a publicly listed company, the Takeover Code (Rule 9) requires the purchaser to make an offer for all the shares in the company. Hence strategic stakes in listed companies tend to be of less than 30 per cent.

Privatisations

A privatisation is a disposal by a government or similar body of a business formerly run by a public body reporting to a government department. The benefit of profits or (more likely) the burden of funding losses of the business would, prior to privatisation, have been the responsibility of the government.

Most privatisations in the United Kingdom had until recently proceeded by way of trade sale or flotation.

The tasks for legal and financial advisers to the government is to package the business for a successful sale and this is likely to involve all or any of the following:

Hire-down of assets

The transfer of the assets and liabilities intended to form the business following privatisation into a new company which will be suitable for sale or listing ('Newco').

Creation of legislation

The creation of the necessary law and/or regulation to privatise the business, including in the case of the majority of privatisations in the United Kingdom the establishment of the detailed regulatory environment in which Newco must operate, which may require the creation of a separate regulatory authority to oversee compliance with the regulatory framework (eg, OFWAT in relation to the water privatisations, OFGEM (formerly OFGAS) in relation to the privatisations of the gas industry).

Retention of rights

Negotiating with those acting for Newco, the retention of such rights as are appropriate for the government to retain in relation to Newco; for example, in many privatisations (including the privatisation of British Petroleum plc (BP) and British Airports Authority, the government considered the importance of these businesses sufficiently important to the national interest to retain a 'golden share'; golden shares vest in the government certain rights, most commonly the right to consent to a third-party acquisition of a strategic stake in the privatised company; golden shares have since been the subject of proceedings by the European Commission on the basis that they are inconsistent with EC regulations on free movement of capital and are less likely to be relevant in the public/private partnership structure which tends to be favoured currently.

In a trade sale, a key issue for the parties will be the employees (as the private sector would expect to reduce headcount either before, after or as part of the privatisation) and any commitments the government is prepared to give regarding regulatory intervention and ongoing business (if the government has been a key client). In both a trade sale and a flotation, a key issue is the price and this will be established in conjunction with an investment bank. This can be a no-win for all parties. Pitch the price too high and in a flotation the offer becomes undersubscribed and is regarded as a failure. If, however, the offer is oversubscribed and/or the company is the subject of a bid shortly after flotation or the initial trade sale, there will be accusations of selling the nation's assets too cheaply.

There have been relatively few full privatisations since Railtrack plc, the current focus being on public–private partnerships (eg, the National Air Traffic Services Limited (NATS) (the air traffic control operator) which is owned by a combination of the private sector (principally airlines and banks), employees and the government (with a 49 per cent minority stake).

However, NATS has experienced financial difficulties following September 11, and the recent events involving Railtrack and British Energy plc privatised in 1996 demonstrate that the government will rarely be able to ignore events involving companies which were formerly public bodies where the company is key to the infrastructure or national security or where there are significant safety issues such that public confidence must be maintained. This may have an impact on the willingness of the private sector to invest in future public/private partnerships and flotations and hence the tactical and strategic considerations of any such transactions.

8
Financial and commercial due diligence issues

Hugh Reynolds, PricewaterhouseCoopers Transaction Services

UK acquisitions – the wider context

UK businesses have always had an international outlook because the United Kingdom's economic and political history has been significantly influenced by its active engagement in international trade. Consequently, although the remit of this book is successful acquisitions in the United Kingdom it will be rare in practice for any sizeable UK acquisition target not to have international operations. A narrow focus on UK-centric commercial, financial and accounting issues is not a recipe for a successful acquisition, particularly as the underlying currents are propelling businesses towards greater exposure to pan-European and global forces. Increasingly, businesses operate in global markets and even if a UK business's customer base is purely domestic it will not be isolated from the impact of global economic conditions. From a legal perspective, discussed elsewhere in this book, European law is progressively having more impact on the operations of UK businesses, particularly as regards labour and competition issues. Capital markets are now *de facto* global and regulation has increased in scope accordingly as evidenced by the separate trends towards the establishment of pan-European listing and merger directives and the moves by the Securities and Exchange Commission (SEC) to extend its control beyond the boundaries of the United States. Even in the rarefied world of financial accounting, the specific nuances of UK GAAP are becoming progressively less important against the background of increased convergence of accounting standards and the specific requirement for EU-listed companies to adopt International Accounting Standards (IAS) by 2005. Accordingly, it can be concluded that one of the key guidelines for making a successful acquisition in the United Kingdom is to ensure that the target evaluation is not purely focused on UK-specific issues.

The United Kingdom is the dominant M&A market in Europe representing (in 2000/2001) approximately one-third of total deals by value – a long way ahead of Germany and France, the second and third placed countries on this measure. This leading position in part reflects the relatively benign environment in the United Kingdom as to execution risk – that is, once a particular transaction has been identified in principle, the chances of actually closing the deal. This relative advantage stems from a combination of factors which have helped to define corporate culture in the United Kingdom, of which the most important are:

– the general acceptance of the primacy of shareholder value and the recognition of M&A as a key tool for achieving that;

– the accepted view that management should be held accountable for the stewardship of a company's affairs and, related to this, that – in the case of public companies – they should be required to explain their actions and decisions and be prepared to answer questions from shareholders, the wider investment community and the press on their record;

– the overriding principle that financial information should be prepared on a 'true and fair' basis – that is, reflecting substance rather than prescriptive rules – and that it should be publicly available; and

– the general availability of comprehensive information (not just financial) on individual industries and sectors and informed analysis and commentary thereon.

In addition to this relatively benign background for assessing M&A opportunities there is the fundamental English legal principle of 'caveat emptor' which places the risk in a commercial transaction squarely on the shoulders of the buyer. Due diligence is the generic term for the means by which an acquirer minimises, to his satisfaction (ie, ultimately through the sale and purchase agreement), the level of transaction and execution risk in a deal. The circumstances outlined above create, in the United Kingdom, both the opportunity and the necessity to carry out effective due diligence prior to making an acquisition. Against this background it is possible to conclude that if successful due diligence cannot be carried out in the United Kingdom then where can it be?

The role of due diligence

Ultimately, minimising the transaction and execution risk on any acquisition, not just in the United Kingdom, depends upon achieving four interrelated objectives:

– satisfactory due diligence;

– an unambiguous sale and purchase agreement with appropriate contractual protection;

– a robust financing structure; and

– timely and effective post-acquisition integration.

As well as aiming to confirm the valuation assumptions on which the price is based, due diligence is the means by which an acquirer identifies both the risks in the proposed transaction against which, to the extent possible, he will seek to protect himself via the sale and purchase agreement and the financing structure, and also the opportunities, which will form the basis of the post-acquisition integration plan. Legal issues, financing structures (including tax structuring) and post-merger integration are the subjects of other chapters in this book but, to the extent it has a direct bearing on the other three objectives, effective due diligence is key to maximising the chances of making an acquisition a success. This is true whether an acquisition is in the United Kingdom or elsewhere, but the relative maturity of M&A in the United Kingdom and the 'caveat emptor' legal principle have resulted in the United Kingdom being relatively advanced in the practice of due diligence.

As it is how due diligence is conducted that ultimately determines how effective it is, this chapter will principally look at the issues surrounding the effective practice of due diligence in the United Kingdom. It will address commercial and financial due diligence and the key theme of integrating these two activities to obtain maximum benefit. (Although an integral part of any due diligence review, tax issues will not be addressed here as they are the subject of a separate chapter.) As M&A activity levels increase in continental Europe and particularly as financial (ie, private equity) buyers become increasingly important participators in that process, these issues are fast becoming just as relevant to the rest of Europe as to the United Kingdom.

Scope and access – the two key due diligence issues

Ask any experienced due diligence practitioner and he or she will tell you that the two fundamental enabling issues to be addressed before due diligence can be successfully carried out are the scope of the review and access to the target, its management and the commercial and financial information. It is obvious but nevertheless important to point out that the setting of the scope is the decision of the acquirer whilst, in contrast, the question of access remains under the control of the vendor. The issues surrounding each tend, therefore, to be qualitatively different – even though some of the means of resolving the issues (eg, the importance of industry expertise) are common – and therefore it makes sense to deal with the two separately.

Scope – the cost/benefit equation

Whilst the due diligence expert and his client will usually agree on the importance of being allowed proper access to the target, they may hold widely different views on the appropriate scope of the commercial and financial review. Too often this difference of view arises from a narrow focus on cost rather than the much more important criterion of value added. A key determining factor of whether or not to proceed with an acquisition is whether it creates or destroys shareholder value; due diligence should be an effective means of helping the client to reach that conclusion and it therefore needs to be a value added activity in its own right. In the right hands, a relatively broad scope – both in terms of the timescale of involvement and the coverage/depth of the review – can facilitate a significant value added contribution to a successful acquisition as compared with the relatively minor incremental cost compared with a restricted scope.

In certain instances, some of the scope of the due diligence review may be determined by third parties or regulations and not by the client directly, including:

- in a leveraged acquisition involving a financial buyer, where the lending bank will want to be directly consulted on the scope of the due diligence as it will expect to be able to (contractually) rely on it as a basis for its lending decision and subsequent syndication;
- in a public company takeover involving the issue of shares where, for example, a statement as to working capital adequacy is required or a profit forecast is given or a statement of merger benefits is made – all of which need to be reviewed by reporting accountants;
- where the structuring of the acquisition – usually in a leveraged situation – constitutes financial assistance for the purchase of a company's own shares under UK Companies Act legislation and, in order for the assistance to be given clearance (a whitewash, as it is colloquially termed), requires a statutory declaration by the directors as to the ability of the company to pay its debts as they fall due, which in turn needs to be reported on by the auditors.

In the past, financial due diligence was viewed largely as an isolated activity within the overall context of the evaluation of the deal and was restricted to a confirmatory role – that is, confirming, as far as possible, that the historical numbers as presented by the vendor were free from material misstatement. Increasingly, however, demand-pull and supply-push factors have widened the remit of financial due diligence and more closely integrated it with the overall commercial evaluation of the acquisition opportunity – demand-pull in the sense that clients, led by financial buyers and their lenders, have increasingly viewed the financial due diligence as core to the overall deal evaluation and required an enhanced service accordingly, and supply-push in the sense that the major accountancy firms with both the specialist resource at their disposal and their wide experience of both industry sectors and M&A transactions believe they can offer a more value added service and have developed their capabilities and marketing propositions accordingly. The key outcome of this has been the re-balancing of financial due diligence away from an historical confirmatory activity to the much more complex evaluation of a business's prospects. This is now much more than the traditional confirmation that forecast financial numbers have mechanistically been put together correctly on the basis of some stated assumptions. To be done effectively, this evaluation of prospects requires a much closer integration of the financial due diligence with the overall commercial due diligence and, of necessity, the use of experts with a specialist knowledge of the industry sector in which the target operates and the competitive forces bearing upon it; this is discussed further below.

Particularly in the wake of recent financial scandals such as Enron, Worldcom and so on, where the basic fault lay with the underlying financial accounting, it may be argued that now more emphasis needs to be given to the traditional basic financial due diligence. However, with the increasing complexity of commercial transactions this reinforces rather than diminishes the need for the use of experts with deep industry knowledge of the commercial activities of the target and sector expertise in best practice accounting for those transactions. Together, the requirements of a value added approach and the need for industry sector expertise on deals has de-commoditised financial due diligence and the cost has risen accordingly; as with all things, you get what you pay for.

> Although industry knowledge is, we would argue, a pre-requisite for successful due diligence, there are certain sectors where deep expertise of specific industry matters is absolutely fundamental. For instance, in the banking sector, a thorough understanding of derivatives and the way in which they should be accounted for is essential. Similarly, in the utilities sector, an underlying knowledge of regulatory (eg, price control) mechanisms is essential to understand key trends in reported revenues.

The importance of focus

Timetable, cost or other factors (eg, the familiarity of the acquirer with the target) will determine whether a broad or restricted scope is chosen for the commercial and financial due diligence but the key determinant of whether it will be value added in the context of the acquirer's assessment of the opportunity is focus. Even if these factors determine a limited review approach it is vitally important that the review should target those areas which have a material bearing on the acquirer's assessment of value.

In this context, it is important that the financial and commercial due diligence advisers should be involved at an early stage of the proposed transaction, preferably before a formal bid is submitted, to be able to impart any specific knowledge they may already have on the target and/or its sector and to provide their views as to the key risk areas that will need to be addressed in the due diligence review which will usually take place once the bid is accepted. They can provide valuable advice to the acquirer on issues that may affect the price or conditionality of the offer as well as setting a framework for the full due diligence that will need to be carried out (and, by implication, the essential information that the vendor will need to provide) to get from acceptance of the offer to deal completion.

Given the relatively short timetable that usually exists between identification of an acquisition opportunity and submission of an offer – at least in the increasingly prevalent scenario of managed auctions – neither the purchaser nor his advisers can afford the luxury of an extended learning curve. Accordingly, due diligence advisers should be selected on three core criteria; these are (i) their expertise in the particular industry sector (ii) their familiarity with/ability to execute the type of transaction envisaged and (iii) their credibility with other influential parties involved in the transaction (particularly lending banks if they will have access to the reports) – which itself is usually a function of the first two criteria.

Expert advice in these early stages of a transaction can provide initial validation for the value-creation assumptions underlying the proposed bid and also identify the necessary conditionality that should accompany the offer. It can make the difference between a successful and an unsuccessful bid in terms of the credibility it gives to the offer thereby enhancing, in the eyes of the vendor, the purchaser's intention and ability to execute the transaction in as smooth and efficient a fashion as possible. Alternatively, expert advice at the beginning may well identify vulnerabilities in the business case which may well lead to the proposed offer being significantly modified or even abandoned – not an ideal outcome but infinitely preferable to finding these out a long way down the road at significant cost both in terms of money and the time involvement of senior client personnel.

Integrated due diligence

Too often in the past the various due diligence workstreams – commercial, financial, postmerger planning, legal, tax, human resources and so on – have been compartmentalised with each workstream operating largely in isolation with little interaction between them. It is often left to the client to identify the cross-over implications both for valuation purposes and also in terms of negotiating the sale and purchase agreement. Given the tight deadlines within which M&A transactions run and the often frenetic pace with which they develop up to the point of signing the deal, this type of approach is fraught with risk both in terms of the knock-on implications of one team's findings not being fully understood or evaluated by others, and in terms of key areas falling into the gaps between one team's scope and another's. In order to ensure that both the maximum benefit is obtained from the due diligence – in terms of identifying and validating value-creation opportunities – and also that all risk areas are satisfactorily covered and addressed, a more integrated approach is required.

The key areas where an integrated approach is fundamental to the overall effectiveness of the review are as follows:

– review of historical and prospective financial information;
– commercial and financial due diligence;
– financial due diligence and synergies/cost savings evaluation;
– financial due diligence and human resources (principally pensions/benefits) due diligence;
– financial due diligence and the structuring of the transaction; and
– commercial/financial due diligence and the sale and purchase agreement.

The first of these areas – review of historical and prospective financial information – is different in nature to the other five in that whereas in the latter the point concerns the integration of the work of two teams (perhaps from different firms), the former is concerned with the need to ensure that a bridge is constructed between two of the main areas of review undertaken in the financial due diligence – namely the past/current results and the future business plan. In the absence of other compelling factors, how a business has performed in the recent past is still the best indication, *prima facie*, of how it is likely to perform in the short to medium term going forward. For this bridge to be constructed effectively, the financial due diligence must, in addition to corroborating the accounting basis on which the historical financials have been stated, identify and conclude on the following:

– what have been the key commercial drivers of the target's past and current performance?
– what are the underlying assumptions concerning these key commercial drivers going forward and how realistic are these?

and more problematic:

– what new commercial forces are likely to impact on the business in the future?
– how robust is the business plan in terms of the strategy it proposes for meeting the commercial challenges going forward?

In the United Kingdom, the major accounting firms can (and are expected to) opine on the commercial drivers of a business's performance and its prospects, as well as providing comfort on the underlying financial accounting. They tend to have specialist M&A (Transaction Services) departments experienced in providing this value added service. However, notwithstanding individual capabilities, it can only be done properly if the review is project managed in such a way that the findings and conclusions of the financial and commercial due diligence are cross-checked against one another to ensure a consistent and mutually supportive view of prospects, which is the second area of integration referred to above.

In practice, this means that the commercial due diligence team and the financial due diligence teams should work closely with one another – with the complementary expertise of each combining to provide a fully rounded view of the target to the client. In cases where a financial buyer is the principal this often means an accountancy firm on the financial due diligence side working alongside a strategy consultancy undertaking the commercial due diligence. The specialist skills of each tend to be complementary with the sector operational and financial expertise of the former aligning with the broader market and strategic capability of the latter. However, prompted by the perceptible benefits of getting ever-closer integration of the two activities, one current trend is for the specialist M&A departments in the major accountancy firms to recruit experts with a strategic consulting background to complement their own industry skills in order to provide clients with a one-stop shop for commercial and financial due diligence.

In the case of a corporate acquirer, where often the commercial due diligence is conducted in-house, integration is achieved in practice by close liaison – sometimes joint working – between the client teams and the external adviser throughout the course of the assignment. However, even in cases where a corporate acquirer has detailed knowledge of the target's sector and operations, there are often benefits in commissioning an external commercial review as well – if only to benchmark the client teams' assessment of the prevailing market trends and the target's competitive position against externally sourced information. For example, an external consultancy may be able to conduct open interviews with the target's competitors and customers – a procedure which may not be possible for the corporate to undertake on its own behalf.

As noted above, a key area of value-creation opportunity in most acquisitions is the prospect of synergies and/or cost savings when the target business is either integrated with the existing business of the acquirer or restructured to deliver operating efficiencies, better working capital management, capital expenditure savings and so on. There may well be a separate team charged with assessing the post-acquisition opportunity and planning the implementation but here again it is important that the post-deal team should work closely with the financial and commercial due diligence teams during the pre-deal phase. Some of the most important areas where the due diligence and post-deal teams can liaise to good effect are:

– benchmarking projected efficiency improvements against other businesses in the sector;
– validating projected cost savings against actual costs being incurred by the target business and identifying the costs of/impediments to achieving these;
– identifying potential revenue and/or working capital synergies from combining customer and/or product portfolios or, conversely, forming contingency plans for dealing with potential dis-synergies (eg, customer fall-out where one business services customers that are in direct competition with customers of the other); and

–   quantifying potential purchasing synergies from adopting the best practices in each business and maximising purchasing leverage.

Given that the quantification of the potential benefits will have a direct impact on the valuation the acquirer ascribes to the target, it is important that the interaction of the due diligence and post-deal teams should take place before completion of the deal rather than after, preferably again by way of the teams working alongside each other (in the case of a financial buyer, the due diligence adviser working with the prospective management team and in the case of a corporate, the due diligence adviser working in conjunction with the client's integration team). As has occurred with the progressive integration of the financial and commercial due diligence activities, another recent trend has been for the M&A departments of the major accountancy firms to recruit experienced personnel from industry who have backgrounds in managing operational change and business integration to provide an enhanced service. The combination of financial and operational expertise enables them to offer clients practical help in identifying, quantifying, planning and even – as discussed below – implementing post-acquisition business integration and restructuring opportunities.

The impact of UK accounting standards aimed at outlawing abuses of acquisition accounting in the past (eg, prohibiting the creation of big bath provisions on acquisition which could later be released to profit) has increased the focus on acquisitions having to deliver real economic benefits – through cost savings, synergies and so on – as opposed to cosmetic earnings enhancement through financial engineering and/or accounting licence. It is clear from the lack of investor support for and consequent dismantlement of the financially driven conglomerates created in the 1980s and early 1990s that their acquisition activities did not create long-term shareholder value. Once one acquisition had been concluded the emphasis was on finding the next one to generate continued reported earnings growth. Today, the emphasis is on core activities and the ability of management teams to deliver real economic value from an acquisition – post-deal integration and/or restructuring are key to this.

The other three areas noted above where an acquirer can minimise the deal execution risk by ensuring proper integration of these workstreams with the financial and commercial due diligence are: human resource due diligence (principally pensions and benefits), structuring and the sale and purchase agreement. Pensions and benefits, particularly in the context of the financial implications of recent stock market performance on funded defined benefit schemes (still common among UK corporates notwithstanding recent trends towards closing these schemes to new entrants in favour of defined contribution schemes), is an increasingly important area of due diligence given the significant liabilities involved. As well as the key matter of ascertaining underlying liabilities and funding position, there will often be ongoing funding implications (ie, increased employer contribution rates) which clearly have to be taken into account when preparing any financial projections. Consequently, to minimise the risk of oversight, in many cases the pensions and benefits due diligence is also undertaken by the relevant specialist departments of the firms carrying out the financial due diligence.

The same argument can be applied to taxation due diligence and structuring (discussed elsewhere in this book). Ensuring that all potential liabilities and their financing implications are properly reflected in the financial projections model is particularly important in leveraged acquisitions where the financial projections form the basis for setting banking covenants. It is now common for the providers of senior bank debt and mezzanine finance to be given access to (and be entitled to place reliance on) the financial and other due diligence commissioned by the acquirer. One of the key areas these lenders will wish to see reviewed in the financial due diligence is an assessment of the deal financing – specifically, they will want the reporting accountants to give comfort on the ability of the acquired entity to manage within proposed facility headroom and to comply with debt repayment obligations and banking covenants. Again, the major accounting firms are used to providing this comfort but in order to do this, not least for their own risk management purposes, they will need to have a full understanding of (i) the commercial risks inherent in the business plan (ii) issues raised in other areas of due diligence (as well as pensions and benefits, insurance and environmental are two other key risk areas) and (iii) the financial and tax implications of the proposed deal structure. Inevitably, this provides further impetus to the trend towards greater integration of the various deal execution workstreams and, increasingly, the tendency for one adviser – usually the major accounting firm carrying out the financial due diligence – to provide some, most or even all of the other due diligence services – except legal, as discussed below – required by the acquirer to execute the deal.

It is unlikely, however, at least in the near future, that the major accounting firms will also act as legal advisers to an acquirer on a large transaction as well as provide other due diligence services (although in most cases they do have in-house legal firms forming part of their practices who could provide this service). However, the argument for closer integration of the financial and legal due diligence remains valid. In the past, once the financial due diligence had been completed, usually in advance of the detailed contractual negotiations, the active involvement of the financial due diligence team ceased. Again, this risks the situation of key issues in the financial (and other) due diligence not being picked up and satisfactorily addressed in the contractual negotiations. Nowadays, therefore, it is common for the financial due diligence adviser to be closely consulted on the relevant provisions of the sale and purchase agreement – purchase price adjustment mechanisms, completion accounts processes, pension provisions, warranties and indemnities and so on. The goal of this is not aggrandisement of the role of the financial due diligence adviser for its own sake. It makes practical sense as the most effective way of ensuring that the financial, commercial and other issues identified during the course of the due diligence review as having a material impact on value to the acquirer are satisfactorily addressed in the contract which, after all, is the only really effective means by which an acquirer protects and secures his own interest in executing the transaction.

Value added across the deal continuum

As argued above, it makes sense for the financial and commercial due diligence advisers to be involved at an early stage of the bid process. Similarly, from a value added perspective, it is also important – as long as that adviser possesses the appropriate skill-sets and resources – to be involved in post-deal completion in order to assist the acquirer to realise the benefits which formed part of the valuation ascribed to the target. As noted above, two of the areas which will undoubtedly be looked at closely in the pre-bid stage are the related ones of cost-savings/synergies and post-acquisition integration – the former because it is often the key reason justifying any premium to be paid to acquire the target, and the latter because careful planning here will in large part determine whether the identified cost savings and synergies are realised. However, although identifying and planning for these is a critical step in preparing a bid, in practice the real work starts when the deal has been closed and the time has come for delivering. Here again, the role of the due diligence adviser is crucial. Detailed knowledge of the target gained from the due diligence exercise allied to his own sector knowledge puts the due diligence adviser in an ideal position to help his client extract the value opportunities identified both before and during the bid. Given that a key factor in determining the success of post-deal integration and/or restructuring is the need to act fast, there is a greater chance of being able to do this if use is made of those people who already have detailed knowledge of the target and its operations. As noted above, the major accounting firms now tend to have specialist personnel within their M&A departments who have backgrounds in industry and experience of delivering these in practice – they are therefore well-qualified to provide this service. Increasingly, the involvement of the due diligence adviser tends to extend beyond the financial close of a transaction.

In summary, therefore, a value added due diligence service pre-supposes the adviser being closely involved with a transaction throughout its lifecycle both before a bid is submitted and after it has closed – not just for a discrete period in the middle leading up to the signing of the sale and purchase agreement which has been the traditional model.

Access – getting more difficult

As mentioned earlier, apart from setting an appropriate scope for the due diligence, the other key determinant of how successful it is going to be in meeting the objectives of the acquirer is the level of access granted by the vendor. In some situations, for example a hostile bid for a UK publicly-quoted company, there may well be no access at all to commercial and financial information on the target other than that already in the public domain – for example, annual and interim reports, presentations to analysts, brokers research and so on. Even in public bid situations where the approach is friendly, the target may well be wary of providing the acquirer with commercially or financially sensitive information as, under Rule 20 of The City Code on Takeovers and Mergers (the 'Takeover Code'): 'Any information … given to one offeror or potential offeror must, on request, be given equally and promptly to another offeror or bona fide potential offeror even if that other offeror is less welcome'. A bidder for a public company may, therefore, find himself in the difficult situation of having relatively little information with which to corroborate commercial and financial assumptions underpinning his bid and at the same time bound by the rules of the Takeover Code which require that all conditions attaching to an offer must be identified at the earliest stage – under Rule 2.5, when a firm intention to make an offer is announced. As this rule also requires the acquirer's financial adviser to confirm that resources are available to the offeror to finance full acceptance, it follows that in the case of a cash offer being funded other than out of the acquirer's internal cash reserves (the usual situation for so-called public to private transactions) the acquirer's bankers and other providers of finance must also have given a firm 'subject to' (ie, the conditions set out in the offer) approval to the offer.

In cases where two listed companies have agreed to merge, a key reason or justification for the merger may be expected merger benefits – for example, cost savings and/or synergies. Where a quantified reference is made to this then Rule 19.1 of the Takeover Code requires it to be reported on by the financial adviser and accountants. This may cause problems where, in order to do this, either or both parties have to disclose sensitive information about their businesses to the other side and thereby run the risk of another (hostile) party requesting that same information under Rule 20. One way round this has been for companies in this position (ie, having agreed to merge) to disclose information to the other side's reporting accountants on the strict proviso that it is not in turn disclosed to their principal. The accountants can then review the statement of merger benefits and give their opinion without the principals being deemed to have disclosed that information to each other and hence a hostile third party would not be able to demand it under Rule 20.

In these situations, undertaking no access due diligence has become a familiar concept in the United Kingdom. The desired output of the exercise is the same – corroboration, as far as possible, of the principal assumptions on which the offer is based to the extent sufficient to allow equity and debt providers to be able to place reliance on it for the purposes of financing the acquisition. Inevitably, in the absence of proprietary information, some of the analyses and conclusions may be more circumspect. However, given the relatively open corporate culture in the United Kingdom concerning the provision and basis of preparation of financial information (the true and fair basis referred to earlier) lack of access should not, of itself, be an insurmountable problem unless the potential acquirer suspects a fundamental problem which has not yet been adequately disclosed by the target nor identified by independent commentators. However, in this context it should be noted that a UK publicly-quoted company has a continuing obligation (under paragraphs 9.1 and 9.2 of the Listing Rules issued by the Financial Services Authority) to disclose without delay:

a) any major new developments in its sphere of activity which are not public knowledge which, by their impact on the business or its financial position, could lead to a substantial movement in the price of its listed securities; and

b) all relevant information that is not public knowledge concerning a change in financial position, performance or prospects which, if made public, could lead to a substantial movement in the price of its listed securities.

To a certain extent, therefore, this provides some comfort to acquirers contemplating public offers that any really bad news should have been publicly disclosed.

Vital to the success of no access due diligence are the same qualities required of the diligence advisers generally – as noted earlier, industry expertise, experience/resources and credibility – they just become even more important in a situation where there is an inherently higher level of risk in the transaction, as is the case with public bids. Industry expertise is particularly important as a no access assignment places an obligation on the due diligence adviser to identify up-front the key risk areas and be able to interpret the limited commercial and financial information available on the target in such a way as to conclude effectively on these. Because the situation does not allow the adviser to request the relevant specific information from the target, there is usually a greater need for large resources on these assignments in order to carry out research of alternative sources from which to extract and/or piece together the necessary data. The high profile nature of most public company bids increases an already high level of risk – not least to reputations – and consequently it is imperative that the best qualified advisers are used on these transactions. They are likely to cost accordingly.

Vendor due diligence – a good compromise

Although they tend, by their nature, to get the lion's share of publicity, public company acquisitions comprise only a relatively small minority of the total number and value of UK

M&A transactions in any one year. By far the majority of M&A transactions are private – where the conduct of the sale process is entirely at the discretion of the vendor.

The prevailing trend in recent years, where the sale of a business or activity is likely to generate some degree of competing interest, is for such disposals to be handled by an investment bank or corporate finance adviser in the form of a managed auction process. This usually follows the following course:

– notification of proposed sale to selected parties inviting expressions of interest;
– interested parties provided with an information memorandum – having previously signed some form of confidentiality agreement – and requested to submit indicative bids;
– shortlist of potential bidders selected and invited to conduct due diligence on the basis of management presentations and/or site visits, data room disclosures and, increasingly, a financial and commercial due diligence report commissioned by the vendor – and requested to submit final offers together with a legal mark-up of a draft sale and purchase agreement; and
– one or more bidders selected to enter into exclusive/short-listed negotiations with the vendor with a view to concluding a definitive sale and purchase agreement.

One of the most high profile such auctions in 2002 was the sale by American Electric Power of its subsidiary SEEBOARD, a major electricity distribution and supply business based in the South-East of England. After a competitive process, SEEBOARD was eventually acquired by EDF, via its subsidiary London Electricity, for £1.4 billion.

In general, in the context of due diligence, the inclinations of the acquirer and the vendor tend to run in opposite directions – the acquirer, in the interests of reducing as far as possible his exposure to the unknown, will press for as much access as possible, whilst the vendor, in the interests also of reducing as far as possible his exposure to unknown facts (insofar as they may influence price) but also of managing the disclosure and/or presentation of unfavourable information, will seek to restrict the level of unfettered access as much as possible. To accommodate these diametrically opposed positions in order to facilitate the transaction being completed, some form of acceptable compromise is needed and, in the United Kingdom, what has fulfilled that need is the concept of vendor due diligence.

Data room disclosures are rarely sufficient as a basis for a potential acquirer agreeing to make a binding offer. This is largely because the acquirer will suspect the vendor of only disclosing that information which he regards as, at best, neutral or more realistically, conducive to the sale process. Accordingly, in order to protect his interests, the acquirer will press for substantive warranties and indemnities which, in turn, may be unacceptable to the vendor.

An independently prepared due diligence report, commissioned from a credible source, is an accepted means of bringing the two sides together. The vendor will have prior knowledge of the matters and conclusions being highlighted in the due diligence report – and therefore be able to adjust his price expectations and/or negotiating strategy accordingly – whilst the acquirer will be able to take comfort from the fact that the due diligence has been undertaken by an adviser whose responsibility (and, ultimately, liability) is to the eventual acquirer.

All this sounds very good as a basis of bringing two sides together. However, a vendor due diligence report, regardless of the independence, expertise and credibility of the person who has prepared it, should not be the sole basis of financial and commercial due diligence on which a potential acquirer makes a binding offer, for four main reasons:

– the vendor due diligence report will have been commissioned by the vendor and scoped to address the likely areas of interest to the majority of potential acquirers – not necessarily all of the material areas of interest to each potential investor;
– the presentation of the findings in the vendor due diligence report will have first been reviewed and commented upon by the vendor and his advisers – there is therefore a possibility that unfavourable matters may well have been given a spin which presents them in a better light;
– the adviser preparing the vendor due diligence report will stipulate that he only owes a legal duty of care to the eventual acquirer – not to any other potential acquirer who may have submitted an unsuccessful offer, which may, to a lesser or greater degree, be due to erroneous or incomplete information in the vendor due diligence report; and
– although the adviser providing the vendor due diligence report will owe a contractual duty of care to the eventual acquirer, the normal £25 million (for larger transactions) limitation of liability – even assuming a successful negligence action can be brought – is not a sufficient insurance policy for the damaging effects of a flawed acquisition if some of the basic facts or assumptions underlying the acquirer's valuation turn out later to be wrong.

Accordingly, it is still imperative, even in circumstances where a comprehensive vendor due diligence report has been prepared, that a potential acquirer engages his own due diligence adviser to:

– review the contents of the vendor due diligence report and give his own, independent interpretation of the information contained therein;
– distill the key findings of the vendor due diligence report – which, by their nature, tend to be voluminous documents – and present them in a more easily digestible form to the potential acquirer and his providers of finance; and

– identify those areas not covered in the vendor due diligence report which are of material interest to the acquirer and recommend areas for additional due diligence disclosures/review prior to a binding sale and purchase agreement being concluded.

Again, these requirements reinforce the need for selecting a financial and commercial due diligence adviser on the basis of the three core criteria mentioned above – industry expertise, transaction experience and creditability. Given the tight timetables inherent in managed auctions for attractive properties, the need for due diligence advisers who can hit the ground running is even more acute in these situations – regardless of whether a satisfactory vendor due diligence exercise has been performed or not – than in those, increasingly rare, situations where a potential acquirer is granted exclusive access to a target.

Summary: maximising the return on your deal

It is a well-publicised fact that a significant proportion of acquisitions by corporates are considered to be unsuccessful – either because the acquirer pays too much for them and thereby destroys shareholder value or the hoped for synergies/benefits from the acquisition fail to materialise in practice. The goal of the financial and commercial due diligence should be to minimise the risk of this happening and, from a positive perspective, to help the acquirer to maximise his return on the deal. To do this, the due diligence adviser should be involved throughout the deal process. From three key perspectives, time is of the essence in delivering value in an acquisition:

– firstly, with increasing limitation over access, advisers cannot afford a lengthy learning curve in coming to terms with the nature of the target's business and the ramifications of the type of transaction being contemplated;

– secondly, with the increasingly frenetic pace of M&A transaction timetables, due diligence needs to be closely coordinated to ensure that all key issues impacting the acquirer's perception of value are satisfactorily addressed in the construction of the offer and the contractual negotiations; and

– thirdly, realising targeted post-acquisition synergies, cost savings and performance improvements depends on well-planned actions being implemented quickly once the deal has closed.

The time factor accentuates the need for an acquirer to adopt three key strategic objectives when planning his due diligence on a target:

– firstly, the use of appropriately qualified advisers both in terms of industry expertise and transaction experience;

– secondly, close integration of all the due diligence workstreams during the course of the target evaluation and contractual negotiations; and

– finally, involvement of the financial and commercial due diligence advisers throughout the course of the deal lifecycle – that is, to ensure the best possible chance of successfully identifying, evaluating and delivering the value-creation opportunities which underpin the proposed acquisition.

It follows that the involvement of the financial and commercial due diligence adviser should not be regarded as simply a tick-the-box requirement in the acquirer's process checklist, but instead as integral to the delivery of value. The best due diligence practitioners in this area already regard this as the fundamental basis for their client relationships.

Financial buyers are steadily increasing their presence in M&A activity – both in number and value of transactions – and their successes can be measured in terms of both their ability to win auctions in the face of competing bids from corporates and also the number of well published spectacular returns from individual investments (eg, Permira's exit from Homebase when it was sold to GUS for about £900 million in 2002 having acquired it for about £700 million two years previously). Part of this success reflects the leveraged nature of the acquisitions but also, in large part, an overall approach to their deals which embraces the ideas and strategies set out above.

Postscript: back-to-basics

As noted above, with the recent spate of accounting-related scandals and numerous (non-fraudulent) requirements for results restatements in the United States, it can legitimately be asked whether it is time for the financial due diligence to be more explicit in providing comfort on whether reported financial results and balance sheets can be relied upon.

As an underlying source of comfort in this area it should be pointed out that UK financial accounting is underpinned by twin concepts of true and fair and substance over form rather than a prescriptive set of rules as used in the United States. However, if one distills most instances of accounting irregularities down to their essence, they fall into one or more of four categories:

– reported income either overstated or recognised on an injudicious basis;

– expenses either not reported or carried forward/capitalised in an imprudent manner;

– overvalued/non-existent assets or understated liabilities; and

– overly-complex transactions primarily designed to hide their real financial nature or commercial impact.

Arguably, these can only go undetected – in the absence of a comprehensive cover-up or web of deceit – if the person reviewing them is either unfamiliar with the business concerned and the type of transactions involved, or is unfamiliar with the best practice method of accounting for them. Given the restricted levels of access in most due diligence assignments nowadays it is unlikely that a review will uncover well-conceived and executed fraudulent activity. However, someone who is experienced in the industry sector – both in terms of the nature of the transactions and benchmark accounting for them – will be in a better position to identify potential areas of concern and make recommendations (eg, for additional disclosure) to his client accordingly.

It may well be that acquirers will press for more explicit comfort than hitherto from their financial due diligence advisers on the underlying robustness of a target's financial accounts. However, the value of this comfort will crucially depend on it being given by due diligence advisers who are experts in the industry sector concerned – in this respect, the requirement is no different from that for the three key strategic due diligence objectives discussed above.

9

The key people – a background investigation?

David Hutchinson, managing director, Box89

'Nearly every mistake we've made has been in picking the wrong people, not the wrong idea.'
Arthur Rock, venture capitalist, *Harvard Review*

Introduction

When making an acquisition within the United Kingdom there are many variables and idiosyncrasies to consider that may be different from other countries. There will be specific requirements in law, particular regulatory demands, climatic and environmental concerns and certainly differences between industry and culture. However, one factor that will not be different, will be that the company 'will be run by people, staffed by people and owned by people'. What does change is that all people are different. Most people are motivated in different ways and everybody has a past.

In order to enter into and complete a successful acquisition the people – that is their background and histories – must be known and understood. This 'knowing and understanding' will fall within the remit of the investigative due diligence.

Over the past 10 years the world of successful acquisitions has seen investigative due diligence evolve as a vital intelligence discipline that is both distinct from and also uniquely complementary to traditional legal and accounting due diligence inquiries.

Investigative due diligence has become an indispensable tool that enables corporate decisionmakers and their legal advisers to reduce the chances of entering into a suspect or risky transaction.

Whilst it is agreed that there may appear to be a certain degree of overlap in terms of analysis of books, records and contracts, investigative due diligence exposes crucial information that these books, records and contracts may not disclose or even contain.

The results of investigative due diligence can generate inside track information that can prove absolutely critical when assessing the credibility of the subject and the viability of an acquisition.

Today's legal, financial and commercial decisionmakers responsible for transactions and consequent business relationships, increasingly rely on investigative due diligence in their evaluation of investments, acquisitions, joint ventures, board appointments and key executive hires.

This chapter focuses on how the investigative process relates to looking into the backgrounds of key people. After all how many of us have said that if we had only known more about the people then we could have avoided situations leading to embarrassment, loss of integrity or commercial failure?

In the light of recent events involving rogue traders, executives altering performance figures and directors hiding monies, the perceived need to check out the key people prior to any investment has become imperative.

So why is it often not carried out properly and comprehensively? This chapter deals with this worrying question.

Terminology

The term due diligence has a widely understood meaning in the context of public offerings of securities, under the Securities Act of 1933. It has also assumed other connotations. It often describes the process that involves one of the parties in a transaction – often an acquisition – undertaking to investigate the other.

Invariably businesses consider the people side of due diligence to fall within the remit of the accountants and lawyers. Sometimes it is considered the responsibility of the market strategists, human resources and the corporate finance people. In fact people-based due diligence requires specific expertise that the traditional members of a due diligence team would not possess.

Within the transactional phase of an acquisition or investment there may not be the appropriate professionals available with the necessary skills to perform due diligence on the people and it is for this reason that such a crucial part of the process is often neglected, side-lined or even forgotten. By understanding the application, implication and intrinsic value one must initially understand the meaning of what it is to investigate a key person.

People due diligence should not be confused with the area of human resource due diligence. The latter relates to matters of compensation, remuneration, succession planning and employee integration.

When the process of investigating is handled by human resources the information generated is often by means of verification rather than investigation. The differences can be explained as:

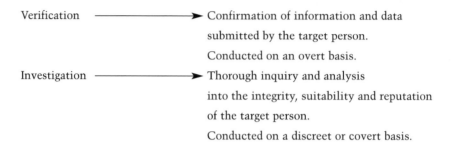

Verification   ⟶   Confirmation of information and data submitted by the target person. Conducted on an overt basis.

Investigation   ⟶   Thorough inquiry and analysis into the integrity, suitability and reputation of the target person. Conducted on a discreet or covert basis.

A definition of the people side of due diligence may be viewed as:

The thorough investigation of legally accessible information in order to provide true insight into the past performance, professional ability and personal and professional integrity of a targeted individual.

Once this requirement is agreed as being a crucial part of the acquisition process the next stage is to understand when and how this component applies.

The scope of investigative due diligence

Using the acquisition example as a model, how do companies and investors benefit from investigative due diligence? The desired result should be that the client will gain a high quality and timely insight into the key people and how they relate to the existing and intended business. This should be done discreetly, often covertly, and should in no way reflect badly on the integrity or reputation of the client or their investors.

To produce the desired results, the database and public records research must be conducted professionally, proficiently and exhaustively. The investigator must know what to look for, where to look, how to look, and almost as importantly when to stop looking.

In addition to his or her competence in public records and on-line research, the investigator must also be able to conduct in-depth and intelligent interviews; evaluate the credibility of information; develop leads and make connections; and extrapolate intelligence from industry and government sources.

Currently many companies and organisations rely simply on the referencing of key management within the acquisition process, which is often limited to the verification of professional history, conversations with known contacts and references, and face-to-face meetings. (Such information is normally provided by the target individual themselves!)

These are usually conducted by commercial managers, accountants and lawyers. Rarely does a professional with specific investigative experience participate as part of the due diligence team. When one does, the findings can provide significant value and insight.

In many professional disciplines it is often considered an unsafe business practice for inexperienced or unqualified individuals to conduct sensitive and important work.

An interesting question is that if investigators should not be conducting legal or financial due diligence as part of an acquisition, should it be wise for lawyers and accountants to be conducting checks on the key people?

The importance of checking key people

In the investment community, especially in dealing with acquisitions, equity injection and investment in relative start-ups, very serious questions must be addressed concerning the circumstances, quality and reputation of the key players as well as the business itself.

In many cases the reliance on on-line information and databases is heavy. Such data resources are valuable primary information tools, but it must be warned that they mostly provide data submitted by the target company, or individual, itself or media information from second or third-party sources.

It will be important to gain some real insight into the backgrounds of the people who are associated with the target company because they are likely to be the ones who will be effectively using the capital and running the business. In many cases total reliance on database sources may prove unsafe.

Historically, businesses and individuals seeking investment can be superb self-promoters whose conduct can range from simple exaggeration to omission, deception and misrepresentation, to outright fraud and criminality.

Since the goal is to entice investment or purchase, the standard operating procedure tends to invariably accentuate the positive and downplay or conceal the negative. In-depth background information about the individual within and behind the company will prove extremely useful if such misrepresentation is to be avoided.

An active and high profile investor was known to have said: 'we only really get to know a person once they have received our money or once they have left us and gone somewhere else!'

Which key people to watch out for?

Although written somewhat 'tongue in cheek,' this section may be extremely useful when watching out for what investigators call 'red flags'. Red flags in relation to people represent danger that may require careful scrutiny, sensitive management or in extreme cases elimination by the investor.

For the purpose of this book, the red flags have been described as character types in a manner similar to the way in which a forensic profiler may refer to subjects when examining personalities within a criminal inquiry.

The lead role CEO

This person has a curriculum vitae to rival all others. He/she will be admired within business school case studies and infatuated over by undergraduate economists. The lead role CEO will always be on the best shortlists for positions in the largest and boldest companies. He/she will have an inexhaustible repertoire relating to the past, but never really expanding into the future.

The background of the lead role CEO may never have been checked out in the past 15 years. He/she has literally ridden on their own coat tails and forged such a strong personal branding that few people feel it necessary to look beneath the veneer. Such a CEO can bring an initial profile to a company but as time passes the inevitable rhetoric turns to murmurs of dissatisfaction, a golden severance package and a short journey on into his/her next awaiting throne room!

This person needs discreet and sensitive checking. A true CEO, with nothing to hide, may even feel flattered that someone is taking more than a fleeting interest.

The celebrity CFO

The celebrity CFO tends to be the more academic cousin of the lead role CEO – less extrovert than his cousin, slightly more cautious with the media but nonetheless very accepting of praise and adoration. If the lead role CEO has ridden his/her own coat tails then they were firmly holding hands with their CFO cousin at the time. They tend to come as a pair. The celebrity CFO may almost never be subject to an independent background check due to the fact that their cousin will have already entered the company and specifically requested his presence as resident CFO.

It is the track record and integrity of the celebrity CFO that must be carefully and sensitively clarified before any firm decision is made during an acquisition or investment.

As important as looking into the celebrity CFO's background will be to look into what happened to the finances of the celebrity CFO's previous companies, particularly during the six-month period after his/her departure.

The cosmetic non-executive

People often ask: 'what does a non-executive director actually do?' It was once said that a non-executive director is very similar to having a bidet in one's home: 'it serves no particular purpose, but definitely brings a touch of class!'

To be fair, a well-researched and wisely-placed non-executive director can bring immense value, wisdom and leverage to an organisation. A misplaced or rashly recruited one such as the cosmetic non-executive can be at best ineffective and at worst a commercial, financial and emotional disaster.

The deal hopper

The deal hopper may in reality be an almost complete creation of his/her own doing. The deal hopper is usually seen as a 30-something high achiever who may, in the past, have been instrumental in a well-documented major transaction or complex sale.

The sense of worth and status gained from this time created a 'drug' for the deal hopper that gives purpose and drive to his/her entire professional existence.

The deal hopper will have built outstanding curriculum vitae that read more like an M&A calendar than a sequential list of companies, positions and dates. The craft of the deal hopper is to get close enough to a major transaction to be able to plausibly credit it to his/her CV. When checking into the background of this individual do not assume that all is what it seems.

The shouter

The shouter is a very unusual creature. Normally, the shouter is a very outwardly confident person with a supreme air of control and worth. When challenged, he/she will tend to infer that the challenger may have their facts wrong. If presented with factual evidence to support the challenge the shouter will claim that the facts are untrue. If challenged further, the shouter will begin to shout until the challenge resides.

The shouter often appears in the role of sales or business development. His/her pattern of behaviour is invariably to promise large targets, have huge amounts of business in the pipeline and just as final deadlines approach, move on to a higher paid position in a different, often competitive, company before the fruits of his/her promises materialise.

When checking the background of the shouter it will be crucial to look beyond the job title, target sales revenues and prospective clients.

Combining key-people due diligence within the acquisition process

When performing due diligence for an acquisition or investment it will be important to follow a schedule and have an agreed process and calendar in place so that all parties are effectively working with the same set of standards and that important information can be compiled and decisions made in a smart and timely manner.

The checking of the key people, although a crucial part of the process, can be performed later than other components. After all, if the target company does not have a viable business model then the need to check out its people becomes irrelevant.

It is, therefore, considered best practice to perform background checks following the financial and commercial due diligence but before the transaction itself. By doing it at this stage it will allow for necessary personnel changes or alterations prior to actual closure of the acquisition.

Regulatory requirements and corporate governance issues

Many compliance officers and people designated as responsible for the purposes of regulatory matters often sign documents relating to the employment of individuals, and acquisition-related contracts, without truly understanding the regulatory requirements, or reading the small print. Often, the requirements will demand that the responsible person conduct certain checks in relation to the background, performance and integrity of such employees. (Some of the other requirements may relate to issues such as anti-money laundering.)

When, for want of a better phrase, the 'corporate wheel comes off,' as we have been seeing more recently, the ability to demonstrate that these checks were performed properly will become crucial within the area of governance.

It is recommended that any person holding a position of compliance look at the people issues and consider whether appropriate checks need to be instructed.

Communicating the findings of background checks

The nature of the information generated as a result of investigative due diligence targeting key people is usually crucial decisionmaking data. As such, the information should be in the hands of the decisionmakers as soon as practicable once it is known.

Agreeing and keeping to a communication strategy enables important intelligence to be effectively captured and used within the overall decision process. It will also ensure that the scope is kept to and that, if needed, the investigation can be quickly and easily redirected or refocused.

A common, and foolish, mistake made by investigators is to wait until a final report is produced and then deliver it in its entirety. The final report is of course a valuable reference document; however the true value of using an investigator will come from the continuous feedback of intelligence over the course of the investigation.

It is, therefore, important to agree on a specific investigative scope, and an effective framework or channel for the feedback of information found.

It has been established that when the investigator remains flexible and responsive to the client's changing requirements the real value of the intelligence generated is clearer and more likely to be used.

Security and integrity of information will also be an important consideration.

Invariably the due diligence will be a sensitive process prior to the transaction taking place. As such it will be important to protect the integrity of any communicated information. This can be enhanced by the use of code names, passwords and encryption.

It is normally advisable to assign code names to projects and target individuals. This will ensure that real names are not inadvertently mentioned during conversations that may be overheard, or indeed eavesdropped upon, either innocently or deliberately.

Passwords and encryption are secondary forms of protection and specific advice should be sought prior to using them.

One of the most effective ways of understanding the value of investigative due diligence is by working through a case study or a sample investigative report.

Case study: Onyx Corporate Finance, London

Matthew Broaden, director of acquisitions, was heading up the strategic acquisitions section of Onyx Corporate Services Group in Boston when he was asked to move to the United Kingdom to set up an operation for Europe, initially by making a strategic acquisition. Matthew had previously worked for other banking groups in London, Paris, Brussels and Prague and relished the opportunity to develop and head Onyx outside the United States. The first task was to acquire a targeted company and recruit a marketing director, a compliance officer and a big hitter in the area of fund management. Matthew had an existing relationship with a trusted headhunter in The City and after some time received a short-list of apparently good people.

Following recent press reports of people not declaring truthful commercial information and also remembering the story and events surrounding the rogue trader Nick Leeson in Singapore, Matthew thought that he should at least look at some form of vetting for everyone prior to employing them within the new company and giving them access to Onyx customers and accounts.

Matthew remembered reading in the press in New York about Box89 discovering a potential rogue trader on behalf of a Wall Street investment firm a couple of years ago. Matthew therefore made contact and requested a meeting to discuss some potential issues. He discussed his concerns relating to the risks associated with not vetting people properly and the legal implications of not taking diligent steps in knowing exactly whom he was going to employ. Box89 explained the legal requirements of vetting and what the process would actually look like, from verifying education to checking professional qualifications, to identifying track records and looking at how the person interacted with colleagues and clients. Matthew wanted to make sure that he was legally and procedurally covered and so engaged Box89 to perform vetting on the three key candidates. As a result, the prospective marketing director was rejected based on repeated falsification of academic achievements. The other two positions were filled satisfactorily.

Since the vetting, Matthew has engaged Box89 to look into the motivations of three directors of a company in a recent acquisition in Scotland. He is also speaking with Box89 about investigating accusations of a fraud associated with a fund based in the Czech Republic.

Sample investigative due diligence

The names of people, places and companies in this report are changed to protect the integrity of those involved. This sample does, however, reflect the findings of a real background investigation conducted by Box89.

Sample Investigative Report

Nicolas TOUKAKIS

Backgrounds Check

For

ABC Capital Partners Limited

11 James's Street
London
SW1 5TT

Month 2002

All information gathered and presented by Box89 is done so legally and ethically. Box89 takes the utmost care to ensure that the information, which we provide, is correct; however, we cannot take responsibility for the accuracy of information provided by or through third parties.

Executive summary

It appears that Nicolas Toukakis is a rather elusive and private individual, with homes in London and Monaco and a rented commercial mail box in New York. It is known that Mr. Toukakis has used the forenames Nicholas, Nicos and Dimitri.

From a professional perspective, it has been established that in the 1980s, there were a number of instances in which circumstantial evidence linked him to the involvement in illicit trading of junk bonds.

It appears that his main income has been generated from the activities of a Monaco-based investment company called Lifeboat.

It is believed that his current income is generated from 'personal trading' through a Texas-based company called Jupiter Systems Inc.

It is understood that both Mr. Toukakis and the company 'Lifeboat' have been the subjects of an official inquiry in relation to possible money laundering activities. (In these instances, however, no apparent enforcement action took place.)

The past issues surrounding money laundering and subsequent investments made by the company 'Lifeboat' are considered to be an area of concern for a prospective investor.

For further clarification or any assistance in relation to this inquiry or any other matter please feel free to contact Box89 directly.

All information gathered and presented by Box89 is done so legally and ethically. Box89 takes the utmost care to ensure that the information, which we provide, is correct; however, we cannot take responsibility for the accuracy of information provided by or through third parties.

Introduction

A due diligence check was instructed to look into the integrity and background of Mr. Nicolas TOUKAKIS.

Mr. Toukakis has approached ABC Capital Partners as part of an investment scenario. Very little is known about his background at this time and it was considered wise to conduct a formal background check.

Subject of investigation

Name: Nicolas TOUKAKIS

Date of birth: 12th April 1942

Known addresses: 123 King Street
                       London
                       SW1T 3RT

                       800 State Place
                       Oceania Buildings
                       Monaco

                       238 Park Avenue
                       New York
                       NY 100036

Nicolas Toukakis is a Greek name that appears to have been anglicised. In order to cover all areas of risk, permutations of the given name were searched within the investigative process.

The forms: Nicos, Nicolas and Nicholas were all considered.

Initial inquiries

Inquiries were conducted in relation to the known addresses and it was established that Nicholas Toukakis is the owner and current occupier of the address in London. Discreet inquiries in the area established that he 'keeps himself to himself and appears to mostly use the address at weekends'. A neighbour believed that 'he travels a lot and always appears to be in a hurry'.

Discreet inquiries in Monaco revealed that the property at Oceania Buildings is owned by Mr. Nicos Toukakis, (verified by date of birth as Nicholas Toukakis), and was purchased for cash in 1982. Discreet inquiries in the neighbourhood established that Mr. Toukakis uses the property mostly for entertaining but has rarely been seen there over the past year.

It was verified that the address in New York is a serviced office building with a prestigious address. Further inquiries revealed that Mr. Toukakis retains a mail box in the basement of the building which is paid for on a monthly basis. The mail box is registered in the name of Dimitri Nicos Toukakis. Discreet inquiries with staff at the office verified that Mr. Toukakis appears to be 'a very well-groomed and private man'.

It was confirmed that he and another male called Clifton Harris have mail forwarded from this location to an address at 123 King Street, London. (It was verified that Mr. Harris is a past colleague and specific details are found later in this report.)

Using all permutations of Mr. Toukakis's names, extensive credit checks were performed with a number of agencies.

It was confirmed that <u>there are a number of creditors</u> who have served claims at the New York postal address of Nicholas Toukakis. The particulars were further examined and it was found that they related to unpaid rentals on limousine hire and hotel conferencing facilities.

No adverse financial data became apparent in relation to the addresses in London or Monaco.

Further checks were also made through legal resources to establish whether any past or current litigation is associated with Mr. Toukakis.

<u>Other than the previously mentioned creditor issues in New York nothing further of concern was found.</u>

Searches were conducted in relation to bankruptcy data.

Nothing of concern was found.

Discreet checks with official bodies, both domestically and internationally, were conducted into the political and social integrity of Mr. Toukakis.

It was discovered that in 1984 Nicholas Toukakis had been named in a Europol 'target list' in an intelligence initiative focusing on money laundering enforcement action. It was confirmed that in December 1983 such a list had existed to monitor people suspected in laundering activities. The initiative was set up to look into the possibility of enforcement action in relation to money laundering activities through The Balkans. The 'initiative' was curtailed in November 1984 and no actual action had taken place in relation to Mr. Toukakis.

It is believed that he may still remain on a European database for use by anti-money laundering bodies.

Extensive international media searches, with specific focus on the US, Greece, The Balkans and Monaco, were conducted to evaluate whether any negative PR exists that may cause concern, embarrassment or conflict, to either Mr. Toukakis or for a prospective investor or business partner.

In the countries mentioned, local financial and business press sources were also contacted directly, to establish whether Mr. Toukakis has been involved in any illicit domestic issues.

Nothing of concern, conflict or embarrassment was found.

Company and business searches

Checks were conducted into the involvement of Mr. Toukakis with any business within the US, UK and Europe.

It was established there are no listings of directorships or any other corporate position within any known UK or US company in relation to Nicolas, Nicos, Nicolas or Dimitri Toukakis.

There is, however, a listing for a Monaco-registered company called LIFEBOAT FUNDS, under the name of Dimitri Nicholas Toukakis, date of birth 12 April 1942.

The registered address for the company is at 800 State Place, Oceania Buildings, Monaco – the residential address of Mr. Toukakis in Monaco.

It was confirmed that Lifeboat Funds is a privately-owned company run by Nicholas Toukakis and two other partners, Paul Connor and another individual called Ali Al Rajhid.

Discreet inquiries established that the company is listed as a 'private fund' and currently has £50 million under investment. It was also verified that it focuses primarily on 'mining ventures in The Balkans' and has been successfully involved with a number of government contracts through the Greek Development Council.

Inquiries both in Monaco and Greece have revealed that Lifeboat has not made any new investments since 1999.

Confidential inquiries with industry bodies

Discreet checks were conducted with the following bodies to see if Nicolas Toukakis has come to notice either in the US, UK or from overseas.

The following bodies were checked:

- SEC – Securities and Exchange Commission;
- COB – Commission des Opérations de Bourse, France's securities regulator;
- HCMG – Hellenic Capital Markets Commission;
- ASE – Athens Stock Exchange; and
- FSA – Financial Services Authority.

It was found that in the early 1980s COB had initiated an investigation into allegations of money laundering, by a company named as Lifeboat Funds.

It was verified that this is the same 'Lifeboat Company' as that owned and run by Nicholas Toukakis.

Further discreet inquiries established that no enforcement action had taken place and it is understood that there are no current investigations focused on this company.

Other commercial activities

It was believed that Mr. Toukakis may also be involved with a company called 'Jupiter'. (Information supplied by ABC Capital.)

Based on his background and experience, inquiries focused on identifying a probable company.

Two possible organisations were found:

Firstly, 'Jupiter Trust and Jupiter Capital' – which are Hong Kong-based investment funds operating mostly within SE Asia and managed by a group called Techpac.

Discreet inquiries established that Nicolas Toukakis was <u>not known to the group or the fund over the past 10 years.</u>

The second option was with the company/organisation called 'Jupiter Systems Inc', based in Austin, Texas. Jupiter Systems Inc is a company that provides software and advisory support to independent traders.

It was established that the company was formed by an individual called Paul Downs who states, 'In the 80s and 90s, it was appropriate to let mutual funds do your investing for you, with many funds posting gains of 15 per cent to 30 per cent per year in one of the greatest bull markets we have ever seen. All of that changed in 2000. The Nasdaq, bolstered by the Internet and technology sectors, reached a peak of 5,000 in March. In the sell-off that followed, 'Buy-and-Hold' investors were hurt as their mutual funds declined in value with the fall of the Nasdaq, followed by the other exchanges.' To assist investors Paul Downs developed a software tool called JupiterTrader.

JupiterTrader was first released in 1994. The software is designed for one purpose – to help find and trade prime candidates in the least possible time. JupiterTrader achieves this goal by automating the analysis process using a technique called the Adaptive Realisation Model. JupiterTrader's easy-to-understand charts contain automatic information such as trend lines and key patterns to help further refine the trading candidate list. With the built-in portfolio and trading simulator, JupiterTrader is a complete, affordable platform for individual investors who want to engage the markets.

It is believed that Nicolas Toukakis has not actually been employed by a fund or company called Jupiter, but instead has been using the 'Jupiter Services' for personal trading and is in reality part of what is known as 'The Jupiter Club' of investors.

Discreet sources within Jupiter confirmed that the 'marketing address' they have for Nicholas Toukakis is a Monaco address at Oceania Buildings.

At present, other than the activity with Jupiter, it appears that Nicholas Toukakis is not actively pursuing any new commercial interests.

Professional background

It is known that Nicolas Toukakis has worked with the companies, Dace Brennan Smith and Prominent Securities.

It is also known that at this time he was a senior metals industry analyst covering gold-mining stocks.

Due to the time of his employment being in the late 1980s it was not possible to clearly ascertain his actual employment at these organisations. This was due to the fact that employee records have been archived and purged.

In order to gain some insight into his activities at that time of employment it was decided that the investigation should focus on the 'activities associated' with the positions held by Mr. Toukakis during the dates given.

It was discovered that the dates and jobs he held with Dace Brennan Smith and at Prominent Securities coincided with both companies being involved in scandal and subsequent prosecutions.

Dace Brennan Smith – New York

At the time when Nicolas Toukakis was at the company there was an ongoing and very highly publicised scandal involving the junk bond trading of an individual called Mr. Michael Joblin.

It was established that at this time Mr. Joblin had apparently used the resources and people of the company to conduct complex and significant fraudulent transactions. It is known that Nicholas Toukakis, then known as Nicos Toukakis, was a close working colleague of Mr. Joblin.

At the time Nicholas Toukakis was not named by any official inquiries, although sources reveal that he 'was very close to Joblin' and 'at times they were as thick as thieves and very nervy'.

Prominent Securities – London

At the time of his employment, a department known as the 'Private Investment Group' of Prominent Securities was known to have been involved in similar illicit activity to that of Dace Brennan Smith, mostly instigated by the individuals Jim Carr and Clifton Harris. (It is believed that Clifton Harris is the individual who is registered at the New York mail box also used by Mr. Toukakis.)

Most prominent in this activity was Mr. Harris, who apparently used a network of brokers and analysts to support a web of insider trades.

Confidential sources have revealed that it is understood that Harris, on occasions, used contacts out of Monte Carlo, specifically in Monaco to assist with such trades.

A number of fraudulent trades were known to have been performed through the non-precious/precious metals markets and it is also known that he preferred to use a network of contacts from predominantly Jewish and Anglo-Greek backgrounds.

It has been documented that during this time of the mid-1980s, certain individuals involved in the illicit activities literally made hundreds of millions of US dollars.

As a result of what took place a number of individuals were prosecuted, some from a high profile perspective, and others were not.

Inquiries with people associated with the scandals have revealed that <u>an unnamed Greek national had used a Monaco-based investment vehicle to 'move cash away from the hands of regulators'.</u>

It was also stated that <u>'much of the money had entered The Balkans through the hands of some very powerful and well-connected people'.</u>

It is known that Harris enjoyed and 'revelled in' a luxury lifestyle and was a regular guest at the Monaco home of Nicholas Toukakis. (At the time employees of Prominent Securities believed that the Monaco base was a property inherited from Nicholas's family.)

<u>It was confirmed that Harris was eventually prosecuted and jailed for his involvement in the scandals. Much of the illicit money was never recovered.</u>

Executive summary

It appears that Nicolas Toukakis is a rather elusive and private individual, with homes in London and Monaco and a rented commercial mail box in New York. It is known that Mr. Toukakis has used the forenames Nicholas, Nicos and Dimitri.

From a professional perspective, it has been established that in the 1980s there were a number of instances in which circumstantial evidence linked him to the involvement in illicit trading of junk bonds.

It appears that his main income has been generated from the activities of a Monaco-based investment company called Lifeboat.

It is believed that his current income is generated from 'personal trading' through a Texas-based company called Jupiter Systems Inc.

It is understood that both Mr. Toukakis and the company 'Lifeboat' have been the subjects of official inquiry in relation to possible money laundering activities. (In these instances however no apparent enforcement action took place.)

The past issues surrounding money laundering and subsequent investments made by the company 'Lifeboat' are considered to be an area of concern for a prospective investor.

For further clarification or any assistance in relation to this inquiry or any other matter please feel free to contact Box89 directly.

All information gathered and presented by Box89 is done so legally and ethically. Box89 takes the utmost care to ensure that the information, which we provide, is correct; however, we cannot take responsibility for the accuracy of information provided by or through third parties.

Conclusion

An acquisition can be a very frustrating and complex arrangement of activities, procedures and requirements; or it can be an exciting, productive and ordered process for the advancement of commercial growth.

The development of the acquisition will, to a large extent, depend upon whether a smart and distinct framework of procedures, checks and timeframes are agreed upon and adhered to. Due diligence will play a major role within such a successful framework and no other factor may be more important these days than the due diligence on the key people.

10
Legal issues

James Gubbins, partner and Nick Thody, senior associate, Weil, Gotshal & Manges

The mergers and acquisitions market in the United Kingdom is one of the most sophisticated in the world, with a legal framework that assists the process of M&A activity. The UK legal system consists of three jurisdictions: England and Wales, Scotland and Northern Ireland. Though the concepts remain similar in each jurisdiction, this chapter addresses issues in respect of legal practice in England and Wales. Competition, environmental and tax issues relevant to M&A activity are not covered in this chapter and are separately covered in Chapters 12 and 13, *Regulatory issues* and *Tax issues*, respectively.

Public or private deal?

The method by which a company or business is acquired in the United Kingdom is determined by whether the Takeover Code (the 'Code') governs the transaction. If the Code applies, the bidder will generally be required to make a public offer to the shareholders of the target and both the bidder and the target will have to comply with the timetable and other requirements of the Code. Where the Code does not apply, the acquisition will be made by means of a negotiated sale contract between the buyer and the seller.

Irrespective of whether the acquisition is made by a public offer under the Code or by a negotiated sale contract, the Listing Rules of the UK Listing Authority (the 'Listing Rules') may also introduce a public element (or, in the case of Code-governed acquisitions, a further public element) to the transaction, as the Listing Rules require companies listed on the London Stock Exchange (LSE) to obtain shareholder consent to any acquisition or disposal of a company or business where the transaction size exceeds certain thresholds.

As a consequence, the application of the Code or the Listing Rules will have an impact on the structure and timetable of the transaction and on the amount of information that becomes publicly available. Where neither the Code nor the Listing Rules apply, the parties involved in a private transaction will have a freer hand, although the articles of association of the target or contractual arrangements between its shareholders may still require shareholder consent to be given to the transaction.

The Takeover Code

The Code applies to any offer for a UK public company, whether or not it is listed on the LSE, and also to offers for UK private companies whose shares have been subject to public dealing or marketing arrangements in the 10 years prior to the offer. The Code is issued and administered by the Panel on Takeovers and Mergers, a non-statutory body made up of representatives from various financial and professional organisations. Although the Code does not have the force of law, there are a variety of sanctions available to the Panel and compliance with the Code is in practice compulsory.

The principal purpose of the Code is to ensure fair and equal treatment of all shareholders and to provide a framework within which takeovers are to be conducted. The Code comprises general principles (see box, 'General Principles of the Code') supplemented by specific rules. Some of the rules are effectively expansions of the general principles and others are provisions governing detailed aspects of takeover procedures, such as dealings in the target's shares during the offer period and the contents of documents circulated and announcements made by the bidder and the target.

A key requirement of the Code is that where any person or persons acting in concert acquires 30 per cent or more of the voting rights of a company (or where, when a person or persons acting in concert already holds between 30 and 50 per cent, he acquires more shares), he is obliged to make a cash offer for the remainder of the company. That offer must be conditional only upon the bidder obtaining control of 50 per cent or more of the voting shares of the target. This loss of control over the terms of the offer means that having to make such a mandatory offer will rarely be attractive to a bidder unless other strategic considerations supervene.

Company law provides that once the bidder has acquired at least 90 per cent of the shares to which the offer relates, the bidder can buy out compulsorily the remaining shareholders who have not accepted the offer. This ability to 'squeeze-out' minority shareholders is particularly important in the context of a leveraged acquisition, where a central part of the financing of the bid will be the grant of security to the lenders over the assets of the target. The sanctioning of this grant is made easier if the bidder is able to control 100 per cent of the target following completion of the offer.

General principles of the Code

1   All target shareholders of the same class must be treated similarly by the bidder.

2   During an offer no party (including their advisers) can provide information to some shareholders which is not made available to all shareholders.

3   A bidder should only announce an offer after the most careful and responsible consideration and only when it has every reason to believe that it can and will continue to be able to implement the offer.

4   Shareholders must be given sufficient information and advice to enable them to reach a properly informed decision and must have sufficient time to do so.

5   Any document addressed to shareholders containing information from the bidder or the target must be prepared with the highest standards of care and accuracy.

6   All parties must use every endeavour to prevent the creation of a false market in the securities of the bidder or target.

7   At no time after a bona fide offer has been communicated to the target board (or after the board has reason to believe that a bona fide offer is imminent) can any action be taken by the board of the target, without the approval of shareholders, which could result in an offer being frustrated or shareholders being denied an opportunity to decide on its merits.

8   Rights of control must be exercised in good faith and the oppression of a minority is wholly unacceptable.

9   Directors of the bidder and the target must always, in advising their shareholders, act only in their capacity as directors and not have regard to their personal or family shareholdings or to their personal relationships with the companies.

10 Where control of a company is acquired by a person or persons acting in concert, a general offer to all shareholders is normally required.

A bidder may wish to build up a stake in a potential target before entering into the offer. Stakebuilding is a highly regulated area and any such acquisitions need to be carefully considered as they may, for example, inadvertently establish a minimum offer price or impact on the 90 per cent threshold for the minority squeeze-out mentioned above. The Panel issues and administers the Rules Governing Substantial Acquisitions of Shares, whose primary purpose is to control the build-up of stakes of between 15 and 30 per cent in the target company by, with certain exceptions, restricting the speed at which a stakebuilder can increase his stake between these levels. Once the stakebuilder holds over 30 per cent, the requirement under the Code for a mandatory offer for the target to be made will apply.

In terms of due diligence and warranty protection, on most public takeovers in the United Kingdom due diligence is limited compared with private acquisitions. In recommended bid situations, the amount of information disclosed by target companies varies considerably. In a hostile bid, due diligence will usually be restricted to publicly available information. (Where there is more than one bidder, it is a condition of the Code that any information given to the bidder or potential bidder must, on request, be given equally to any other bidder or potential bidder.) In addition, in a public takeover, the warranty protection received by the bidder will be limited to the accepting shareholders warranting that they have good title to their shares and so the bidder will not receive the extensive warranty and indemnity protection that is typical of a private transaction.

The Listing Rules

When a company listed on the LSE proposes to make an acquisition or disposal where the transaction, calculated by reference to specified ratios, exceeds certain thresholds then shareholder approval must be obtained prior to completion of the transaction. This approval is sought by circularising shareholders with details of the transaction and by a shareholder vote in general meeting. As a result, completion of the transaction must be made conditional upon shareholder approval being given. The Listing Rules also require that a transaction which would result in a fundamental change in the business or in a change in control of the listed company, or which is between a listed company (or any of its subsidiaries) and a related party (typically a director or major shareholder), is approved by shareholders.

If the consideration for the transaction involves an issue of shares by the listed company, it may be necessary for shareholder consent to be obtained to an increase in the company's authorised share capital, for shareholder authority to be given for the directors to issue the relevant shares and for a disapplication of the pre-emption rights of existing shareholders to be made. As a result, shareholder approval may be effectively required even where there is no specific requirement for the transaction to be approved under the Listing Rules.

Public-to-private transactions

The effect that the requirements of the Code and, to a more limited extent, the Listing Rules can have on an acquisition transaction is illustrated by the example of public-to-private transactions. Such a transaction usually involves a medium or smaller sized company de-listing and returning to private ownership. Public-to-private transactions are typically structured as takeover bids governed by the Code or as court-approved schemes of arrangements.

As with conventional management buy-outs, public-to-private transactions are backed by private equity money as well as supported by debt financing. However, whereas in a conventional management buy-out the acquisition would be made by private contract, in a public-to-private transaction there has to be a public offer to shareholders in the listed company and so the Code will determine the timetable and contents of the offer document and regulate the acquisition process. Other differences from a conventional management buy-out include:

- the target and its directors will need to comply with the Code and Listing Rules requirements on directors dealings in the target's shares;
- because of Code requirements in relation to secrecy and announcements, the private equity investors and lenders to the acquisition vehicle are likely to get more limited rights to conduct due diligence than in a private transaction and limited, if any, exclusivity;
- as the acquisition of the target's shares will be made by way of a public offer, there will not be an acquisition agreement containing warranties given to the bidder. As a result, the private equity investors will look for warranties from the management buy-out team in a separate agreement;
- there is more financing risk for lenders as the Code requires that there is committed funding for an offer before it is announced; and
- in a public-to-private transaction there is a greater risk than in a private deal, due to the public nature of the offer, that a competing bidder may be prepared to offer more for the target.

What is being bought: shares or assets?

One of the first decisions to be taken in buying a business is whether to buy the shares of the company that owns the target business (a 'share purchase') or whether to buy only the assets which make up the business (an 'asset purchase').

Share purchase

If the transaction is structured as a share purchase, all of the target company's assets, liabilities and obligations are acquired. The risk is that the buyer will acquire liabilities and risks of which he is unaware at the time of completion. The seller's ongoing liability will be limited to the extent of the warranties and indemnities which it gives to the buyer.

Asset purchase

If assets are purchased, only the identified assets and liabilities which the buyer agrees to buy are acquired. This will be the preferred method of acquisition of a buyer who is concerned about particular liabilities in the target business, such as product liability claims or other unquantified or unknown liabilities, and who therefore prefers to 'cherry-pick' assets and only assume known liabilities.

Statute imposes one exception to the general freedom of the buyer to acquire only those assets he wishes to on an asset purchase. The Transfer of Undertakings (Protection of Employment) Regulations 1981 (the 'TUPE Regulations') require that, where there is a transfer of a going concern, employees must be taken on by the buyer on their current terms and conditions of employment. The basic test to determine whether TUPE applies is to see whether what has been sold is an economic entity which is still in existence. TUPE imposes obligations on the employer to inform and consult with employees where a transfer is planned. Where, either before or after a transfer, an employee is dismissed, that dismissal is treated as automatically unfair if the dismissal is in connection with the transfer and so the dismissed employee will have a claim for damages. On a share sale, the employment contracts of the employees of the target are unchanged by the sale of the company's shares, subject to any change of control of provisions that may be contained in those contracts.

Transfer of title

On a share purchase, all of the assets and liabilities of the target company remain with the target and so come under the buyer's control without the need for consents to the transfer of individual assets. The principal exception to this will be those contracts which contain change of control clauses that may be triggered by the transfer. Careful due diligence will be required to determine the extent to which any change of control provisions will need to be addressed and a commercial decision taken as to whether completion of the transaction should be made conditional on the consent of counterparties to key contracts to the change of control of the target.

By contrast, more consents and approvals are likely to be required on an asset purchase as each asset will need to be identified and transferred either by delivery or by a specific form of transfer. As there is a change of ownership of the assets themselves, as opposed to just the shares of the target company, the consent of customers, suppliers, landlords and others may be required. If it is impracticable or thought to be impossible to obtain the necessary third-party consents required to transfer the assets, a share purchase may be the only practical way of acquiring the target business.

Financial assistance

On a share purchase, the buyer will need to consider the implications of the statutory prohibition on a company giving financial assistance for the purpose of the acquisition of its

Exhibit 10.1: Summary of a typical private acquisition

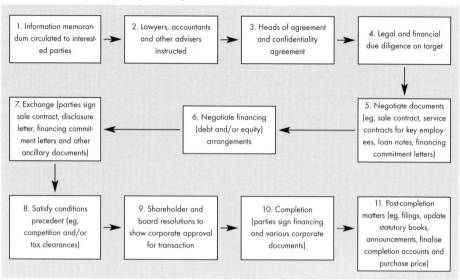

own shares. This is particularly relevant where the buyer incurs borrowings to fund the purchase price of the acquisition and looks to the target to provide either monies to repay, or security in relation to, those borrowings. Financial assistance means assistance given by way of gift, guarantee, security, indemnity or loan and includes any other form of assistance if its effect is to reduce the target company's net assets to a material extent. The prohibition against financial assistance relates both to assistance given before or at the time the shares are acquired and to the reduction or discharge of a liability after the acquisition.

Statute does provide that a private company may give financial assistance for the purpose of the acquisition of its own shares, provided that the net assets of the target are not reduced as a result or, to the extent they are reduced, the assistance is provided out of distributable profits. The directors of the target are required to swear a statutory declaration in a prescribed form and to follow various other procedures. This 'whitewash' procedure is technical and cumbersome. A White Paper recently issued in response to the Company Law Review has agreed with the recommendation for the abolition of the prohibition against financial assistance in so far as it relates to private companies and the revision of some of the existing exemptions from the prohibition. Such a reform would, in particular, recognise and simplify the commercial reality of leveraged transactions.

Risk allocation

Whether the transaction is structured as a share or an asset purchase, the buyer will want to seek to reduce the risk it is taking in acquiring the business. The seller will aim to be left with as few potential liabilities in connection with the sale as is possible. Within this process of risk allocation, the seller starts with a considerable initial advantage. English law implies no terms into a private contractual bargain such as a business purchase. As a result, the doctrine of 'caveat emptor' or 'let the buyer beware' means that, in the absence of specific contractual protection, the buyer will take all the risk connected with its purchase of the business. The buyer will seek to minimise this risk in two ways. Firstly, through a due diligence exercise whose primary purpose is to familiarise the buyer with the business it is acquiring (see box, 'Issues for legal due diligence and warranty protection'). Secondly, it will seek to minimise risk through obtaining warranties and indemnities from the seller in the sale contract.

The due diligence process

Due diligence is an audit of the target business's financial, commercial and legal affairs carried out so that the buyer can decide whether the proposed purchase represents a sound commercial investment. The due diligence process also acts as a bargaining tool as the buyer may use any negative results of the investigation to renegotiate the terms of the transaction, such as a reduction in the purchase price. The process also helps to define the scope of warranty and indemnity protection that will be required in areas of potential risk or weakness.

Commercial due diligence is usually carried out by the buyer or its financial adviser and looks at broad issues such as the market in which the business operates, its competitors and the business's strengths and weaknesses. Financial due diligence, rather than constituting a full accounting audit, focuses on the areas of the target's financial affairs that are material to the buyer's decision to proceed with the transaction.

The legal due diligence will primarily concentrate on three matters. Firstly, on whether the target company has good title to the assets being sold. Secondly, on the full extent of the liabilities that will be assumed by the buyer. Thirdly, the legal due diligence should assist in establishing the value of the target to the buyer by a thorough investigation of the principal areas of the target's business (see box, 'Issues for legal due diligence and warranty protection').

The use of a data room in the due diligence exercise is increasingly common where there is a large amount of information or where, as in an auction process, there are a number of interested parties. Data rooms enable sellers to minimise the disruption to the target caused by the sale process, to maintain physical control of the documents and to provide each prospective buyer with equal access to information. The data room will contain information that is confidential and so a potential buyer will be asked to execute a confidentiality agreement before being given access.

The seller will choose what information to make available in the data room and accordingly the buyer and its advisers will need to identify whether material information has been omitted. It may be that more information is subsequently made available to those buyers who proceed beyond the first round of the auction process. The benefits for the seller of restricting the availability of confidential or commercially sensitive information until a potential buyer has been identified or bidders have been short-listed may, however, be outweighed by the effect that the eventual release of the information may have on the buyers' view of the business and on the amount they are prepared to pay.

Once the investigatory work of the due diligence exercise is complete, the information obtained is summarised in a report. This either takes the form of an executive summary together with a detailed descriptive review of the documentation, or – as is more usual practice in the United States – a more informal report focusing on matters material to the transaction and highlighting problem areas and unusual features. The report should provide the buyer with an indication of those matters that should be covered by warranties or be specifically indemnified in the sale agreement.

Warranty and indemnity protection

A warranty is a promise made by the seller to the buyer that a particular set of circumstances exist. On a typical acquisition, warranty protection will be sought by the buyer to cover the target and the principal areas of its business. Where the warranty is shown to be untrue, the buyer will seek to recover damages from the seller to compensate the buyer for the loss it has suffered. Unless the sale contract specifies some other measure, damages for breach of warranty are calculated by reference to the amount by which the value of the shares or assets acquired is reduced by the breach of warranty. Under these common law principles, the damages received by the buyer will be limited to the extent to which the loss it has suffered was reasonably foreseeable. The buyer will also be expected to take reasonable steps to mitigate its loss. This contrasts with the US practice of warranties being given on an indemnity basis where the seller is liable for all of the buyer's losses. The measure of damages on an indemnity basis is discussed below.

The warranties requested by the buyer will usually cover all aspects of the business being acquired and will often run to 20 or 30 closely-typed pages which will be negotiated in detail by the parties' lawyers (see box, 'Issues for due diligence and warranty protection'). As a result, the warranties come to serve a secondary purpose in addition to their primary purpose of risk allocation, as the process of negotiation and disclosure against the warranties should serve to inform the buyer further as to the condition of the business being acquired.

In contrast to warranties, an indemnity from the seller to the buyer is a promise to reimburse the buyer in the event that a specific loss or liability is suffered by the buyer.

The usual purpose of an indemnity is to address a particular problem of which the parties are aware at the time of completion of the sale contract. This problem may have been brought to light through the buyer's due diligence process and may, for example, concern a potential environmental, employment or pensions liability.

The seller's liability under an indemnity will depend on the exact wording used. Generally, the seller will be liable for all of the loss suffered by the buyer, whether or not that loss was foreseeable, and the buyer is under no duty to attempt to mitigate its loss. The measure of damages on an indemnity basis will often, although not always, result in a higher sum being paid by the seller than under the common law measure of damages. If the buyer wants to be compensated for breach of warranty on an indemnity basis, that must be clearly stated in the sale contract and will usually be strongly resisted by the seller.

Seller protection

The seller will seek to minimise its liability under the warranties that it gives to the buyer. It will do so by disclosing certain facts against the warranties, by negotiating limitations to its warranty liability and by reducing the absolute nature of the warranties by introducing various qualifications as to materiality or the state of the seller's knowledge.

The seller will disclose information to the buyer by means of a disclosure letter provided prior to the signing of the sale contract. To the extent that the disclosures made are fair, they will serve to qualify the contents of the warranties and to bar the buyer from seeking damages from the seller in relation to the breach of warranty that has been disclosed. If the disclosure is material, the buyer should seek to obtain a reduction in the purchase consideration or have the seller rectify the problem prior to signing of the contract.

The seller will seek to reduce its potential warranty liability by limiting both the amount that can be claimed for breach of warranty and the period of time in which the buyer can bring a claim. The financial limitations will typically specify that no claims may be brought unless the aggregate amount claimed is above a certain figure, so seeking to avoid a series of small or spurious claims, and will state the maximum aggregate liability of the seller under all of the warranties. This maximum figure is frequently based on the amount of consideration paid by the buyer and – as with all limitations on the seller's liability – is likely to be the subject of vigorous negotiation between the parties.

The statutory limitation period under which a claim for breach of warranty must be brought is six years, or 12 years if the sale document is a deed. The seller will seek to reduce this period substantially. The period that is normally agreed varies between 18 months and two years, to enable the normal annual audit process to reveal the existence of any problems. The period for claims relating to tax matters is usually longer and should extend to at least the six-year period which the Inland Revenue has for assessing past tax-ation matters.

The qualifications to the warranties that the seller will aim to introduce will, in broad terms, seek to limit its exposure to matters within its knowledge or awareness (which may be particularly relevant if the seller has only owned the business for a short period of time), and by introducing quantitative words that limit the scope of the warranties to what the seller perceives as being of substantial or material importance. Again, the extent of these qualifications will be a matter for detailed negotiation.

Where there is more than one seller

A key issue for both the buyer and the sellers will be how the potential liability under the warranties is apportioned between multiple sellers. The buyer will invariably wish the sellers' liability to be 'joint and several'. This will enable to buyer to pursue any one or more of the sellers for the full amount of damages resulting from breach of warranty, irre-spective of which of the sellers caused the breach. This gives the buyer the important commercial advantage of being able to claim against whichever seller has the greatest financial resources.

Where the co-sellers accept joint and several liability, they may put in place a private contractual agreement between themselves which allows a co-seller who has paid damages for the warranty breach to recover a proportion of those damages from any or all of his co-sellers. Less desirably, a co-seller may have a right of contribution from his co-seller under statute. The buyer need not be concerned about these behind the scenes arrangements between the co-sellers.

Multiple sellers will aim to restrict their liability to a 'several' basis where each co-seller will be treated as having assumed liability solely for his own performances. The sell-ers will also aim to limit their individual several liability to a specified amount, usually being either an equal share of the total consideration paid by the buyer or a specified pro-portion of that total.

Certain types of sellers will frequently make the case that they should give no war-ranties or only very limited warranties. Venture capital investors will argue that they have had no direct management involvement in the running of the business and so do not have the knowledge required to give warranties. Trustee sellers will advance a similar argument and may also be prohibited from giving warranties by the terms of the trust document. Receivers will refuse to give warranties on the basis of the alleged insufficiency of infor-mation available to them and their need to distribute to creditors any funds received. Although buyers are generally accepting of the position of receivers and, to a lesser extent, of trustees, they are increasingly less willing to accept that venture capital investors should cease to have any continuing liability following completion of the transaction. The buyer will maintain that the giving of warranties is a matter of risk allocation and that venture capitalist investors, in return for the consideration received, should give at least some material warranties, albeit often qualified by the state of awareness of such investors.

Warranty insurance

A seller giving warranties may not wish to be exposed to a contingent liability that could exist for a number of years. This will particularly be the case with sales by institutional investors or private individuals. An increasingly sophisticated market has developed in recent years offering warranty and indemnity insurance that, depending on its terms, will provide sellers with a clean break from, or at least a diminution in, post-transaction liabilities.

The insurer will want to see advance drafts of the sale documentation and to be assured that a full due diligence and disclosure process has been conducted. The insurance policy

Issues for legal due diligence and warranty protection

- Company, subsidiary and associated company information
- Memorandum and articles of association, books, records and returns
- Directors details
- Company accounts
- Contracts and commitments
- Terms of trade and business
- Licences
- Data protection
- Insurance
- Assets
- Properties
- Environment
- Employment
- Pensions
- Competition and trade regulation law
- Litigation and compliance
- Bank accounts, borrowings and liabilities
- Grants and subsidiaries
- Insolvency and winding-up
- Tax

will not cover known issues, such as existing litigation, and may exclude some areas of risk, such as environmental claims or bad debts, altogether. There is also often a self-insured excess level and this may be substantial. Nevertheless, warranty insurance can be a useful bridge between a seller who is unwilling to provide warranties on an exit and a buyer who is not comfortable completing without adequate warranty protection.

Further buyer protection measures

The gap between exchange and completion

There is frequently an interval between the signing of a sale contract ('exchange') and the completion of that contract. This gap is usually to facilitate some event upon which completion has been made conditional, such as the obtaining of a competition clearance or of shareholder consent to the transaction. The buyer, unless the sale contract specifies otherwise, will bear the risk of the business from exchange. There is also a risk for the buyer that the seller, no longer being interested, will allow the business to suffer a loss of direction or even that the seller will strip assets out of, or load liabilities onto, the business prior to completion. As a consequence, it is usual for the sale contract to stipulate that the business must be run in the ordinary course between exchange and completion and to specify in detail what actions the seller and the business are allowed to carry out before completion, with, for example, the consent of the buyer being required to expenditure or borrowings in excess of a stated amount and to other matters that would materially affect the business.

The buyer will also commonly insist that the warranties given at exchange be repeated at completion, with the seller requesting a corresponding right to disclose against the warranties up to completion. The buyer will want to be able to rescind the sale contract – and so not do the deal at all – if the seller discloses a matter of such materiality after exchange that the buyer is unwilling to proceed with the acquisition.

Restrictive covenants

The buyer will often aim to restrict the seller's freedom to compete with the business sold following completion. To be enforceable, any such restrictions placed on the seller or its group in the sale contract must be reasonable for the protection of the buyer's legitimate interests and so will be limited in their scope, duration and geographical extent. Restrictions determined by the court to be excessive for the protection of the buyer's interests and excessive in restricting the activities of the seller may be struck out in their entirety by the court and so careful drafting of these restraint of trade clauses is required. In addition to restricting the seller from competing with the business being sold, the buyer will also seek to prohibit the seller from soliciting existing customers of the business, from using the name (or a similar name) of the business and from soliciting key employees of the business.

Financial promotion

Private share purchase transactions

On a share purchase transaction, the seller and its advisers will need to ensure that the sale process does not offend the rules regulating financial promotion contained in the Financial Services and Markets Act 2000. The basic prohibition on financial promotion is that no person may, in the course of business, communicate an invitation or inducement to engage in investment activity (in this case, the purchase of shares) unless the contents of the communication have been approved by an authorised person, such as an investment bank, or the communication is made by an authorised person or is covered by an exemption.

As a consequence of this prohibition, any information memorandum that is circulated by the seller or its financial adviser to potential buyers will either need to be authorised or, alternatively, sent only to certain recipients so that advantage can be taken of one of the exemptions to the financial promotion regime. Where all the recipients are investment professionals or sophisticated investors or high net-worth companies or individuals, such an exemption will be available. The contents of a data room will normally be limited to factual information and so would not be regarded as forming an invitation or inducement. The circulation of sale documentation such as the sale contract is similarly not normally regarded as constituting a financial promotion.

In addition to the financial promotion regime, statute makes it a criminal offence to make a statement, promise or forecast in connection with a sale of shares which the person making the statement knows to be misleading, false or deceptive or recklessly to make such a statement, promise or forecast. The seller and its advisers will need to be aware of this throughout the course of negotiations.

Public takeovers

A public takeover offer is, naturally, more heavily regulated by the rules on financial promotion than a private transaction as the bidder will be communicating its offer to the public at large. Many communications relating to an offer for the shares of a target company are likely to fall within the financial promotion regime and may therefore need to be issued or approved by the bidder's (or the target's) financial adviser. Advice should be taken before any proposed 'communication' is made.

The gathering of irrevocable undertakings to accept an offer from key shareholders will clearly constitute financial promotion although, as those shareholders will frequently be investment professionals, sophisticated investors or high net-worth companies, exemptions from the authorisation regime should be available.

The Financial Services and Markets Act 2000 also created the civil offence of market abuse in relation to securities traded on a UK stock exchange. The offence applies where behaviour has occurred which has involved misuse of information, or behaviour has resulted in a misleading impression being given to the market, or there has been market distortion and such behaviour is below the standards expected of a hypothetical objective regular user of the market. Directors should ensure that their conduct in relation to the offer does not fall short of the standards to be expected of a director of a company and that they do not give a misleading impression either of the value or of the price of the securities of the bidder or of the target. Compliance with the Code will in some cases (but not in every case) avoid market abuse as compliance with parts of the Code has been given safe harbour status under the market abuse regime.

Restructuring and insolvency

Directors of English companies have both general duties and specific duties under various statutes. When a company is solvent, the directors have a common law duty to act in the interests of the company and its shareholders taken as a whole. Directors also have a statutory duty to consider the interests of the company's employees. Where a company is insolvent or potentially insolvent, the duty of directors changes as they are then required to consider the interests of creditors. In the meantime, the directors remain subject to their usual fiduciary duties.

There are various provisions in the Insolvency Act 1986 which provide liquidators with extensive, additional powers, not otherwise available, to attack prior actions and transactions and to claim compensation for creditors. The provisions that may be used to attack M&A transactions by insolvent companies are those relating to transactions at an undervalue and to preferences. Directors of companies in financial difficulty or having dealings with a company in financial difficulty, need then to be aware of these provisions generally and in particular where disposals and acquisitions of company assets or businesses are proposed.

Transactions at an undervalue

A transaction entered into by a company with any other party can be ordered to be set aside by the court if the court is satisfied that it was entered into at an undervalue. This provision is of potential application where a company disposes of assets or where a parent company sells shares in a subsidiary.

A transaction will be capable of being attacked if it was entered into within two years prior to the commencement of the insolvency and, at the time of the transaction, the company was insolvent or became insolvent as a result of the transaction. A company is automatically presumed to be so insolvent where the transaction has involved a connected party, unless it is proved otherwise to the court. A connected party here, broadly, means a director of the company, a member of that director's family or another company if under common control with the company making the disposal.

The court will not make an order for a transaction at an undervalue to be set aside, or compensation to be paid, if it is satisfied that the company entered into the transaction in good faith and for the purpose of carrying on its business, and at the time of the transaction there were reasonable grounds for believing that the transaction would benefit the company.

In practice, where there is a danger of insolvency, it is important that the directors proposing to enter into a transaction:

— are satisfied that appropriate valuations, where available, have been obtained in respect of the relevant assets (so as to provide evidence that no undervalue transaction has taken place); and
— have recorded the business case and reasons for entering into the transaction (so as to assist in establishing that the transaction has been entered into in good faith).

If the court believes that a transaction was at an undervalue, it may make whatever order it sees fit to restore the position to what it would have been had the company not entered into the transaction.

Preference transactions

The court can also set aside a transaction if the transaction has the effect of putting a creditor or any person who is a surety or guarantor for any of the company's debts into a position which, in the event of the insolvent liquidation of the company, will be a better position than if the company had not done such thing. The purpose of this power is to prevent one creditor from unfairly stealing the march on other creditors by, for example, being paid out in full or receiving other assets of the company and leaving other creditors to share in the remaining proceeds.

The court will not, however, make an order under this power unless it is established that the company was influenced by a desire to give such a preference. Such an intention will be presumed if the transaction is with a connected person. Longstop dates apply to those transactions which are capable of challenge – the preference must have been given within six months prior to the commencement of the insolvency, or two years in the case of a connected person, and, as with undervalue transactions, the company must have been unable to pay its debts at the time or have become unable to do so as a result of the preference.

In determining whether a creditor or surety has been preferred, the test is whether the particular action in question has improved the position of such person relative to the other creditors in the statutory order of priorities compared with the position in which he would have been if such action had not been taken. Again, if the court believes that a transaction was a preference transaction then it can make whatever order it sees fit to restore the position to what it would have been had the company not entered into the transaction.

Conclusion

This chapter seeks to do no more than give an overview of the issues that may arise in the context of a UK M&A transaction, whether public or private. Inevitably, the issues which come to dominate a particular transaction will depend on the nature of the transaction and the parties involved.

11

Intellectual property and information technology

Barry Fishley, partner, Kevin Smith, senior associate and Paula Doyle, associate, Weil, Gotshal & Manges

Introduction

As the focus of business has shifted from industrial manufacturing to information-based technology, the importance and value of intellectual property has reached unprecedented levels. Where perhaps 20 years ago a buyer may have given little consideration to the intellectual property of the target in valuing the business, today every business will own some form of intellectual property, whether in the form of a patent protection of pharmaceutical products or copyright protection of software products. Indeed, a large number of companies are valued almost solely on the basis of their intellectual property. Whether it is Coca-Cola, whose trade mark has been valued at almost US$70 billion, IBM, whose patent licences bring in over US$1 billion every year or Disney's ownership of copyright to protect Mickey Mouse, or any other company, intellectual property is vital to business and can be a core value driver in many acquisitions.

This chapter covers the key issues relating to the acquisition of intellectual property and information technology within the United Kingdom by focusing on three main areas: due diligence, warranties and the issues that must be considered in order to transfer intellectual property and information technology.

Defining intellectual property

First, it is worth very briefly defining the nature of intellectual property and summarising the various types of intellectual property.

Intellectual property is an asset like any other and an owner of intellectual property has monopoly rights to use and exploit the intellectual property. Consequently, the owner can prevent others from exploiting the intellectual property. Whilst most countries protect the most common forms of intellectual property, there are differences between the laws of each country concerning the validity and enforcement of certain types of intellectual property.

The target (ie, the company which is either being sold or which owns or uses the intellectual property and information technology assets being purchased) will either own the intellectual property or will use it in its business by way of a licence or some other agreement by which the owner gives the target the permission to use it. If the target uses the intellectual property without the owner's consent, this will amount to an infringement of the owner's intellectual property.

Overview of intellectual property rights

Patents

These are novel, non-obvious inventions which are capable of industrial application. They have a maximum duration of 20 years. Patents are particularly important to pharmaceutical, manufacturing and electronic companies.

Registered trade marks

These are marks (such as a sign or logo) which distinguish the goods and services of one undertaking from that of another. The registration may be held forever, but must be renewed for 10-year periods at a time, based on the continued use of the mark. They are important in industries where brands are critical, for example the clothing, food and beverage industries.

Unregistered trade marks

These protect the goodwill of an undertaking. They have no finite term. They are most commonly relied upon in industries where brands are important, as mentioned above.

Copyright

This covers literary, dramatic, artistic and musical works and also computer programs. The maximum duration is life of the author plus 70 years. Copyright is particularly important in the entertainment, publishing and computer software industries.

Registered designs

These refer to the appearance of an article (for example, the contours and shape of a product). The maximum duration is 25 years. Registered designs are particularly relevant in the manufacturing industry and to consumer goods companies.

Unregistered designs

These protect original designs. The right arises automatically when the design has either been recorded in a design document or when an article has been made to the design whereas, by definition, registered design rights only arise on registration. The original design protection extends to the shape or configuration (whether internal or external) of an article. The design may be both functional and artistic. An example of an unregistered design is the design of a mobile phone case. The maximum duration is 15 years or 10 years from first marketing. Unregistered designs are particularly relevant in the car parts and fashion industries.

Database rights

These cover all types of databases (whether electronic or manual) where the data or other materials are arranged in a systematic or methodical way and are individually accessible. The maximum duration of the right is 15 years but may be extended for successive 15-year periods if there is a substantial change to the contents of the database resulting in the database being considered to be a substantial new investment. Clearly, this right is significant to organisations that rely on the exploitation of data or information in database form, for example direct marketing and mail order companies.

Know-how

This refers to confidential information such as a business's secret manufacturing process. It has no finite term. It can provide important protection in the pharmaceuticals, electronic, technology and manufacturing industries.

Domain names

Internet domain names have become increasingly important to businesses. They not only allow Internet users to connect to a business's website, which in and of itself provides commercial value, but they also normally incorporate the business's trading name and/or trade mark, which clearly are assets. Indeed, as at 31 December 2002, there were almost 4 million domain names registered using the .uk top-level domain name.[1]

Accordingly, domain names can be important assets and should be considered at the same time as considering intellectual property, even though the domain name systems are different from those relating to intellectual property.

Essentially, an undertaking does not 'own' the domain name, the domain name is merely registered to the undertaking for a period of time. Accordingly, the undertaking's rights are governed by the terms and conditions of the relevant registry. For example, in the United Kingdom a business may have an agreement with Nominet UK, which is the registry that provides .uk domain names. Alternatively (and possibly it is more likely that), the undertaking will have a contract with an Internet service provider which hosts the domain name and obtains the domain name as agent for its corporate customer. The validity, and therefore the commercial value of a domain name, is subject to both the terms and conditions issued by each registry and to the laws relating to trade marks and passing off. For example, if the target uses a third party's trade mark as part of its domain name without the third party's consent, the use of the domain name may be challenged.

Share versus asset acquisition

As regards intellectual property, the key distinction between a share and an asset deal is that in a share deal, generally all of the intellectual property rights of the target will pass to the buyer with the shares (subject to any change of control provisions in licences by which the target uses the intellectual property). In an asset deal, the buyer does not automatically obtain everything the target owns because it is only buying specifically identifiable assets or business. It is therefore imperative that the buyer properly identifies those assets that it needs and understands any attendant risks relating to them. Such risks may have an impact on valuation and whether, ultimately, the transaction takes place.

Due diligence

Purposes

As the maxim 'let the buyer beware' applies to all transactions, it is for the buyer to obtain from the seller information regarding the target and, if it believes it is appropriate, to independently verify information regarding the target so as to make an informed decision about whether to proceed with the transaction and, if so, at what price and upon what terms. The extent of the due diligence depends on a number of factors, including timing, any limits on access to the information by the seller, the resources available to the buyer as the exercise can be expensive, and the importance of the transaction to the buyer.

Buyer's viewpoint

The main purposes of intellectual property/information technology due diligence are as follows:

– identifying the intellectual property and information technology that the target owns or uses in its business;

– determining whether the target has appropriate rights to the intellectual property and information technology that it owns and the intellectual property and information technology that it uses;

– determining whether any third party has been granted any rights to or interests in the target's intellectual property or information technology and evaluating the licences and other agreements by which the target has granted these rights or interests and understanding whether any third party is in breach;

– ascertaining whether the target has implemented proper measures in its business to protect and exploit its intellectual property and information technology;

– determining whether any intellectual property or information technology owned by third parties is used in or is necessary for the operation of the target's business and evaluating whether all licences or agreements granted to the target are valid and enforceable and whether the target is in breach; and

– identifying and evaluating risks which may arise as a result of the buyer's use or ownership of the target's intellectual property and information technology.

Seller's viewpoint

In addition to the general issues which the seller should consider and which are dealt with in Chapter 10, *Legal issues*, specific issues which arise within the context of intellectual property and information technology include the following:

– Protection of target's know-how – as know-how is in the memory of members of the target's staff, clear confidentiality provisions prohibiting the unauthorised disclosure and unauthorised use of know-how by the buyer should be included in the non-disclosure agreement which the potential buyer will normally be asked to enter into with the target before receipt of information from the seller. The seller should also consider asking the buyer to agree to non-solicitation undertakings preventing it from poaching key staff who may be invaluable to the buyer as holders of such know-how, at least until the seller feels that the buyer will definitely proceed with the transaction and where such staff will either not be needed by the seller or will not automatically transfer to the buyer by operation of law.[2] These restrictions will assist in protecting the seller from having its own confidential information used to compete against it should the acquisition fall through.

– The seller should also consider whether, and if so to what extent and when, during the transaction, it should disclose specific information concerning any intellectual property which it knows will be valuable to a buyer. For example, commercially sensitive information relating to technology underlying a new product which the target owns but has not yet launched. If the information relating to the technology is disclosed to a buyer too early in the due diligence process, particularly before the seller feels sufficiently comfortable that the buyer will go through with the transaction, this could mean that the target will lose the competitive advantage of such information.

Personnel

In addition to the advisers or consultants that are normally retained on a transaction, such as bankers, accountants and lawyers, where the target's intellectual property is a key driver behind the transaction, the due diligence process may require the involvement of other individuals, including technical personnel and local counsel in jurisdictions where high-value intellectual property is maintained. They may assist in valuing the intellectual property and/or in carrying out the due diligence.

Furthermore, where intellectual property forms the basis of the target's business, for example a pharmaceutical company, it is likely that it will have internal and/or external intellectual property specialists who will be familiar with the target's intellectual property portfolio and with whom the buyer and its advisers should liaise during the transaction.

Identifying owned intellectual property

The first step in the due diligence review is to identify the intellectual property that the target claims it owns and that it uses in its business. Generally, one would expect that the seller will provide a detailed list of the registered intellectual property that it owns, including the countries in which such rights have been obtained and registered. Such a list may have been provided as a result of a detailed questionnaire being submitted by the buyer. Ideally, the buyer should undertake independent searches to verify the information disclosed by the seller although if it does not (and even if it does), the buyer will normally ask the seller to warrant the accuracy and completeness of such information. Registered intellectual property can be verified by reviewing the various databases held by the relevant registry, for example the UK Patent Office holds information regarding patents, trade marks and registered designs.[3] However, the buyer should note that very recent information concerning an application may not be available from the database. This possibility means that the buyer should also raise enquiries regarding applications for registered rights. Furthermore, physical inspection of these registrations can also be undertaken, usually by intellectual property experts.

The parties will also want to list the unregistered intellectual property owned by the target where it forms a material part of the target's business, or is viewed as a valuable asset. For example, if the target company is a software company, the copyright in each product should be listed. However, in other circumstances by definition, this will be more difficult.

Depending on the value being placed on the intellectual property, due diligence may focus solely on determining ownership and/or may attempt to confirm that all the requirements for obtaining a valid and enforceable right have been met. The extra step of reviewing the validity and enforceability of the intellectual property is expensive and time consuming, but is important if the buyer places a high value on particular intellectual property or the buyer is purchasing the intellectual property with intent to enforce it against third-party infringers, who will undoubtedly attack the validity of the intellectual property.

Trade marks

For trade marks the buyer will want to check the status of the registration, verify ownership, and understand whether all fees have been paid in order to maintain the right and whether any liens or charges have been filed against the right. It will probably be necessary to instruct local counsel or trade mark agents in relation to foreign trade marks which are important to the buyer. The buyer should also raise enquiries of the seller in relation to trade mark applications in order to evaluate the chances of the application being granted, having regard to, amongst other things, existing registrations and whether the mark has the necessary distinctiveness.

Patents

The first step with patents is to review the status of the registration and ensure that the ownership is properly recorded and that all fees have been paid. In the United Kingdom, this is a relatively simple process involving a search of computer databases held by the UK Patent Office. In other countries, the only way to obtain this information is to hire local counsel or a local search firm to go to the patent office and examine the physical records.

In order to track down and uncover additional patents that should be assigned as part of the transaction, the buyer could conduct an owner search at the Patent Office under the target's name and, where dealing with a small company with a few key inventors, an inventor search under the names of the key inventors. The company search should confirm that the target is the registered owner of the patents and applications it claims. The inventor search may uncover additional patents related to the business that were filed prior to formation of the target's business or when any inventor was working with another company. If these patents are owned by the inventors that are major shareholders in the target company, it may be appropriate for the buyer to ask that these patents be assigned to the target and subsequently sold to the buyer. If the patents are owned by a previous employer of the inventor, these patents should be reviewed in detail and compared against any key patents in the target's control invented by that individual to determine whether there is any overlap. This will assist in determining whether there is any risk that the previous employer may claim that the inventions underlying the target's patents were made while the individual was working for it. Obviously, this analysis will rest mainly on the statements of the inventor and his or her ability to confirm the statements with laboratory notebooks and related materials.

Copyright

Copyright is not registrable in the United Kingdom (in contrast to the United States, where copyright materials are capable of registration). The key condition to be met for materials to attract copyright protection is originality, that is, in broad terms, the material must not be a copy of a pre-existing work. Thus, as part of the due diligence review, it is essential to understand whether there have been any claims that the copyright work infringes copyright in another work and, if such a claim has been made, to understand the veracity of any defence. For example, if the claim relates to software, a prudent buyer would ideally want to know to what extent the software was written in a 'clean' room environment, that is, without the use of the claimant's software. This can only be answered by speaking to personnel within the target who were involved in the development process and reviewing preparatory materials relating to the development.

Know-how

The due diligence review will include a review of the confidentiality agreements which the target has executed and its standard terms, as well as the contracts that it has in place with its employees to ensure that there are appropriate clauses prohibiting unauthorised disclosure and use. In addition, discussions with the target's in-house counsel (if any) and commercial staff may confirm that the seller takes appropriate steps in its day-to-day operations to protect such know-how.

Domain names

As mentioned above, the right to use a domain name is a right granted by contract. It may therefore be necessary to review these contracts (or at least samples) as part of the due diligence.

Employees and internal policies

Generally, intellectual property which is created by employees in the course of their employment will be owned by their employer, but it is important to note that, other than in the context of an employer/employee relationship, normally the owner of such rights is the creator even though someone else (eg, the target) commissioned the creation. This typically surfaces when independent contractors are used by the target. For example, if the target is a software company and consultants are commissioned to write software, copyright will be owned by the consultant unless the consultant transfers ownership to the target in writing. As a consequence, it is important to know who developed the software and ensure that all the developers were either employees of the seller or individuals that signed written contracts assigning their intellectual property rights in the software to the target.

Another important aspect to examine is whether the target company has an intellectual property policy that it follows. A detailed intellectual property policy may establish a committee that examines new inventions and determines whether or not to pursue intellectual property protection. It may also require that relevant employees keep records to track the development of any intellectual property, such as scientists keeping lab notebooks in relation to inventions.

The buyer should also try and assess how vigilantly the target polices and enforces its intellectual property. Does it operate a proactive regime of looking out for potential infringers and does it consistently send correspondence warning the third party from such activity, threatening litigation if they continue?

Claims and litigation

Examining third-party intellectual property claims is vital to understanding the validity of the target's intellectual property and whether the transaction could lead to unwanted litigation with a third party. While this is an important step, it is also one that is without any guarantees. For example, as regards database rights, in the absence of a third-party claim, it may not be possible to make sure that the database right will successfully withstand any challenge. Buyers sometimes attempt to cover this situation by requiring the seller to provide an unqualified warranty that the target's business does not infringe any third-party intellectual property rights. However, most sellers will resist such a warranty or will normally require that it be limited to items of which it (or certain named individuals within the company) has knowledge. Accordingly, while due diligence and the proper use of the warranties assist in mitigating the risk and damage of third-party claims, some risk may be unavoidable.

While some risk is unavoidable and not in view, other risks may already be evidenced by ongoing litigation or pre-litigation correspondence. In view of the high costs involved and the possible damages available in intellectual property actions, any ongoing litigation should be thoroughly reviewed so as to evaluate the likely outcome of the litigation. Whether the target company is the plaintiff or defendant, it will face certain risks and be paying costs that the buyer may wish to factor into the purchase price. If the target is the defendant, the buyer should examine its own relationship with the plaintiff (for example, does the buyer have a corporate-wide licence from the plaintiff that would cover the activity of the target after completion or does it have some other bargaining power with the plaintiff?) and determine whether it could resolve the matter. Otherwise, it must factor into the price of the deal the possible level of damages, which may include ongoing royalties, licence fees, or possibly even an injunction preventing the use of the intellectual property.

If the target is the plaintiff, the buyer should closely examine the defences the defendant has asserted because if the intellectual property is critical to the buyer and the defendant is claiming that it is invalid or unenforceable, the prospects of such litigation may adversely affect the value of the target.

Prior to the commencement of legal proceedings, there is normally some pre-action correspondence from the claimant. For example, a third party may send a 'cease and desist' letter informing the target of the allegation of infringement and asking it to cease from using or further exploiting the intellectual property and to pay damages and costs for such use. In light of such correspondence, the buyer must examine whether the target would be sued and the outcome of any litigation.

The completion of the transaction itself may trigger a lawsuit. For example, a small company may avoid litigation because the patent owner determines the cost of commencing proceedings against the target is not worth the expected outcome. However, if the buyer is a bigger player in the industry, the owner may be more likely to bring a suit after completion where there are deeper pockets and potentially wider infringement.

Intellectual property and information technology used by the target

The final aspect of the intellectual property review, which overlaps with the wider due diligence exercise, is a review of the agreements relating to intellectual property and information technology. Companies will have a variety of licences granted to third parties and licences granted by third parties. A thorough review of these licences will provide an indication of how the target is exploiting its intellectual property and how much of the intellectual property it uses, or owns.

As with other agreements, licences must be reviewed to determine the effect that the transaction will have on them. If the transaction is an asset deal, the focus will include a review of the assignability of the licences to the buyer. If the transaction is a share deal, more focus will be placed on whether there are any change-of-control provisions that would be triggered by the transaction. In either case, where the target grants the licence, the buyer should consider any corporate-wide cross-licences or other broad licences. Depending on the exact wording of the licence, on completion of the transaction, the licence may well automatically incorporate the other intellectual property rights of the buyer into the licence granted to the third-party licensee. If there are any such licences, the buyer may direct the seller to attempt to amend them or enter into discussions with the licensee, either as a condition of the transaction or after completion.

Furthermore, the buyer must ensure that the target has not granted exclusive licences (ie, licences which prevent the target from using and granting further licences to third parties in relation to the same subject matter) of the intellectual property to third parties in fields that the buyer is interested in pursuing.

Other items that should be reviewed in the licence agreements are the length of agreement, termination provisions (including change-of-control clauses), limitations on the geographic or technological field, assignment provisions, indemnities and the financial terms. The buyer will need to factor these limitations and rights into the valuation of the intellectual property, both in respect of licences granted to the target, as well as licences granted by it.

Shared intellectual property

Where the buyer is purchasing a business or company which is part of a group of companies, it is quite common for intellectual property which is used by the target to be either owned by or licensed to another company within the group. For example, a software supplier may grant a licence to the target's holding company which allows it to sublicense use of it to the other companies in the group, including the target. If the buyer wants to have the benefit of the intellectual property following completion, in the case of sale of a business or assets, the buyer will need to set up an appropriate licensing structure prior to completion, or, where the sale is of shares, review the group-wide licence to determine whether there are any change-of-control clauses which prevent its continued use. If consent of the licensor is required (which often is the case for software licences) for the transfer of use or change of control, it is not unusual for the licensor to ask for payment for giving consent.

Clearly, the parties need to decide which one will be responsible for approaching the licensor and paying any fee.

Joint intellectual property

In addition to shared intellectual property, the target may jointly own intellectual property. Jointly-owned intellectual property may arise deliberately (for example, two biotech companies undertake joint research and development and formally agree joint ownership of any patents), or inadvertently (for example, where the target and a third party jointly write a book and one cannot distinguish between either party's contribution – they will both jointly have copyright in the book). This presents unique problems and the buyer must carefully examine any agreements establishing a joint ownership relationship and try and set up arrangements which will allow it to exploit the intellectual property following completion. Without clearly established contractual commitments, the rights of each party in a jointly-owned work vary between intellectual property areas and countries. For example, in Europe, a joint owner of a patent can use the invention, but cannot license it without the consent of the other owner, whereas in the United States, a joint owner can fully exploit the patent, including licensing the patent, without obtaining consent from the other owner.

Warranties

As discussed in Chapter 10, *Legal issues*, warranties provide some protection for the buyer to cover principal areas of risk. In the event of breach of a warranty, the buyer will seek to recover damages from the seller to cover its losses. In addition, the buyer may seek to obtain an indemnity to cover breaches of any warranties. Typically, in either case, the sale agreement will limit the damages recoverable to an amount which may be below the purchase price. Accordingly, the buyer needs to understand that warranties may not be a panacea for all risks.

Generally, the buyer will seek as many broad warranties as possible, whereas the seller will seek to minimise the number of, and will place parameters around, any warranties given. The seller will also seek to dilute any warranties given by way of disclosures made in the disclosure letter. As always, each party's relative bargaining position will dictate the outcome of these negotiations.

As a starting point, the buyer should seek to address matters of risk or concern which arose out of the due diligence exercise. For example, if due diligence uncovered the fact that some of the target's valuable trade marks have not been kept up-to-date which could lead to revocation of those marks, the buyer should ask the seller to warrant that all renewal and maintenance fees have been paid and that none of the trade marks will be exposed to revocation as a result of non-payment. The advantage of including this warranty is that, in light of the factual situation, it obliges the seller to fully disclose against it, thereby describing in some detail what the position is regarding these trade marks. In the absence of this warranty, the seller is less compelled to fully disclose this information.

Whilst the warranties should be tailored to each particular transaction, there are some general issues which the buyer will want to see covered in the warranties. Typical warranties include the following:

1 *Seller to list intellectual property to be acquired and warrant that the list is complete and accurate.*

    The seller should be asked to list all the registered intellectual property that the target owns. It is vital that, at the very least, the registered intellectual property is listed as this leads to greater certainty. If the target's unregistered intellectual property is important to the buyer, the materials that attract unregistered intellectual property protection should be listed. For example, if the target is a publishing house, then, at the very least, those publications which attract copyright should be listed.

2 *Target solely owns and has all unencumbered rights over all the intellectual property.*

    Clearly, the ownership warranty is crucial. However, the seller may seek to focus this warranty on registered rights which can be verified by searching the relevant register. By contrast and by definition, there is no register of ownership for unregistered intellectual property, therefore the seller can only give the warranty if it believes that it owns the rights and has investigated the surrounding circumstances. For example, where the target is a software company, the target will need to identify the individual writer of the software and determine whether that person was an employee who wrote the software within the scope of their employment or, if they were an independent contractor, whether there was documentation in place assigning their copyright to the target. Given this greater chance of uncertainty, the seller may seek to qualify this warranty with the knowledge of the target or certain individuals (eg, directors) within it and/or merely give the warranty against 'material' unregistered intellectual property, but not all the unregistered intellectual property which the target owns. This latter device will narrow the area of investigation (and therefore risk) for the seller. So, if the target is a publishing house, the seller may list copyright in its top 10 best sellers as the 'material' intellectual property.

3 *All the target's intellectual property is valid and enforceable.*

    Again, the seller will normally want to qualify this warranty to matters within the actual knowledge of the seller or some named individuals, on the basis that, in the absence of a challenge, they believe (but cannot be absolutely sure) that the intellectual property is valid and enforceable. It is also likely that the seller will wish to narrow the number and type of intellectual property covered by this warranty. For example, the target may own a large portfolio of international trade marks, but deliberately not maintain certain marks because they were not linked to its major brands. The seller will therefore seek to only give this warranty as it relates to 'major' brands – and it will be up to the buyer to satisfy itself as to the meaning and ambit of 'major' brands.

4   *The target's business does not infringe any third-party intellectual property rights.*
Again, it is likely that the seller will want to dilute this warranty with the knowledge qualifier and/or limit its ambit to infringement that would affect the key or material portions of the business.

5   *The list of licences granted by and to the target is complete and accurate and no licensee is in breach of any licence.*
This points to whether the licensee is in breach of a licence. Where the target is the licensee, this could enable the licensor to terminate the licence, thereby preventing the target's use of the intellectual property.

6   *The confidential information of the target has been protected by commercially reasonable methods, including the use of confidentiality agreements prior to any disclosure.*
This relates to the protection of know-how and is particularly important where the target's processes or methods are considered valuable by the buyer.

The above warranties are merely examples and are not exhaustive.

Disclosure letter

The seller will normally attempt to include disclosures against the warranties in the disclosure letter, covering everything that the buyer could have reviewed during due diligence, including all the information provided by the seller. In addition, the seller may attempt to include information from the various intellectual property registries. The buyer needs to review these disclosures carefully and consider limiting the references to registries to items actually uncovered by a specified search on a specified date rather than all matters. For example, only those matters available at the UK Patents office on 20 December 2002.

Completion
Sale agreement

As previously mentioned, in share acquisitions all the intellectual property owned and used by the target will automatically be owned by the buyer without the need for any other formalities, subject to any change-of-control clauses in licences to the target which require the licensor's consent. In contrast, in assets or business deals there must be a specific assignment of intellectual property to the buyer.

Although some business sale agreements contain generic clauses for the transfer of all intellectual property rights, it may be preferable to have stand-alone documents which transfer these rights. This may help with recording the buyer as the new owner with patent and trade mark offices in different jurisdictions.

If there are separate documents which transfer intellectual property, the content of these agreements should be agreed between the parties prior to completion.

The parties also need to allocate responsibility for the upkeep of certain types of intellectual property prior to completion. For example, renewal fees may need to be paid and correspondence and other matters dealt with in connection with pending intellectual property applications. The sale agreement should oblige the seller not to do anything which may have an adverse effect on any of the target's assets, including its intellectual property, before completion.

Generally, it is only the owner or the exclusive licensee who has the right to bring proceedings against an infringer of intellectual property rights. However, the buyer may not be formally recorded as the owner with various registries for some time after completion. This is because the process of formally recording the change of ownership of any registered intellectual property may take up to several months depending on jurisdiction. Accordingly, it would be prudent for the buyer to seek reassurance from the seller that it will assist with any enforcement of the transferred intellectual property during such period, perhaps, subject to the buyer agreeing to indemnify the seller against any costs that it incurs in doing so.

Prior to completion, the buyer should also consider any intellectual property rights licensed to the target. These rights may be terminable upon any transfer of the business (asset sale) or any change of control (share sale). Where the licensor's consent is required for any transfer, the buyer should be pressing the seller to obtain such consents prior to completion, particularly if the licensed intellectual property is critical to the business operation. However, it is not uncommon for the licensor to ask for a fee for such consent, at which point the parties need to decide which one will be responsible for such costs.

The sale agreement should also contain a clause which obliges either party to take steps reasonably necessary to perfect the transfer of ownership of the intellectual property. In the context of intellectual property, this could be extremely important as there may be hundreds of trade marks and patents in the target's portfolio which are both domestic and foreign. The transfer of ownership will be potentially expensive and time consuming because it will involve instructing overseas agents, paying fees and corresponding with different registries in order to register the buyer as the new proprietor. It is therefore advisable for the parties to carefully anticipate these costs and allocate responsibility for them.

Post-completion

The due diligence report produced for the buyer prior to completion will continue (depending on the extensiveness of the due diligence conducted) to be important to the buyer post-completion. Through the due diligence report (or some other detailed information covering the intellectual property), the buyer should be looking to ensure that it has sufficient information in its possession to undertake the proper management of the intellectual property assets transferred.

Typically, the due diligence report should contain information such as maintenance and renewal dates for patents and trade marks; expiration, renewal and option dates for licences; and identification of pending and threatened litigation.

As mentioned above, recording the change of ownership of intellectual property could entail a great deal of work and take some months. For example, it is likely that, for a large portfolio of rights, the recording of the new owner with the various registries will possibly be undertaken by trade mark or patent agents. The buyer should be aware that there is considerable risk if it fails to record ownership in a timely manner. For example, in the United Kingdom, failure to record a patent or a trade mark assignment within six months of completion of the transaction restricts the ability to recover damages for any infringement.

Domain names

The parties should also consider whether any domain names will be transferred as certain formalities will need to be adopted, depending on the particular registry which regulates the domain name. In some Internet registries, the name of the domain name registrant may be changed only with the consent of the current registrant. The rules of NSI (the main registry for .com, .net and .org domain names) provide that the organisation registered as the domain name holder may not be changed. Rather, transfers of the domain names technically require deletion of the old holder and re-registration in the registration authorities' records under the new owner's name. In order to successfully transfer the domain name, the parties must complete the domain name registration transfer agreement. Ideally, this should be prepared prior to completion. The process adopted by Nominet UK also requires the consent of the current registrant.

Licences

If the target has granted options to licensees (eg, to extend the term of the licence), the buyer should ensure that it has or makes a schedule of the dates upon which such options must be exercised by the licensee and should thus determine whether the term of the licence will be extended or whether the term and other provisions should be renegotiated.

Ideally, these decisions should be made during the due diligence process. In relation to licences granted to the target, the buyer should make a list of all critical dates relating to renewal and termination provisions and the buyer's management team will need to decide whether there are any critical clauses that need renegotiating.

Stamp duty

Following the Finance Act 2000, the transfer of patents, trade marks, registered designs, copyright and other intellectual property rights are now exempt from stamp duty.

[1] *Source:* Nominet UK.

[2] By virtue of the Transfer of Undertakings (Protection of Employment) Regulations 1981.

[3] See www.patent.gov.uk.

12

Regulation issues

Douglas Nave, partner, head of international competition law; Juliette Enser and Nick Flynn
Weil, Gotshal & Manges

This chapter deals with two types of regulation that have become increasingly important in M&A transactions: competition and environmental law. In both cases, detailed regulatory schemes can create substantial commercial costs and risks for the parties, who will need to ensure that such costs/risks are properly identified, addressed in a timely manner, and appropriately allocated as a commercial matter.

Competition

A UK acquisition may fall under a variety of competition rules, including those of the European Union (EU), EU member states, and other countries where one or both of the parties do business. Many countries now provide that sizeable transactions cannot be closed until after the parties have filed with the regulator and either waited a prescribed period of time or, in some cases, received formal agency clearance. If a transaction raises substantive competition law issues, the regulators may prevent its completion or impose conditions requiring, for example, divestiture of certain operations, agreement to specific rules on how the combined entities will do business, and so on.

The United Kingdom and a few other countries have laws empowering them to regulate mergers and acquisitions but operate only voluntary notification regimes. In such cases, the regulator may commence investigations on its own initiative, and may intervene in a transaction post-closing (with, for example, possible orders to divest what has been acquired). Accordingly, even where notification is not technically required, parties may decide to consult with a regulatory authority in advance to minimise any legal uncertainties in this regard.

As noted above, mergers and acquisitions in the United Kingdom may be subject to review not only by EU or UK regulators, but also by regulators in other countries where the parties do business (as at February 2003, 68 countries operated some form of merger notification programme). While such other reviews are beyond the scope of this chapter, they typically raise many of the same kinds of issues as are raised in the EU and the United Kingdom. In any event, it is important to make a timely assessment of potential notification obligations in all of the countries in which the parties to a transaction do business, because some jurisdictions have particular reporting deadlines or other rules whose infringement may expose the parties to substantial fines. A failure to report under the competition laws may, in a number of countries, render a completed transfer invalid as a matter of law.

Given the potentially significant impact of the competition laws on the permissibility of various transactions, as well as on the parties' ability to complete their deal in a timely manner, it is generally important to ensure that competition law advisers are brought into the parties' transaction planning at an early stage. Early consideration also should enable the parties to allocate their regulatory obligations and risks as a commercial matter, both to ensure timely compliance with all regulatory requirements and to provide for any unfavourable outcomes that might affect the value of the business being acquired.

The EU regime

Under the EU's Merger Control Regulation (MCR), transactions meeting certain revenue thresholds must be notified to the European Commission for clearance prior to completion. With limited exceptions, transactions may not be closed until clearance is received. Simultaneous signing and closing of a transaction meeting the EU's notification thresholds is rarely possible, and depends on the Commission's discretionary grant of a derogation from the normal suspensory rules.

One-stop-shop

The MCR is intended to provide a one-stop-shop for transactions that otherwise might require notification in multiple national jurisdictions. Notification to the European Commission normally pre-empts the ability of UK or other EU member state regulators to review the same transaction. The parties may find this quite advantageous, since they are not then burdened by the costs and uncertainties of dealing with multiple agencies under regimes that may well have different informational requirements, different timing and procedures, and even different substantive standards of assessment.

Despite the foregoing, notification under the MCR does not ensure that a transaction will receive its sole EU review in Brussels. National regulators, in some cases, may request that the European Commission refer all or part of a transaction having substantial local effects back to the member state for independent assessment.

Notification thresholds

Whether notification is required under the MCR is determined, in the first instance, by turnover thresholds intended to identify transactions between sizeable companies having substantial business activities/sales in the EU. Notification of transactions meeting such thresholds is required, whether or not a transaction might reasonably be expected to have any material effect on competition. Specifically, the MCR requires notification of transactions where:

- the aggregate worldwide sales of the parties are in excess of €5 billion;
- two parties each have EU sales in excess of €250 million; and
- the parties do not achieve two-thirds of their EU sales in one and the same member state.

If this test is not met, a second set of thresholds applies, so that notification may be required where:

- the aggregate worldwide sales of the parties are in excess of €2.5 billion;
- two parties each have EU sales in excess of €100 million;
- the aggregate sales of the parties in each of at least three member states exceed €100 million;
- in the same three member states, two parties each have sales in excess of €25 million; and
- the parties do not each achieve two-thirds of their EU sales in one and the same member state.

The revenues to be included for these purposes are those of the acquirer(s) and the groups to which they belong (insofar as each party may be deemed to be acquiring a control position *vis-à-vis* the business being transferred). On the seller's side, the parties are required to take into account only the revenues attributable to the shares or assets being acquired (and not those of the seller itself, where it remains outside the concentration).

As indicated above, transactions involving parties that each realised two-thirds of their turnover in one and the same member state are deemed to be predominantly local in effect. Jurisdiction over such transactions therefore generally lies with the member states, rather than the European Commission.

Notification and timetables

Transactions meeting the thresholds noted above must be reported to the European Commission in a Form CO, which calls for detailed information regarding the proposed transaction, the parties' commercial operations, and characteristics of potentially affected markets. The filing ostensibly should be made within seven days of the signing of a binding agreement (or announcement of a public bid), though the Commission generally is very accommodating towards requests for extension of the deadline. It is anticipated that, under MCR reforms now being considered, there soon may be no deadline for notification (though the parties still will be required to suspend closing until the end of a post-notification waiting period) and the parties may be able to file notification before they reach a binding agreement (subject to their agreeing that the proposed transaction may be publicised). In any event, parties for whom timing is important are well advised to begin preparation of the notification early in the transaction, as the Form CO often requires quite voluminous and detailed information that may take a matter of weeks, rather than days, to assemble.

Once notification has been filed, the Commission has approximately one month to consider the potential competitive effects of the transaction (unless the parties are prepared to offer commitments at this stage to deal with any substantive issues, in which case the period is extended to roughly six weeks). This period may be extended by approximately four more months if the Commission believes that the transaction raises serious competition issues. As noted above, parties generally are not permitted to complete their transaction during these waiting periods.

Despite the MCR's relatively inflexible waiting periods, parties who wish to close a transaction may be able to shorten the review period by working proactively with Commission staff. Early and thorough pre-notification contacts may enable the parties to answer any initial concerns, and thus avoid the opening of an in-depth review. The timely negotiation of undertakings may prevent a potential challenge or lengthy review. Further, if there is a pressing commercial need for early closing, the parties may seek a formal derogation from the obligation to delay closing, which may be granted upon a showing of sufficient cause. While the Commission is bound to provide a period for the member states and other interested parties to comment on a proposed transaction – and such comment periods constrain it from significantly reducing the waiting period – Commission staff have proven willing to try to shorten the period as far as possible to accommodate serious commercial concerns of the parties.

The substantive review

The Commission's task, under the MCR, is to identify mergers and acquisitions that are likely to lead to one or more companies obtaining a dominant position. In general terms, dominance may result where a company acquires some degree of market power (ie, the power independently to raise prices or to reduce industry output), or where the transaction will leave few competitors with diminished competitive incentives and an enhanced ability to collude. In such cases, the Commission may block the transaction entirely, or may condition clearance on the parties' commitments to various steps (eg, divestiture of competitively sensitive assets and so on) designed to resolve its concerns.

The types of considerations informing a full competitive assessment on the merits are beyond the scope of this chapter. However, in any case raising potentially serious substantive issues the parties are well-advised to assemble their arguments, often with the aid of a professional economist, in advance of notification. If this has not been done, the rapid pace of regulatory enquiry and decisionmaking (which often involves numerous, detailed and burdensome requests for information from the parties) may overwhelm later efforts to marshal an effective defence. It also should be noted that the Commission often relies heavily on representations from the parties' competitors and customers, particularly in deciding whether a transaction merits a full four-month 'Phase II' review. It is therefore important to anticipate any complaints and, as far as possible, to ensure that customers and suppliers understand how a proposed transaction is likely to work to their benefit.

The tight timetables of the MCR leave little room for negotiation with the Commission on commitments in cases where the Commission believes a remedy is required. Indeed, the Commission has, for this reason, put forward some proposals for reform of the MCR which might allow for some extensions of time in this regard. Nonetheless, the parties are well advised to ensure that they have thoroughly explored their options for resolving any serious competition issues in advance, so that they may propose undertakings in a timely manner if that is appropriate. The parties also should be aware that the Commission will seek to verify the effectiveness of any proposed remedies with other market participants.

The UK regime

The UK regime is one of the few European regimes that differs substantially from that of the European Commission, most notably from a procedural standpoint. In particular, parties are under no obligation to notify the UK regulators in advance of a transaction. Rather, the Office of Fair Trading (OFT) has jurisdiction to investigate any transactions which meet certain thresholds (even after a transaction has been consummated), and often opens an enquiry on its own initiative. Where their transaction does not meet the MCR notification thresholds but may raise some UK competition concerns, parties often choose to notify the OFT voluntarily in advance of closing, to reduce the risk of post-closing intervention.

Consistent with the voluntary nature of notification, parties are permitted to close a transaction at their own risk during the course of an OFT investigation (although the OFT will soon have increased powers, in appropriate cases, to prevent business integration while its investigation is pending). Once the OFT's investigation is complete, a decision is taken on whether the transaction should be referred to the Competition Commission for further investigation. If a reference is made, the parties generally are prohibited from closing (if they have not already done so) until the regulatory proceedings have run their course. Where closing already has occurred, an acquirer may be obliged to provide appropriate assurances that it will not take measures impairing the competitive viability of the acquired business pending completion of the review.

The OFT investigation

The OFT currently has jurisdiction over transactions where the parties have a combined share of supply or demand in excess of 25 per cent, or where the target's worldwide assets exceed £70 million. Under the Enterprise Act 2002 (the 'Act'), which is expected to come into force in the second quarter of 2003, these thresholds will be amended so that the asset test will be replaced with a test based on the target's UK turnover.

Parties wishing to notify may do so either using a statutory procedure or by more informal means. In the former case, the OFT is under a binding timetable, which requires that a decision be made within seven weeks (reduced to six weeks under the Act) whether the transaction should be cleared, referred to the Competition Commission for in-depth investigation, or cleared subject to remedial commitments by the parties. In cases of less formal notification, the OFT generally aims to complete its investigation (under non-binding guidelines) within nine weeks. In either case, careful and timely preparation of the notification and related materials may enable the parties to help shape the regulator's thinking before opponents of their transaction have had time to poison the well.

In addition to the foregoing, the OFT offers a confidential guidance procedure enabling parties to a deal that is not yet public to gauge the likelihood of a reference. In that case, the parties provide the OFT with basic information regarding the transaction, the parties' operations, and any affected markets, and the OFT may advise on whether it considers a reference likely to be warranted in the light of the information presented. Because this procedure is confidential, and the OFT does not have an opportunity to market test the proposal with customers and competitors, the regulator's advice is necessarily preliminary and non-binding. Nonetheless, this procedure can be useful for parties wishing to obtain some guidance as to the existence and height of any regulatory hurdles at an early stage in their transaction planning.

As noted above, the OFT is not the final decisionmaker regarding potentially problematic transaction, but refers such deals to the Competition Commission for in-depth investigation. The decision whether to refer currently is made by the Secretary of State for Trade and Industry (the 'Secretary of State'), acting on advice from the OFT, but will lie solely with the OFT, in all but exceptional cases, once the Act comes into force. Under the Act, the OFT's decision must be made purely on competition grounds, and a merger that may cause a substantial lessening of competition generally must be referred. However, the OFT will be empowered to accept undertakings from the parties aimed at remedying the anti-competitive effects of the transaction rather than making a reference.

Unless there has been a statutory pre-notification, a transaction may be referred up to four months after completion (or later, if the transaction is not publicised on completion).

The Competition Commission investigation

The procedure on a reference will be substantially altered by the Act, in that the Competition Commission will soon have the power to reach a final decision on almost all references (whereas its powers currently are limited to clearing transactions and, where that is not appropriate, advising the Secretary of State on any remedies/injunctions). In cases where the Commission concludes that a proposed transaction may substantially lessen competition, it will be able to block the deal or to condition its completion on appropriate commitments from the parties to divest overlapping businesses or otherwise remedy the pertinent competition concerns. In the case of a completed merger, the Competition Commission will be able to order divestment or other measures to remedy its anti-competitive effects.

The Act provides that the Competition Commission's investigation should last for a maximum of 24 weeks (with the possibility for an eight-week extension in exceptional circumstances). During this period, the parties to a proposed transaction are prohibited from purchasing each other's shares, and the parties to a completed merger cannot carry out any further integration, without the Competition Commission's consent.

In deciding how to exercise its new powers, the Competition Commission clearly is seeking to improve its procedures, and, in particular, to make them more transparent. The Competition Commission also appears to want to respond to concerns raised about the sheer quantity of information that parties currently are required to provide in a very short period. Nonetheless, the parties to a merger that has been referred should expect to devote substantial management time and resources to the proceedings. This, coupled with the desire to avoid the prolonged uncertainty associated with an investigation, can provide a powerful incentive to negotiate with the OFT for undertakings in lieu of a reference.

Allocating regulatory risk

It is increasingly common for parties to a transaction that might raise competition law issues to include relatively detailed clauses in their agreements allocating any regulatory risks between them. Indeed, even if a transaction raises no substantive issues, contracts generally must address any mandatory notification regimes in order to ensure that the parties can properly meet their obligations in this regard and are not contractually obliged to close in breach of such rules.

To the extent that a transaction is subject to the MCR or other suspensory regimes, the parties generally will insert provisions conditioning closing on the expiration/termination of all mandatory waiting periods and receipt of all necessary anti-trust clearances. This can be done either through use of a generic 'all material filings' clause or by specifying the jurisdictions in which filing is required. While such provisions are necessary to ensure that the acquirer or, in some cases, both parties are able to fulfil their regulatory obligations, they also mean that, if the transaction is blocked, the seller will bear the risk that the value of the target business has fallen in the meantime, unless the parties provide otherwise (eg, through some form of indemnity).

In transactions falling under the United Kingdom's jurisdiction, and other voluntary-filing regimes, the parties must decide whether to include regulatory clearance as a closing condition. In the absence of such a provision, the regulatory risk essentially lies with the buyer who, if the proposed transaction raises serious competition issues, might be forced to divest some or all of an acquired business post-completion, under fire sale conditions. In these circumstances, confidential guidance and similar informal contacts with the regulator may provide some assurance for the buyer that any risks being assumed are reasonable. Where such contacts cannot be agreed in advance, the buyer may wish to ensure that its obligation to complete the transaction is contingent on its receipt of satisfactory regulatory assurances that the transaction will not be challenged or referred for in-depth investigation.

Parties to potentially problematic transactions also are well advised to address and allocate, in advance, the possibilities and potential costs of regulatory intervention. For example, the parties may agree that they must close (or, if closing is prohibited, arrange sale of the business to a third party), and that the acquirer must bear all costs and risks of any regulatory action (including any diminution in value from divestiture, or the difference between the agreed purchase price and the amount realised on sale of the subject business to a third party). In contrast, the acquirer might limit its exposure by conditioning completion on the absence of material intervention or the imposition of regulatory requirements up to no more than an agreed value. Likewise, the parties should agree, through a drop dead or other mechanism, how far through a regulatory process they are required to go – whether through only a first-stage notification and review, through any in-depth agency investigation, or through all potential appeals from a potentially unfavourable decision.

Conclusion

Parties to a transaction that may involve application of the EU or UK competition rules (or rules of similar regimes) should address such issues early in their transaction planning. Early consideration should enable the parties to complete their deal in a timely manner, with minimal disruption. More importantly, it should enable parties to understand and intentionally allocate any regulatory risks that might exist, while positioning the parties most favourably to reduce those risks in the thorough preparation of a regulatory defence.

Environment

Introduction

It is only in the last few decades that environmental issues have become a strategic issue in mergers and acquisitions. This trend began in the 1980s when the United States introduced laws imposing the threat of large fines, significant clean-up costs and the possible closure of sites for industrial polluters. By the late 1980s, the potential environmental liabilities which an acquirer could inherit on completion of an acquisition had become a mainstream corporate concern in the United States. Since then, much of Europe has followed suit and, in the early 1990s, the United Kingdom introduced new legislation to address clean-up of historic contamination and the licensing of industrial operations with an environmental impact. It is now essential in any corporate transaction with a UK land element to take steps to: (i) quantify environmental liabilities and costs, both actual and contingent, which affect the target business or company, (ii) consider their impact on both value and, where relevant, the availability of finance, and (iii) to apportion responsibility for or insure against them. Failure to do so can leave an acquirer, in particular, exposed to large-scale unexpected liabilities. A sophisticated array of advisers and products has sprung up to service these needs.

This section will focus on the environmental issues which the parties to a typical M&A transaction need to address. The emphasis will be on the acquirer's perspective because his lack of knowledge about the target is a key factor in the negotiations and is also a concern of any lender which is providing funding. Environmental costs and liabilities can be significant and the acquirer should conduct adequate due diligence to discover their likely extent and then consider the various contractual protections which may be appropriate to allocate the environmental risks arising from them. Although the emphasis will be on the acquirer, the seller's exposure to environmental risk does not automatically come to an end at completion and the seller's strategy should also include anticipation of the issues which the acquirer is likely to raise.

Likely environmental liabilities and costs

Environmental liabilities and costs typically arise in the context of (i) the remediation of existing contamination and/or (ii) compliance with licence conditions and laws regulating the day-to-day operation of any facility.

Clean-up liability

The Confederation of British Industry (CBI) estimates that there are 100,000 contaminated sites in the United Kingdom which will cost approximately £20 billion to remediate. The likelihood of clean-up liability arising from such sites is significantly greater now than in the past because local authorities are under a recently imposed duty to search for contaminated land in their jurisdictions and to require it to be cleaned up. Most local authorities began this search in earnest in late 2002, which means that an increase in the incidence of liability is likely for both actual polluters and innocent owners and occupiers of polluted land.

Compliance costs

Operations which affect the environment are likely to be regulated by laws limiting their emissions to air, land or water, and these laws are tending to become more onerous and costly over time. In particular, facilities that fall under the new Pollution Prevention and Control (PPC) licensing regime face significant costs. PPC is an integrated approach to licensing whereby the aggregate impact of an operation's emissions to air, land and water are considered together rather than in isolation. Compliance involves regular equipment upgrades to ensure the use of best available techniques to avoid damage to the environment and the clean-up of any new contamination caused by the operator during the licence. In addition, operations subject to PPC have to submit benchmarking environmental audits with their PPC licence applications and these audits may actually provide the regulator with the information needed to prompt it to exercise its various clean-up powers.

Environmental regulation continues to grow inexorably and clean-up and compliance costs are an increasingly important issue affecting the bottom line for many businesses. Acquirers and sellers need to ensure, as far as possible, that these are anticipated and factored into negotiations.

Key environmental issues to address in due diligence and negotiation

Clean-up liability for historic contamination

Historic contamination means contamination resulting from the release or disposal of hazardous materials prior to completion. The disposal or release may be the result of actions of the seller, a predecessor, or migration from another site. Liability to remediate such historic contamination in the United Kingdom does not exclusively depend on either (i) guilt being established for a breach of law, (ii) participation in the relevant release or disposal, or (iii) whether the pollution occurred before or after the introduction of the environmental liability regime. The key factor in triggering liability is simply the presence of a sufficient threat to the environment and, once this has been established, government policy is that the costs of clean-up should be dealt with by the private rather than the public purse.

The relevant legislation[1] provides that the 'causer' or 'knowing permitter' (each a 'Class A Person') of the presence of the substances giving rise to the contamination or, if such a person cannot be found, the innocent current 'owner or occupier' (each a 'Class B Person') will be required to remediate if the regulator becomes aware that either (i) significant harm is being caused, or there is a significant possibility of that happening, or (ii) (in the case of Class A Persons only) pollution of controlled waters is being, or is likely to be caused.[2]

One of the defining characteristics of contamination is that it can remain hidden for long periods and, therefore, the time between the deposit of a substance in the ground and the realisation that there is a problem requiring remediation may be very lengthy. During that period the original causer of the pollution may or may not have disappeared and the relevant property may have changed ownership and/or occupancy a number of times. In such a scenario, there are various ways in which clean-up liability may impact upon an acquirer of a target after completion regardless of how long ago the original pollution occurred.

After completion of an asset purchase, the acquirer may incur direct liability for historic contamination in three ways despite its usually not being the original causer of pollution. First, over time it may acquire knowledge of the pollution and have sufficient control over it to be regarded as a knowing permitter of the presence of the relevant substances and therefore become a Class A Person. Second, if no Class A Person can be found, liabilities can be imposed on the acquirer as an innocent owner or occupier or Class B Person. Thirdly, the applicable statutory guidance states that in transactions between large commercial parties, if the seller gives the acquirer permission to carry out his own audit and the seller and acquirer are both classified as Class A Persons, the seller is to be excluded from liability. In this specific circumstance, the seller's liability is transferred by operation of law to the acquirer.[3]

After completion of a share purchase, the acquirer may find that the target already is or may become a Class A or Class B Person in respect of historic contamination with a consequent impact on its value. Unlike in an asset sale, the acquirer is purchasing a corporate entity along with its history, including any liability it may have for its past actions. As discussed above, environmental liabilities may only manifest themselves after a lengthy period and the target may be found liable after completion for pollution which it caused a long time beforehand. The target may even incur liability after completion in respect of pre-completion events at facilities which it used to own or occupy but which it has since sold or ceased to occupy.

As part of the due diligence sale and purchase negotiations, the parties need to ascertain and allocate environmental liabilities that may arise post-completion because in the absence of such an agreement, the allocation of liability will reflect public policy considerations rather than the commercial intent of the parties.

Operational compliance costs

A distinction should be drawn between (i) costs for maintaining continued compliance with licences or laws and (ii) costs to remedy non-compliance, that is, breaches of licences and laws. Costs to maintain compliance are a normal ongoing business expense which any acquirer should expect to shoulder. Such costs can be significant, however, and because this area of regulation is a dynamic and constantly changing one, they can escalate rapidly. Any acquirer should investigate what these costs, such as under the PPC regime discussed earlier, are likely to be in the future and factor them into its financial models.

Material non-compliance prior to completion can also involve the acquirer in significant expense which should not be characterised as merely an ongoing business cost for the acquirer to bear. It can lead to the imposition of large fines and penalties and/or the need to achieve compliance by the installation of equipment such as, for example, emission stack scrubbers or waste water treatment plant. In the worst-case scenario, if the relevant breach cannot be fixed, the operation may need to be shut down and production brought to a halt until a solution is found. Needless to say profits will suffer in that event.

In an asset purchase the continuation after completion of any pre-completion non-compliance will directly expose the acquirer to the risk of incurring fines and penalties itself or being required to incur expenses to avoid them. In a share purchase, such liabilities and expenses are not directly incurred by the acquirer but may affect the value of the company acquired. The acquirer, and, where relevant, its lender need to understand the risks faced in this area so that they can factor them into the negotiations on price, warranties and indemnities.

Environmental due diligence and negotiation

Due diligence

Environmental issues are often scientifically complex and need technical expertise to fully understand and analyse them. This means that they can become deal-breakers because neither party to a transaction feels able to take a view of the nature of the risk it is being asked to accept. It is therefore vital that the parties obtain information and advice to enable them to understand their real exposure to risk and the pre-acquisition due diligence process is crucial to this. The acquirer usually knows far less about the target than the seller does and is most in need of information. However, environmental costs are ultimately an issue affecting price and both parties need to be able to negotiate on the basis of fact rather than speculation. Accordingly, both the seller and acquirer should consider the extent of the audits which may be required and who should commission them. The acquirer wants as much information as possible but needs the cooperation of the seller who may not be prepared to consent to the level of disruption to its business which would be required to comply with the acquirer's wishes.

Types of audit

Various companies offer desk and public record-based searches which are comparatively inexpensive and give basic data about the environmental setting of a site but with little or no interpretative analysis. Such a report can form the basis for deciding whether a site is of sufficient concern to merit further investigation.

Often a more extensive evaluation is warranted. There is a broad range of specialist environmental consultants who offer a more sophisticated service which will include the collection and interpretation of raw environmental data and an interpretative analysis of the issues. A Phase I assessment by such a consultant involves desk-top research of publicly available information and a site visit with interviews of site staff. The focus is often limited to the risk of contamination, although for an additional fee a compliance audit can be added to the scope of work. The resulting report provides a reasonable idea of the environmental sensitivity of the site and the relevant operational issues.

Such a Phase I often identifies issues but recommends additional intrusive investigations to confirm or quantify potential risks. If further investigations are appropriate, and agreed to by the seller, a Phase II assessment should be performed. It will involve bore-holing, testing and laboratory analysis. The seller may be reluctant to allow a Phase II before the acquirer is committed to the purchase because the consultant might discover a condition that requires an immediate response. If the acquirer pulls out of the transaction as a result, the seller's position is prejudiced.

If permitted, a Phase II assessment can require several weeks to complete and any type of assessment requires preparation and time. Therefore, it is very important for the parties to consider environmental due diligence as early as possible in the transaction to ensure that it fits with the deal timetable. If there are many sites to visit spread through many jurisdictions, the completion of the environmental due diligence will be a major logistical effort in its own right.

In addition, the acquirer's lender, where relevant, will have its own view on the scope of due diligence required and will expect to be able to rely on the final report regardless of who has commissioned it.

Transfer of liability

The performance of audits by the acquirer has consequences for the allocation of liability at law of which it and the seller should be aware. Acquisition of knowledge in the auditing process can lead to an acquirer becoming a Class A Person as a knowing permitter following completion if the audit leads to the acquirer becoming aware of a problem over which it has sufficient control for it to be said to be permitting the presence of the relevant substances. In addition, as seen above, the mere act of a seller giving permission to an acquirer to perform environmental investigations can lead to the transfer of the seller's clean-up liability to the acquirer by operation of law in the specific situation where the acquirer and seller are both Class A Persons. Permission from the seller to the acquirer to perform a Phase I assessment is likely to be sufficient to have this effect in most cases. As seen above, there are reasons why the seller may be reluctant to go further and consent to Phase II assessments. However, if it is asked for permission to perform such assessments, the seller should satisfy itself that a refusal of permission does not mean that the opportunity to transfer its liability is lost.

Despite the fact that an audit may lead to the transfer of liability or acquisition of knowledge described above, it is advisable to do one because the acquirer should make important investment decisions when in possession of the relevant facts. Ignorance is not an effective protection from liability because, once in occupation, the acquirer may acquire the relevant knowledge to become a Class A Person as a knowing permitter in any event or it may incur liability as an innocent owner/occupier (a Class B Person) even if that does not happen. It is better to consider the liability implications before, rather than after, completion so the acquirer can use this information to negotiate an appropriate contractual allocation of the legal liabilities.

Negotiation

If the results of the above due diligence indicate that significant environmental liabilities and costs for remediation and compliance are likely, the acquirer and seller need to factor this into the discussions about price and to agree contractually how to allocate such costs. Some of the tools which the parties may use to resolve these issues are discussed below.

Contamination

The parties to any transaction may find it very difficult to agree the amount of any likely clean-up liabilities and therefore also find it difficult to negotiate a typical allocation of risk by way of purchase price reduction, warranty and/or indemnity. The difficulty of quantifying such liabilities can easily become a deal-breaker. However, there are alternatives which the parties can explore and some of these are discussed below.

Insurance Historically, insurance has typically been available only for clean sites. However, there are now specialist insurers who are prepared to offer insurance on contaminated sites. The nature of the cover and the size of the premium will depend on the facts of each case but, in principle, insurance is available to put a definite cap on the extent of a party's liability. It can therefore assist the parties where the fear of unknown and unquantified liabilities is preventing agreement. It is not, however, a perfect solution as it merely gives the insured a right to sue the insurer on the terms of the policy and full recovery is not guaranteed.

In order to quote, the insurers will need to review the due diligence and formulate a proposal. The terms of the insurance policy may need negotiation with the insurer and this solution should be considered as early as possible in the transaction timetable.

Exclusion of property/pie-crust lease If a purchaser is not prepared to accept environmental risk in relation to a particular property, and insurance is not an acceptable solution, the relevant land could simply be excluded from the deal if the seller is prepared to retain it.

An extension of this concept is for the acquirer to take a pie-crust lease of the site causing concern. This involves the acquirer taking leasehold title of only the surface of the site while the seller retains full title and responsibility for the land bequeath that layer. The intention is that, if the relevant pollution is underneath the acquirer's surface layer, the acquirer cannot be said to be the causer or knowing permitter of its presence or be classified as the owner or occupier of the land where the pollution is located. The pollution remains in land retained by the seller and is its responsibility. However, the validity of this concept has not been tested in the UK courts.

Clean-up pre/post-completion Another solution is for the parties to agree the terms of a clean-up programme to address the relevant problem. This gives rise to issues which require careful consideration such as, inter alia, how the parties will determine that the work has been satisfactorily performed, who will control the contractors and how will the costs be borne?

Contamination and operational compliance – warranties and indemnities

Warranties and indemnities are the traditional way of allocating risk in any transaction. The drafting will be governed by the facts in each case but certain issues commonly arise. For example, in the context of contamination, it is important to establish whether all relevant environmental audits have been disclosed, whether contaminants are or have been used, stored, disposed of or merely present on the site (for example, in underground storage tanks) and whether there are any circumstances which have or are likely to give rise to any regulatory action. In the context of operational compliance, the seller should be prepared to warrant, without qualification by reference to its awareness, that the target has the licences required for its operations, that there have been no material breaches of such licences or any applicable laws and that, so far as it is aware, there are no circumstances likely to give rise to such breaches.

Warranties are an effective means to flush out information by way of disclosure. Properly drafted, they prompt the seller to describe the true condition of the target because his protection from being sued for breach of warranty is adequate disclosure to the acquirer. Ideally the acquirer will use the disclosed information to secure further contractual protection and/or a price adjustment. This is preferable to suing for breach of warranty which is likely to involve court proceedings (within what is likely to be a reasonably short warranty claim period of one to [three] years) and will be subject to the rules regarding remoteness of damage and quantification of loss which may mean the acquirer's recovery is inadequate.

If a particular environmental concern emerges from the due diligence and disclosure process, it should be dealt with by way of indemnity. Payment under an indemnity does not depend on establishing breach of any term and disclosure is irrelevant. If the indemnity's terms have been satisfied, the seller is contractually obliged to pay on the basis of whatever formula the parties have chosen, whether this is pound for pound of loss or any other arrangement. The time period for claims will also often be longer than for the warranties. Due to the nature of contamination problems, the acquirer ideally wants an indemnity for clean-up liabilities which is unlimited in time and amount although a well-advised seller should never agree to such uncapped liability.

However, an indemnity is only as good as the financial standing of the indemnitor and can be heavily caveated. For example, there may be limitations on paying out if the acquirer has volunteered information to the regulator and/or its own actions have led to the situation becoming sufficiently serious for a regulator to require clean-up, for example by bore-holing or changing the use of the site.

Conclusion

Environmental issues are often complex and are increasingly the subject of extensive and costly regulation. The cost implications of this increasing regulatory burden are likely to grow in significance as a proportion of any target's overall budget and any unexpected material clean-up liability could have a significant impact on a target's financial strength.

An acquirer needs to provide for enough time to perform adequate due diligence and to factor the results into the negotiation process to ensure that the likely costs and liabilities are understood and allocated properly before committing to a purchase. The seller also needs to protect its own interests. Environment is now a key strategic concern and the parties to a transaction cannot afford to ignore it.

---

[1] Environmental Protection Act 1990: Part IIA.

[2] A Class B Person can only incur liability if the liability arises because of the significant harm referred to in item (i) above and not in respect of pollution of controlled waters referred to in item (ii).

[3] DETR Circular 2/2000 Annex 3 paragraphs D59-61 Test 3 – 'Sold with Information'.

13

Tax issues

Gary Richards, tax partner, Weil, Gotshal & Manges

Introduction

When carrying out an acquisition, a key UK tax issue is how the transaction should be structured. In some cases, commercial or regulatory factors will dictate that an acquisition is carried out in a particular way. In many cases, however, there will be scope to structure a transaction in a way which provides significant tax benefits to both vendor and purchaser. Accordingly, in order to provide a framework for UK tax structuring, this chapter initially summarises key aspects relevant to UK acquisitions:

- corporation tax;
- capital gains tax; and
- income tax and social security contributions.

Apart from value added tax (VAT), discussed briefly below, and stamp duty, there are no other direct taxes generally applicable to corporate profits in the United Kingdom: in particular there is no trade tax.

Corporation tax

Corporation tax is charged on the profits, as computed for tax purposes, of companies resident for tax purposes in the United Kingdom (a 'UK resident' company) and companies which, even if not UK resident, carry on trades through a permanent establishment in the United Kingdom.

A company is UK resident either if it is incorporated in the United Kingdom or, even if incorporated in another jurisdiction, it is centrally managed and controlled in the United Kingdom. A company is centrally managed and controlled where key strategic decisions are taken, often but not invariably where board meetings take place. The place where a company is centrally managed and controlled can be a different location to where a company's main business operations are carried out. (Note that if a double tax treaty contains a tie breaker provision providing that a company is to be tax resident in the country where its place of effective management is located and the place of effective management is in fact within that country, the company will be regarded for most UK tax purposes as resident in that jurisdiction and not the United Kingdom.) A company has a UK 'permanent establishment' if it has a fixed place of business through which business is carried on, such as a branch or office, or if a UK-based agent 'has, and habitually exercises, authority to do business' on behalf of the company.

A company which is UK resident is liable to UK corporation tax on its worldwide income and gains, although a UK resident company liable to tax in another jurisdiction may be able to obtain credit (but not exemption) for local tax paid against UK tax under the UK's double tax relief legislation.

A non-resident company carrying on a trade through a UK permanent establishment is liable to corporation tax on (i) income attributable to the permanent establishment and (ii) chargeable gains in respect of assets situated in the United Kingdom held in connection with the permanent establishment. Accordingly, a non-resident company is not liable to corporation tax on income derived from assets unconnected with the permanent establishment (although it may be liable to UK income tax, for example, on rental income from UK land). Nor is it liable to UK taxes on chargeable gains on disposals of assets unconnected with a UK trade or where that non-resident does not carry on a trade through a UK permanent establishment.

A UK resident company's profits for tax purposes can be significantly different from profits computed in its financial statement, in particular:

– depreciation (or amortisation) in a company's financial statements is ignored but a UK resident company is given tax relief, particularly on industrial buildings, and plant and machinery, under the capital allowances regime. (In many cases this regime provides for more generous relief than would be available if amortisation in a company's accounts formed the basis for tax deductions on capital equipment);
– the UK thin capitalisation and transfer pricing regime may limit the deductibility of expenditure, including financing costs;
– the tax legislation may spread, defer, or deny tax relief for certain types of expenditure which is deductible in computing for profits accounts purposes.

Capital gains tax

Individuals (and trustees) who are resident or ordinarily resident for UK tax purposes can be liable to capital gains tax (CGT) if they dispose of chargeable assets whether or not the assets are located in the United Kingdom. Chargeable assets include shares and loan notes which are not qualifying corporate bonds (QCBs): gains or losses on QCBs are exempt. Where assets situated outside the United Kingdom are disposed of by individuals who, although not domiciled in the United Kingdom, are resident or ordinarily resident in the United Kingdom, they will not be liable to CGT (unless at a time when they are still UK resident or ordinarily resident they subsequently bring the proceeds of sale into the United Kingdom). For these purposes, shares which are registered in a shareholder register which is maintained overseas will ordinarily be treated as situated outside the United Kingdom.

The reorganisation of share capital provisions in the CGT legislation provide for many forms of corporate transactions not to involve a disposal of the original shares but instead for those shares and any shares resulting from such a reorganisation to be treated as the same asset. This is particularly relevant to acquisitions involving the issue of shares and/or debt (discussed in more detail under 'Making the acquisition' below).

Income tax and social security contributions

Income tax is particularly relevant to employee shareholders and employees who are, or as a result of a change of control become, entitled to exercise share options in the context of acquisitions. The UK tax legislation distinguishes between Inland Revenue approved arrangements under which, if operated as expected, no income tax charges arise at all (or are at least deferred until receipt of cash) and unapproved arrangements which can give rise to tax charges on receipt of shares or where the value of shares already held is enhanced. While, in general, if an employee holds options and on a takeover or other change of control he exchanges options over the target company for options over shares in the acquiring company with an equivalent value there is no immediate tax consequence, the exercise of an unapproved option (or an approved option in certain circumstances) can give rise to a tax charge. In many cases, any income tax due is required to be collected under the UK payroll withholding tax system (PAYE) by the employing company, or in some cases, the acquiring company. To avoid providing employees with a taxable benefit, arrangements will therefore need to be made by the person responsible for paying the tax under the PAYE system to be reimbursed by employees.

Broadly similar principles govern any liability to national insurance contributions (NICs), the UK social security contribution system, in respect of the exercise of options and receipt of shares by employees, although different rules have applied to options and shares provided at different times. The NIC regime imposes liabilities on employees (up to certain monetary limits) and on employers (uncapped) to pay contributions, an employee's share of contributions usually being deducted from remuneration. With one exception – for NICs payable on the exercise of unapproved options where it was agreed after 18 May 2000 by an employee that he would meet the liability – the legislation prevents an employer shifting the employer's liability to make NICs to an employee. Accordingly, particularly on the exercise of unapproved options, NICs can be a significant transaction cost of an acquisition.

Structuring the transaction

Recent changes to the UK tax legislation have made it even more important to consider how a transaction is structured, both from the viewpoint of vendor and purchaser. However, clearly there may be commercial or legal considerations affecting how acquisitions are carried out: for instance in the acquisition of a company whose shares are publicy traded there is little scope for acquiring the underlying businesses or groups in a different way.

Vendor issues

If the transaction involves a corporate vendor of a business which is carried on in a subsidiary, ordinarily the vendor will want to sell the shares in that subsidiary. This is because, provided the requirements of the substantial shareholdings exemption (SSE) are satisfied, any gain (or loss) on the shares will be exempt. The SSE will usually apply if the vendor or, if in a corporate group, the vendor group has held a 10 per cent plus shareholding interest in the company being sold for at least a year and both the company or group being sold and the vendor or vendor group are (wholly or mainly) carrying on trading activities. (Note that if the vendor is controlled from overseas, any gain exempted by the SSE may be deemed to be received and taxable in the parent company's jurisdiction, so on a global basis, the SSE may be less valuable to such a group as compared with an attractively priced offer for the subsidiary's assets. This is because tax payable in the United Kingdom on an assets disposal may be creditable in the overseas jurisdiction.)

If the vendor had to procure the sale of the assets of the subsidiary, gains on the underlying assets of the subsidiary could be taxable (or losses on those assets allowable) and the vendor left to extract the proceeds from the subsidiary. While in many cases dividends can be paid intra-group without a UK tax liability, such a dividend could give rise to overseas tax consequences if the vendor is owned by one or more non-resident shareholders. Further, the extent to which dividends can be paid to reduce the value of a limited company is restricted to the distributable profits (a UK company law concept) of the payer.

Purchaser issues

A significant disadvantage to a purchaser of a company's shares is that generally the assets of that company will not be revalued. Accordingly, tax reliefs available to that company, particularly capital allowances, will be based on historic acquisition costs and not their current value. Additionally, any actual or contingent liabilities, whether tax or commercial, of the company acquired, will indirectly be transferred to the purchaser group.

Accordingly, a corporate purchaser will often prefer to acquire assets. This is particularly the case if the corporate business being sold has a high proportion of its assets in the form of goodwill and intellectual property, as in general a UK purchaser of assets from an unconnected third party can obtain tax relief by reference to amortisation of that intellectual property in the purchaser's accounts or, in certain cases, annually at a rate equal to 4 per cent of acquisition cost. (The tax benefit from such relief can be clawed back when the intellectual property is sold). Even if the intellectual property content of the business is low, to the extent that value is properly attributable to assets eligible for capital allowances, relief ought to be available by reference to the acquisition cost of plant and machinery. Different rules apply to calculate the relief in respect of plant and machinery located in or on land or buildings which have become 'fixtures' and on 'industrial buildings' (as defined). Further, the stamp duty cost to a purchaser of a purchase of assets may not differ significantly from the cost of acquiring the company's shares. This is because UK stamp duty is chargeable principally on the consideration attributable to interests in land, rights under contracts, certain types of debts and where the acquirer assumes or becomes liable for liabilities of the vendor, but in particular is not now chargeable on consideration attributable to intellectual property and goodwill. (See Example I.)

Tax losses

An acquisition of assets does not cause tax attributes (such as losses of the company) to transfer to the acquirer. To have access to tax attributes such as carryforward tax losses, capital losses and so on, a purchaser would have to acquire the shares in the company itself. As mentioned above, this would involve, via the acquisition of the company's shares, indirect acquisition of the company's tax and commercial history. So a purchaser will need to balance this consequence against the extent to which the company is likely to be able to use the losses and so on against profits or gains of that company. This is because there can be restrictions on the use of losses against profits where there is a change of control of the company. In the case of trading losses, these can only be used against future income of the trade carried on by the company being acquired although, unlike other jurisdictions, there is currently no time limit within which such losses must be used provided the company continues to carry on that trade. Capital losses in a company gen-

Example I

Vendor has £50 million base cost in a target company which has a market value of £200 million.

The Target has goodwill with a market value of £100 million which was self-generated; stock/inventory with a market value of £25 million but a production cost of £20 million; and plant and machinery that has a tax written down value of £42 million but a market value of £75 million. It rents premises on arm's length terms (and so only a negligible amount would be paid for the lease).

If Vendor sells the Target for £200 million (ie, a share sale), the Purchaser will pay stamp duty of $\frac{1}{2}$ per cent on £200 million; obtain no tax relief on the intellectual property; if the Target subsequently sells the inventory for £30 million, it will pay tax on £10 million of profit and obtain capital allowances by reference to £42 million. The Vendor will pay no tax on chargeable gains if the SSE applies. If there were to be a sale of a Target out of a group where the SSE did not apply, even if the holder of the shares in the Target had a low tax basis in those shares, there might be a company further up the group with an adequate base cost to ensure that no, or a reduced, gain arose. Assets in higher-tier companies that the Vendor wished to keep could be extracted prior to sale using the technique in Example III. Alternatively, a new company might be inserted into the vendor group which could acquire the Target's shares in exchange for newly issued shares. The new company, with an enhanced tax basis in the Target, could then sell off the target to a third party.

If the Target sells its assets, Purchaser should pay no material stamp duty by reference to Target's assets, potentially obtain annual tax relief by reference to the higher of £4 million or the actual rate of depreciation of the goodwill, if it sells the inventory for £30 million, it will pay tax on £5 million profit (assuming £25 million was paid for the inventory); and obtain allowances by reference to £75 million (assuming £75 million was attributed to the plant). Target would face a gain of £100 million on the goodwill; £5 million profit on the inventory and a potential tax charge (or reduction in the value of future tax relief) on the plant.

Whether the Vendor/Target would be prepared to structure the sale in this way would depend on the availability of losses and other reliefs to it, particularly losses and other tax attributes in the Target that, following a share sale, would have restricted use to a Purchaser but that the Target could use to shelter profits on an asset sale; and/or the extent to which the purchase price took account of tax benefits accruing to the Purchaser.

erally cannot be used (or used to any significant extent) against profits on assets transferred into the company which were acquired from other companies in the acquirer group.

Example II

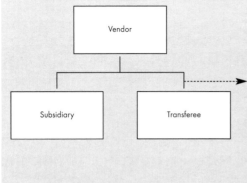

Asset acquired by Vendor for £10 million, transferred to Transferee when worth £17 million and has a current market value of £25 million.

If Vendor sells Transferee for £30 million (reflecting £5 million of trading assets in Transferee and £25 million for the asset), the degrouping charge would be £(17-10) million, giving rise to tax payable of £2.1 million. If the SSE applied, there would be no gain on the share sale, leaving net proceeds of £27.9 million.

If Transferee sold all its assets, the chargeable gain on the asset would be £(25-10) million, giving rise to tax payable of £4.5 million. Even if there was no tax charge on the £5 million attributable to other assets, net proceeds would be £25.5 million.

Degrouping charges and pre-sale group restructuring

To combat attempts indirectly to transfer assets enveloped in a company which, if they had been disposed of directly would have given rise to a chargeable gain, a degrouping charge can arise in a company when it leaves the corporate group if there has been an intra-group transfer of a capital asset to the company within the previous six years. Until 2002, this was a liability of the company being transferred, and a purchaser would either attempt to reduce the price payable to reflect the tax and/or seek warranties and indemnities from the vendors. Now it is possible for the degrouping charge, by election between the vendor group and the company that would otherwise face the liability, to be borne by the vendor group of companies. There are certain exemptions from the degrouping charge, principally when the company owning the asset that was transferred intra-group leaves the group at the same time, and in a group relationship with the company from which the asset was transferred. Note that (see the diagram in Example II) the amount of the exit charge may differ from the liability that would have arisen had the

Example III

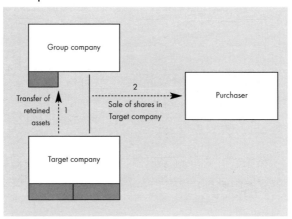

asset been sold direct, and this is particularly significant following the introduction of the SSE (see Example II).

One way of avoiding the degrouping charge that could arise were assets transferred into a Transferee company formed or used for the purposes of the sale, while ensuring that the purchaser acquires only the assets that it wishes to acquire, is to transfer part of the Target company's assets intra-group to another group company, as in Example III.

After such a transfer, the Target could be sold to the Purchaser. In principle the Purchaser would acquire the benefit of some or all of the Target company's losses; the Target would still have its tax and commercial history and, carefully structured, no significant tax charges could arise on the intra-group transfer prior to sale. A purchaser would still want to check and seek warranties/indemnities against degrouping charges on assets transferred into the Target where the transfers had not been connected with the planned sale.

As it is often commercially inconvenient for assets to be transferred direct between the company carrying on the business and the Purchaser, and the Purchaser may not wish to acquire the company with its tax and commercial history, a common strategy is for the relevant assets to be transferred intra-group and for the new company's shares then to be transferred to the Purchaser, as in Example IV.

This could obviously give rise to a degrouping charge but now it is possible to elect for that charge still to be borne by the vendor group which, if the transaction gives rise to a degrouping loss, means that the loss accrues to the vendor group and, if it gives rise to a gain, may enable the vendor group to have control over negotiations of the amount of the gain. (The vendor group may have losses or may be able to reinvest in assets enabling the tax to be reduced or deferred.) Such a transaction should, if carried out in such a way that the new company is beneficially owned by the vendor group, enable capital allowances and

Example IV

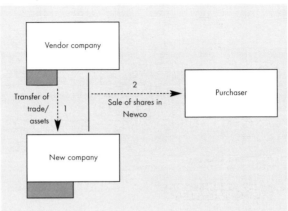

tax losses attributable to the assets transferred to be available to the new company. However, to the extent that liabilities connected with the trade are not transferred to the new company, this may preclude or restrict the availability of tax losses, quite independent of the restrictions which can also operate where there is a change of control of a company with tax losses and where there has been a major change in the nature or conduct of the trade or business of the company concerned. If the transfer to the new company occurred a year or more before the sale of that company's shares, potentially any gain on the sale of the new company's shares could be exempt under the SSE. The overall stamp duty on the intra-group transfer of assets to the new company and then the sale of its shares may be lower than the duty payable on a direct sale of its assets, although new anti-avoidance provisions in relation to stamp duty on the transfer of interests in UK land may limit the saving.

A degrouping charge, calculated in a slightly different manner, could also arise in relation to the new relief in respect of goodwill and other intangible assets if there had been an intra-group transfer of such assets prior to a sale of a company. As this relief only commenced with effect from 1 April 2002, either as regards new intangible assets or intangible assets acquired from unconnected third parties, for the next few years this is less likely to be an issue than the degrouping charge referred to above.

Depending on the relative bargaining power and identity of the vendors and purchasers, normally on a private acquisition of a UK company, a tax covenant and extensive tax warranties are sought. Rather less extensive tax warranties are obtained in relation to making an asset acquisition as most of the tax liabilities would remain with the vendor and not, unlike the case in a corporate acquisition, remain in the company being acquired. Where there is a sale by an insolvency practitioner, a receiver or other person acting in a representative capacity, more limited warranties can be expected. In the case of a sale of a company whose shares are listed or traded on a recognised stock exchange, the purchaser is unlikely to be able to obtain any meaningful contractual protection in relation to tax.

Financing the acquisition vehicle

If the acquisition vehicle is a UK limited company, no UK tax relief is available on dividends paid on its equity and, before dividends and distributions can be paid, it has to have distributable profits for the purposes of the UK Companies Acts. In contrast, tax relief can be available for interest and other returns to lenders, and there is no need to have distributable profits, before principal and interest can be paid to lenders.

The UK tax system limits the deductibility of accrued interest and other returns to lenders in various ways, either by a restriction on deductibility altogether or by deferring relief until payment or redemption of a discounted security. In more detail:

- it limits tax deductibility on borrowing, even from third parties, to the extent that the debt carries more than a reasonable commercial return;
- it prevents a deduction for interest or other returns on certain types of convertible debt securities where the convertibles are neither listed on a recognised stock exchange nor issued on terms reasonably comparable with listed convertibles, unless the holder is liable to UK corporation tax on the interest or other return on such convertibles;
- it prevents a deduction for interest etc on certain limited recourse debt or equity notes, unless the debt is held by a company liable to UK corporation tax;
- no relief is available for interest on debt where it is necessary or advantageous for a holder of the debt to transfer, in addition to the debt, a proportionate amount of any shares it holds in the company, unless the interest on the debt would accrue to a company liable to UK corporation tax;
- relief is restricted to the interest or other return that would have been paid had borrower and lender been unconnected persons where 75 per cent or more of the ordinary share capital in the borrower is held directly or indirectly by the lender or both borrower and lender are directly or indirectly '75 per cent subsidiaries' of a common parent (see Example V). There is an exception to this rule where the lender is liable to UK corporation tax on the income;
- there is a restriction on relief, where the UK transfer pricing rules apply, to the amount of interest or other return that might have been expected to apply had the loan (if it would have been made at all), been made on arm's length terms between unconnected persons. This can apply both where directly or indirectly the lender controls the borrower or where two 40 per cent plus shareholders jointly control the borrower.

Example V

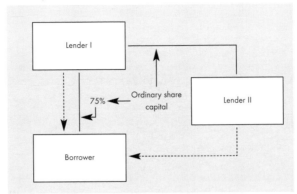

Generally, except where one or both of the parties enjoys certain specified tax benefits, the transfer pricing legislation does not apply between two UK persons;

– interest relief can be deferred in certain circumstances where interest has not been paid within 12 months of having accrued unless the lender was fully taxable on the interest as it accrued;

– relief for an accruing premium on a discounted or zero coupon bond can be deferred until redemption where a borrower and lender are connected or where the borrower is a 'close company' and the lender (or associates of the lender or companies that it controls) are also shareholders in the borrower. Relief for the cost of the accruing premium will, ordinarily, still be available if the corresponding accrual is fully taxable in the hands of the lender;

– there can be a restriction on tax relief for debt, whether domestic or cross-border and irrespective of whether it is between related or unrelated parties, if a loan is taken out for an unallowable purpose (including if a main purpose of taking out the loan was a tax avoidance purpose).

As will be apparent, many of the restrictions on tax relief do not apply to borrowing from corporate lenders liable to UK tax, although they could be relevant to the terms of any loan notes issued as consideration to former shareholders in a company. (As discussed below, limiting these restrictions to persons not liable to UK corporation tax may infringe EU law and so be capable of challenge by borrowers). Therefore, subject to issues about the need for parent company guarantees, a common acquisition structure involves one or more new companies being set up as part of the acquisition structure and borrowing in the United Kingdom. One reason why more than one borrowing company is needed is to achieve structural subordination, that is, the lenders to a lower-tier borrower having access to cash

Example VI

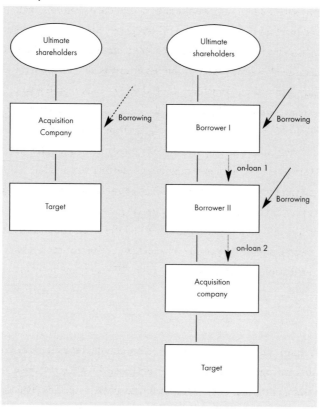

before any remaining cash is paid up to a higher-tier company and so available to the higher-tier company's lenders. See Example VI.

Withholding tax

A borrower is required to withhold tax at the rate of 20 per cent from payments of annual interest, that is on loans capable of lasting for more than 364 days. There are exceptions for payments on advances made by banks in the ordinary course of their banking business and to other institutions which bring the interest into charge to UK tax. There is also an exception for interest paid on a quoted Eurobond, that is a debt instrument listed on a recognised stock exchange issued by a company, whether it is in registered or bearer form.

No withholding obligation applies to short interest or to other rewards to lenders, for example the premium paid to a holder of a discounted security. There is, however, a withholding on PIK bonds, that is where, rather than paying interest, additional debt instruments with a value equal to the interest otherwise payable are issued to the lender. In such circumstances, a certain proportion of the debt instruments should be delivered to the Inland Revenue (in lieu of any withholding that would have applied had cash been paid).

If the borrower is financed by third-party lenders to whom payments of interest could be subject to UK withholding tax (see below), the Inland Revenue maintains that where an overseas parent company guarantee has been given to the lenders, it is able to apply transfer pricing legislation in deciding the extent to which the Inland Revenue would give permission for the interest to be paid without withholding if the Inland Revenue consider the borrower to be thinly capitalised. If the overseas lender (or guarantor) was an affiliate, the Inland Revenue would invoke the transfer pricing legislation and, depending on the terms of any relevant double tax treaty, the 75 per cent subsidiary-related party lending rules described above, if it thought the borrower group was thinly capitalised. This challenge would often arise at the time that any application to pay interest gross to a non-UK lender was made, given the need for Inland Revenue permission before interest can be paid gross. A recent decision of the European Court of Justice on German thin capitalisation rules suggests that the UK rules may be capable of challenge, at least if an EU company is involved.

Effective relief for debt

A key issue for an overseas acquirer is whether it can (and, if so, should) take effective tax relief for interest and other borrowing costs in its jurisdiction or seek to use the relief in the same jurisdiction as the target company. One factor for buyers of UK targets will be the effective rate of tax relief in the overseas jurisdiction compared with the relief in the United Kingdom (broadly 30 per cent), but any constraints on amount and timing in the acquirer/buyer's jurisdiction also need to be compared. So a purchaser group located in a high tax jurisdiction might choose to borrow locally and inject equity into a UK acquisition vehicle, rather than borrow in the United Kingdom and obtain 30 per cent tax relief, if the effective rate of relief locally was higher than in the United Kingdom. Where there is an offshore parent, a decision will need to be made whether to borrow in sterling or in local currency and, if the latter, in which jurisdiction potentially taxable currency gains or losses arise.

Unlike the US consolidated group concept, UK companies are taxed on a company-by-company basis (with exceptions for VAT and group payment arrangements for corporation tax). So the borrower will either need to generate taxable income which the interest and borrowing costs can be set against or surrender the tax loss attributable to finance costs to the target company under the UK group relief rules. Very broadly, this requires a surrendering company (the borrower in this case) to have a 75 per cent holding in shares that carry an effective 75 per cent plus interest in income and assets of the claimant company (in this case, the target). So a key issue in acquisition planning is to ensure that an offer for a company's shares does not become unconditional below 75 per cent (where group or consortium relief is necessary). Where the two companies are not in a group relationship throughout the relevant period, for example where an acquirer is formed and acquires a target halfway through the year, ordinarily only a proportion of the target's profits will be capable of being reduced by group relief. Moreover, if any borrowing costs accrued prior to the date when the surrendering company acquired a 75 per cent interest in the target, a proportion of that cost may not be capable of surrender. So careful planning is needed for drawdown dates, entry into commitment fees and so on, particularly as surplus interest and other finance costs that, via group relief, cannot be set off against other companies' current year profits have to be carried forward in the borrower. The carried forward surplus is not available for group relief surrender in the following year.

Note that if a borrower is incorporated outside the United Kingdom but intended to be UK resident for tax purposes, it may constitute a dual resident investing company (DRIC). If so, it is critical that it on-lends into the acquisition structure, so having the opportunity to off-set interest income against its financing costs, as a DRIC cannot surrender losses (including finance costs) to shelter profits of other group companies. There are various techniques intended to permit a tax deduction for financing costs in more than one jurisdiction or for a deduction in one country without a corresponding taxable receipt in another jurisdiction but as these are very structure and jurisdiction specific, they cannot be summarised here.

Although the UK rules for deduction of interest and financing costs are perceived to be generous compared with other jurisdictions, there are restrictions which can defer relief. This is important, as relief which accrues for a particular period but which cannot be used in that period, either by the company concerned or via group relief, can only be carried back by the company and used against certain income and gains (for example, interest or profits on derivative instruments) or foreign exchange profits which accrued in the previous year or carried forward in that company and used against similar profits. As mentioned above, there is a restriction on the borrower obtaining tax relief if interest is paid more than 12 months after it accrued (unless all of the interest is liable to corporation tax in the hands of the lender as it accrues) where either (i) the creditor is connected with (ie, broadly, it controls) the borrower, or (ii) the borrower is a close company and the lender of an affiliate is a participator (a shareholder or holder of options to acquire shares in the borrower), or (iii) there are two 40 per cent shareholder lenders to the borrower; or (iv) certain pension schemes are lenders. Where a discounted security has been issued by the borrower, relief can be deferred until the period of redemption, rather than as the redemption premium accrues, if the borrower is controlled by the lender or vice versa (or both lender and borrower are controlled by the same person) or the borrower is a close company and the lender or an affiliate is a participator in that company. For this reason, shareholder debt is often introduced at a different level in an acquisition structure than the level of the equity holdings.

Making the acquisition

Tax deferral

The principal tax difference between a cash acquisition and an acquisition involving shares or loan notes is that receipt of shares or loan notes offers selling shareholders the opportunity to defer a gain (or a loss). The tax position will depend on the tax position of the shareholders concerned and, to the extent that shareholders receive cash, some of the gain or loss may not be deferred. If the acquirer company already holds, or as a result of a share exchange comes to own, more than 25 per cent of the ordinary share capital of a target company, shares newly issued by the offerer to former shareholders will be treated as the same asset as the shares in the target company that such shareholders used to own. The same no disposal treatment applies if shares in the target company are exchanged for newly issued shares in the offerer as a result of a general offer which only becomes unconditional if the offerer acquires control of the target company.

Unlike roll-over regimes in some other countries, no relief would be available to UK shareholders if one company acquired the target company and a second, affiliated company, perhaps a parent company with listed shares or debt, issued the consideration shares. To achieve deferral in such circumstances, either the listed parent company could acquire the target in exchange for newly issued shares (or debt) and then transfer the target company to the relevant subsidiary; or the offer would provide for the offerer company to acquire the target company in exchange for newly issued offerer company shares on terms that former shareholders in the target could be required to exchange their newly issued offerer shares for newly issued shares in the parent company, as in Example VII.

With the exception of certain kinds of convertible/exchangeable loan notes and loan notes linked to the value of chargeable assets, generally, on an exchange of shares for loan notes, any gain or loss will be calculated at the moment of exchange and then crystallised only on redemption or on certain transfers of the loan notes. (This different treatment does not apply where UK corporates hold such notes, principally because in most cases the gain or loss on the notes will be taxed as income on the exchange.) However, where the loan notes carry certain rights, for example to be repaid in another currency or to subscribe additional securities, they may be treated as the same asset as the shares they replaced and, therefore, no gain or loss is calculated until redemption or disposal. While it is common to structure the notes so that they offer complete roll-over treatment for former shareholders in the target, rather than just deferral, some classes of shareholder may prefer deferral because of the UK taper relief rules applicable to individual shareholders.

The roll-over provisions discussed above involve the transfer of shares in the target to the offerer company which, if the target has a UK shareholders' register, will give rise to stamp duty ordinarily payable at the rate of $^1/_2$ per cent. Another deferral relief involves a

Example VII

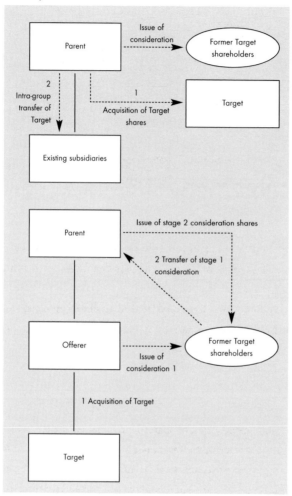

scheme of arrangement under which, if approved by the UK courts, shares in the Target company are cancelled, newly created shares in the Target are issued to the Acquirer and shares in the Acquirer are issued to the former shareholders of the Target. If all the conditions for such a scheme are satisfied, the Acquirer comes to own the Target without UK stamp duty being payable. Where there is an agreed bid such a scheme, although it has an incidental stamp duty benefit, can provide significant corporate law benefits (for example, a lower percentage of shareholders needing to vote in favour), compared with a conventional offer to acquire shares.

It is customary for confirmation to be sought from the Inland Revenue to the effect that such transactions, whether involving share exchanges or schemes of arrangement, are

Example VIII

bona fide commercial transactions. If the Inland Revenue were not convinced, persons holding more than 5 per cent of any class of shares or loan notes in the target might find that no disposal treatment was challenged.

Note that where assets – rather than shares – are transferred to an offerer in consideration of an issue of shares or debt by the offerer, there is no deferral relief to a vendor, despite the vendor having received non-cash consideration.

Shareholder issues

A direct acquisition by a company in one jurisdiction of shares in a Target which is tax resident in another jurisdiction may be unattractive to Target shareholders resident in that other jurisdiction for reasons including a more favourable tax treatment for dividends from the Target's jurisdiction or restrictions on certain shareholders being able to invest in shares of companies from another jurisdiction. (For example, in the United Kingdom, a UK corporate shareholder would prefer a (tax free) dividend from a UK company than a potentially taxable dividend from a non-UK company. UK individuals obtain a tax credit on UK dividends that reduces the income tax payable compared with an identical dividend from an overseas company.)

Accordingly, various other structures need to be considered such as stapled stock arrangements (see Example IX), mergers/acquisitions at the operating company level (see Example X) or dual-listed company structures. A stapled stock arrangement entitles a shareholder in one jurisdiction to continue to receive dividends on shares in the same jurisdiction which are linked with shares in a company in another jurisdiction. The stapling means that the shares in both companies have to be transferred and that the holder of the unit from time to time can elect whether dividends flow on one share or the other share,

Example IX

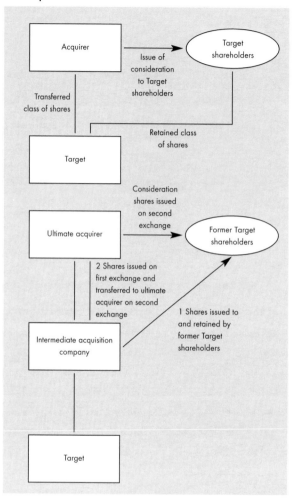

as the holder's circumstances change. This could be achieved either by the Target reorganising its shares and then acquisition by the Acquirer of only one class of shares of the Target, followed by stapling to the shares retained by Target shareholders of the shares issued by the Acquirer or by an intermediate acquisition company issuing two classes of shares to former Target shareholders on terms that shares of one class were then to be exchanged for newly issued shares in the ultimate Acquirer.

There are potential technical tax difficulties with stapled stock structures, for example, under the US tax code. Also, over time there seems to have been a consistent pattern of arbitrage, causing the stapled units to trade at different prices in different markets so many stapled stock arrangements have subsequently been unwound.

Example X

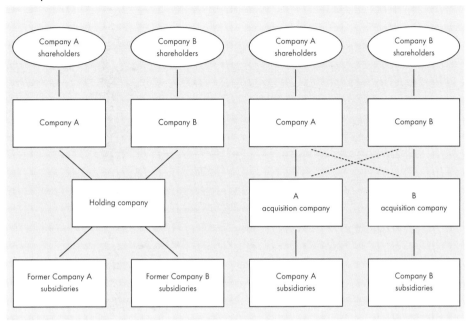

The merger at operating company level partly addresses the shareholder flowback issue, as shareholders can continue to hold the shares in the company which is most beneficial from a tax viewpoint and is permissible as an investment. (Some investors may have only a limited mandate to hold shares listed or incorporated in other jurisdictions). To minimise arbitrage opportunities, it is normally necessary to equalise dividend payments on the two shares, usually taking account of any tax credits available to shareholders.

From a tax viewpoint, steps can often be taken to minimise corporate taxes on the merger of operating companies more readily than ensuring that shareholders in all principal jurisdictions in which companies are listed can satisfy local tax free reorganisation rules. So in this structure, shareholders in Company A and Company B do not make a disposal of their shares, although there is a change in the assets underlying their shares. The first structure in Example X envisages a holding company jointly owned by companies A and B to which they have contributed subsidiaries, rather like the Reed:Elsevier structure. The second structure envisages access shares or simple contractual arrangements without a cross-holding to ensure that companies A and B can both make equivalent dividend payments even if there is a cash or profitability deficiency in any particular company's subsidiaries, based on the Shell and Unilever structures.

The dual-listed structures, of which that involving the companies RTZ and CRA is one example, are broadly a variant on the second type of structure in Example X.

Other issues

Private equity

A key feature of a successful private equity transaction is to maximise the internal rate of return (IRR) of the fund investors. This normally involves introducing as much debt as the investee group can service commercially. Another key requirement is to avoid, or at least minimise, any tax charges arising at the fund level before exit. So while the acquisition structure is likely to be relatively simple, with existing shareholders ordinarily being paid cash for their shares (or possibly loan notes and a minimal residual shareholding), the complex tax issues derive from structuring the debt to maximise finance cost accruals and consequent tax relief yet avoid or minimise recognition of interest or other accruals to the lenders, often involving the use of discounted securities. Another tax complication arises out of the need to maximise the possibility that increases in the value of shares and rights to receive shares conferred on management are liable to CGT rather than income tax.

Deal costs

UK stamp duty can be a significant transaction cost, usually borne by the acquirer (not least because of the UK restrictions on a company providing financial assistance on the acquisition of its shares, which would be the case were stamp duty to be borne by the Target). A particular point to watch is whether arrangements whereby shares can be held through intermediaries (excluding for these purposes CREST) could amount to a clearance service or depositary receipt arrangement, so giving rise to higher rate ($^1/_2$ per cent) stamp duty or SDRT costs.

Where transactions involve the issue or transfer of shares to EU persons generally there will be no, or only limited, recovery of VAT on advisers' costs: the position can be different if there is a non-EU element to the transaction. Companies need to appreciate that while many services provided by investment banks can benefit from VAT exemption, certain advisory services attract standard-rated VAT, currently chargeable at the rate of 17.5 per cent and the VAT recovery.

Conclusion

The UK tax code provides many opportunities for structuring transactions in a way which will minimise tax charges on an acquisition, so increasing the post-tax consideration recieved by the vendors. It also facilitates a purchase maximising deductions and other reliefs so increasing the post-tax return on the investment made by the purchaser in the company or assets acquired.

14

Post-merger integration – maximising the return on your deal

Jonathan Andrew, PricewaterhouseCoopers Transaction Services

Introduction

As companies come to the end of their financial year and begin the process of setting budgets for the next and refining any five-year strategic plan, one problem is becoming a recurring theme for many. How do they engineer significant growth in revenues, profits and ultimately cash?

It seems unlikely that businesses will return to the 10 to 20 per cent profit growth figures of the 1990s, but for many, any positive growth seems difficult to accomplish at the moment. However, with bullish, expectant shareholders continuing to demand a return, the pressure remains to deliver stellar improvements in profits. It is therefore no surprise that many CEOs reach for the automatic alternative: 'if I can't deliver organic growth I'll have to go out and acquire it'. With such an approach, the CEO sees revenues dramatically shooting up and once obvious synergies are realised, profits jumping by an even bigger margin.

Of course it is not that easy. Finding a deal in the first place is difficult enough. This is because the ideal target no longer exists. Companies with solid profits and cash flows, a decent management team and yet with enough potential in the business for genuine operational improvement to be achieved are now no longer easy to find. Even after finding a business that fits well with yours, there is still work to do to get the deal through due diligence and financing. Most vendors are getting smarter at using advisers in advance – to groom the business for sale. This makes the sale and purchase negotiations long and drawn out. Securing the financing is just as perilous. Lending banks are setting tighter working capital restrictions, tougher covenant arrangements and very aggressive debt repayment profiles.

This all means that a typical deal of, for example, £100 million can take over nine months from inception to completion. At the end of such a long and drawn-out process which has absorbed significant amounts of board members' time, it feels like the hard work has been done. It is, in fact, only the beginning. In many situations the deal has meant that the directors have bet the company – now they have to deliver. It is a gamble and it is not easy. So much so that anyone familiar with mergers and acquisitions will tell you that 60 to 85 per cent of deals fail to deliver a return on investment. The challenge remains a truly difficult one – to make a merger or acquisition work to deliver maximum return.

So after all that doom and gloom, how are integrations carried out successfully? What improves the odds? This is the theme of this chapter. Whilst every acquisition is different and there is no one size fits all solution to integrations, there are a number of key areas that should be addressed to deliver benefits from the deal. This chapter will set out our experiences of post-merger integration and share the processes that we have found to be instrumental in maximising the returns on your deal – in short, what works and what does not and, in particular, the eight things to do that will improve the odds of success.

So what does indeed improve the odds?

We are often asked to list the most important attributes of a successful integration. Whilst there can never be a definitive checklist which applies to every integration, our experience is that we do see a number of recurring success factors. Having these clearly embedded in the mind of the senior management at an early stage does help integrations to succeed.

The list is made up of eight actions or statements of intent that should characterise any integration. They can be categorised into three sets of imperatives:

– *Stability* – two businesses coming together require immediate stability for them to function. A combined entity will take some time to come together no matter how quickly the integration goes – it will not be integrated by day one, week one or even month one. So it is imperative for the two separate businesses to run in parallel in as normal a way as possible.
– *Speed* – do not hang about – any integration should be done as quickly as possible as it always involves change and change is a painful experience. The quicker the pain can be stopped the better. Think of a sticking plaster over a wound – when you come to take it off, you know it is going to be painful – rip it off quickly and the pain is over quicker. The same applies to an integration – dawdling with integration activities is a recipe for failure and a lot of pain.
– *Focus* – there are always lots of tasks that need to be done during an integration. However, no company has the appropriate level of available resources necessary to make sure they all get done. A focus is required – resources need to be deployed on the

20 per cent of actions that will deliver 80 per cent of the value with the greatest probability of success.

These three – Stability, Speed and Focus – drive our list of statements of intent. Note, however, that the list of eight imperatives below is not a guarantee, nor is it a buyer's protection plan – it is, in our experience, a list of the key attributes which, if completed satisfactorily, increase the chances of success. Do these well and you are on the way to a successful integration. It can be viewed as a sort of integration checklist. These will be covered in the remainder of this chapter.

The eight post-merger integration imperatives

Stabilise the business

1. Communicate often and early
2. Take control immediately
3. Do not ignore potential culture clashes

Speed makes the difference

4. Appoint the top team as soon as possible
5. Integrate quickly

Focus on the value driving actions

6. Plan, then manage the integration
7. Apply scarce resources to where the greatest benefit will be gained
8. Set clear targets, incentivise and measure

Stabilise the business

Why is stability important? The answer lies in the fact that a merger or an acquisition invariably leads to a significant amount of change for a business. Such change can bring an endless list of destabilising effects which can undermine the longevity and profitability of the new entity. It is therefore essential that in the days and months immediately after completion, the two entities remain stabilised. That is why you hear so many CEOs talk about 'business as usual' when announcing a deal. It is an attempt to keep people focused on what they were doing before the deal was announced. A stable business means that the people are behaving rationally and consistently and are more likely to cope quicker with any proposed changes. A destabilised business means chaos, lack of clarity and confusion, which makes acceptance of change much more difficult and in the end can cause an integration to fail. Therefore, in order to maintain a stable business in the immediate days following an acquisition or merger, the management team must ensure effective and regular communication and secondly, quickly take control of the combined business. Thirdly, any potential clashes in the way two businesses operate cannot be ignored.

1. Communicate often and early

Let us begin with communications. The premise here is simple: during a time of such significant change, the expectations of stakeholders need managing. If they are not, then the stability of the new combined business is severely threatened. Anyone who has an interest (or stake) in either the acquired business or the purchaser is a stakeholder and any stakeholder needs managing.

The typical stakeholders are employees, customers, suppliers and investors. However, the list is normally more complex – unions, regulators, sub-contractors, and neighbouring businesses to name only a few more. All of them will have questions that they would like answering, largely around: 'How does this deal affect me?'

One of our assignments involved assisting two media businesses with their integration. In the last two weeks before the deal was to be announced, we discussed with the directors of the acquiring business how the deal was going to be announced. During the discussions, it became clear that because the majority of management's time and attention had, quite rightly, been focused on getting the deal done, no-one had really thought carefully about what they would do once the deal had actually happened. Further, all the questions that stakeholders were predicted to ask needed answers. Management toyed with numerous questions. For example: 'What were the main strategic reasons for the deal and how much detail should be provided to employees?' Secondly: 'What is our response if an employee asks about their pension plan'? (No final decision had been made about pensions at the time); and thirdly: 'Who's going to announce the deal to the Head Office staff and who's going to do the same (with the required level of consistency) to the warehouse staff 40 miles down the road?'

All in all, the announcement of any deal to employees (we call it Day One Communications), the City and the wider world is difficult – it has the potential to haunt any CEO who makes rash promises or if the whole exercise has not been planned and executed with careful precision. Further, a lack of a coordinated and well-planned Communications Plan to manage the ongoing expectations of stakeholders throughout the integration process can seriously affect the success of any integration. People will have more questions than answers, will not believe or trust the answers that they have heard and the 'coffee machine effect' will begin. People will gather around the coffee machines, water coolers and canteens of the organisation and speculate about what is really going on

– and this will not just be happening amongst employees. Customers, suppliers and other stakeholders will be displaying similar behaviour. This is where the rumour mill will start up and it will largely be negative and damaging in its content. Answers to awkward questions, for example about people's pension plans, will be made up in the absence of any clear communication from the executive. This will damage morale and accelerate people looking for jobs elsewhere, away from such a highly charged environment.

To prevent the rumour mill festering and destabilising the organisation, a Communications Plan should be developed and executed. There are four key steps to achieving this.

Communicate often and early

(i)   Identify stakeholders in each organisation, their major issues and concerns

(ii) Build a Communications Plan for the integration period

(iii) Communicate a little and often (based on the premise that no news is bad news)

(iv) Establish a two-way dialogue with all major stakeholder groups

---

(i) Identify stakeholders in each organisation, their major issues and concerns

This can initially be a time consuming process but is well worth it in the end. It centres on listing all the different groups of people who have a stake or interest in the combined entity – from suppliers to regulators, unions to local authorities. Then for each group, identify the key concerns and issues that they are likely to have based upon knowledge of the deal and integration plan. For the major stakeholder groups it is often worth meeting with a selection of them to validate your assumptions. This can be done by running a small number of focus groups and is especially useful for employees. Questions to ask include:

– what is your understanding of the deal?
– what is the level of support for the proposed changes?
– what do you think are the opportunities for the new business?
– what are your issues and concerns?
– to what questions would you like answers?
– what are your preferred methods of communication?

From the work we have performed in numerous integrations, it is clear that stakeholders welcome this approach. If managed well, they feel like they are being consulted, treated like adults and that they are important to the success of the integration.

(ii) Build a Communications Plan

Armed with the information gleaned from Step (i), the second step is to build a

Communications Plan. Such a plan identifies the critical issues which need to be communicated and plans what is to be said, by whom, to whom, and when. It also ensures that all communication channels are exploited and, in some instances, additional channels are created. In a Gallup research study, sponsored by pharmaceutical giant Astra Zeneca Plc, employees said they liked receiving merger information by e-mail or voice-mail, but only as a backup to face-to-face communication. Further, Renee Hornbaker, vice president and CFO of Flowserve, the world's premier provider of industrial flow management services based in Texas, United States, has spearheaded 16 mergers and acquisitions in five years. She believes a company cannot communicate too much with employees. She visits each department to explain new policies, procedures and practices. This is then followed up with e-mails and newsletters to encourage feedback and keep employees informed.

(iii) Communicate a little and often

The key to the plan is to communicate a little and often and sometimes even repeat key messages. This is because in some instances it is only on the third or fourth time of repeating a key message that it begins to be heard and acknowledged by the audience. The maxim here is 'no news is bad news' – if the integration is going well but there is really nothing to communicate then the message is ' the integration is going well but there is really nothing to communicate'.

(iv) Establish a two-way dialogue

Of course, some communiqués cannot be planned in advance because events will arise that were unforeseen at the time of communications planning. Knowing that a new issue has arisen during the integration can only be achieved if the integration team knows what is going on in all the integration workstreams. To do that, the best way is to establish a two-way dialogue with stakeholders, normally through existing communications channels such as supervisors meetings or group sessions or alternatively by holding smaller focus groups similar to those in Step (i) at certain, appropriate times during the integration.

The message then is communicate, communicate, communicate. The rumour mill loves to fill a communication gap. By executing a well-planned Communications Plan with no-nonsense, honest and hype-free communiqués, the stakeholders' expectations during the integration will be well managed and the business stabilised.

2. Take control immediately

We have already mentioned that the real hard work begins once the deal is completed. In fact in terms of Taking Control of any new business, the hard work starts at least a couple of weeks before completion. Taking Control essentially involves the CEO and acquiring management team getting to understand the new business as quickly as possible – ideally in the first month after deal completion. There are two elements to Taking Control:

Take control immediately

(i) Plan to address all the 'must-do' actions (Urgent Actions) related to the deal

(ii) Define quickly what is required in terms of management information and key performance indicators (KPIs) for the acquired business

---

(i) Urgent Actions

Whenever two businesses come together through a merger or acquisition there is always an endless list of actions that must be done relating to the deal and the newly formed entity. These actions are not value-creating ones, but ones which simply must get done – they relate to legal and deal execution matters such as changing companies' registered names and addresses or to such matters as security (access of new employees to all new buildings), technology (allowing the two parties to communicate to each other via e-mail) or finance (ensuring that there are sufficient funds in the appropriate bank account to pay wages to the enlarged employee numbers). Other examples include re-setting authority levels and approval limits for middle managers. Further, at the target entity some strategic projects may no longer be appropriate or relevant – some may need redefining; others may need to be stopped altogether. In particular, expenditure relating to such projects may require closer scrutiny from management as a result of the integration. Therefore, procedures need to be put in place to monitor capital and strategic expenditure.

From the examples used, you can see that such actions are hardly exciting or earth shattering. However, if ignored and not done on time, they could potentially cause problems later, drawing on resources otherwise directed to more value enhancing activities. As part of Taking Control we recommend that these actions be done with urgency as close to day one as possible. We call them Urgent Actions and recommend that the majority be completed in the two or three weeks before day one. This goes a long way to ensure that the businesses are stabilised immediately prior to and following completion of the deal.

Clearly this needs to be carefully managed so that management does not end up with a large and unfocused To-Do list. Each Urgent Action should be prioritised between what is *business critical* (ie, the business will be adversely affected if the action is not performed on time), what is *important for the business* and what would be *nice to have* but is not an immediate priority. Having attached a priority to each action, the owners of the action should also assign dates for completion and identities of those tasked with completing the necessary tasks.

This piece of work should involve management covering all operations of the business. Ideally as large a group of managers should be involved as possible as this will invoke a feeling of being involved and part of the process which will help remove uncertainty and create stability. Clearly this is also an excellent first opportunity for counterparts at the two businesses to meet and share information in a non-judgemental way about how each business operates.

(ii) Management information and KPIs

The second area that involves management Taking Control of the new entity is management information and reporting. Whilst the acquiring management team will no doubt know the newly acquired business fairly well, at least as a result of due diligence, it will not necessarily be entirely familiar with how the business is run and managed on a day-to-day basis – how it generates cash, how working capital is tied up, what its treasury position is. Also, the management accounts of the newly acquired company will no doubt be different to the existing business and may involve the monitoring of KPIs that are not familiar to the acquiring management team.

In terms of understanding the new business, this is an essential area for management to sort out immediately on acquisition. They will want to know details about revenues, gross and net margins, cash flows and other key metrics. Understanding what data and analysis is produced and re-aligning it to meet the business requirements of the new entity is very important. This is particularly so where the acquisition has changed the debt profile of the company. Where significant additional borrowings have been made to fund the deal, tighter working capital and covenant restrictions often result, which means that management has to watch its cash flow much more carefully and regularly.

Often changes to the financial information are associated with changes to the computer systems. The key here is to ensure that no large systems changes are required to generate the new information, instead only slight tweaks. Also, the additional workload that is required to generate revised management reports and KPIs must be assessed – it is critical that finance resources are not overstretched in preparing the amended reporting information.

In terms of Taking Control, management should aim to have revised and retuned management information sufficient for them to manage the enlarged business, ideally by day one, but if this is not possible, within one to two months following deal-completion.

3. Do not ignore potential culture clashes

Cultural incompatibility between merging or acquiring companies has become the main reason that is cited for failed integrations. If in doubt, put the blame on an inability to get along with one another. Whilst it is often the scapegoat, there is no doubt that bringing two differing cultures together is extremely difficult. A recent survey by PricewaterhouseCoopers on mergers and acquisitions showed that 49 per cent of respondents reported differences in culture as the most troublesome integration issue.

John Reed, CEO at Citicorp, certainly found this to be the case. Following Citicorp's 1998 acquisition of Travellers Group, he wrote an article for *Business Week* in 1999, entitled: 'The Culture Will Take Care of Itself'. In it he stated: 'The culture will take care of itself. People ultimately learn how to work together. They may not like it. They may complain a lot. But, you know what? Five years from now, they will be quite surprised at how they have learned to get along'.

However, eight months later, writing for *Fortune* magazine, Reed had changed his tune. In the article, entitled 'Reed: Reflection on a Culture Clash', he said: 'We are talking about putting two cultures together that are quite different, quite distinct. I am trying hard to understand how to make this work. I will tell you that it is not simple and it is not easy, and it is not clear to me that it will necessarily be successful. Just as the body sometimes rejects an organ that it needs, business systems can sometimes reject behaviours that are required for a systems success. As you put two cultures together, you get all sorts of strange, aberrant behaviour'.

First, let us define what we mean by differences in culture. There are two main types:

(i) Differences in the way companies get things done – their operating philosophy. This means everything from how decisions are made, how people are rewarded, motivated and incentivised, or how important training and development is to the organisation. This was starkly observed during the merger of Hewlett-Packard with Apollo Computers. During the integration, people were quickly put into two distinct camps based on behaviour at the two companies – Hewlett-Packard staff were nicknamed the 'Stepford Wives' whilst the Apollo people were the 'Hell's Angels'.

(ii) The second type of cultural differences arises because of geographical boundaries. Whilst there are obvious exceptions to the generalisations, the way business is conducted in Japan or France is vastly different to the way it is done in the United Kingdom or Spain, for example. This makes cross-border integrations even more difficult. To support this, a study sponsored by DaimlerChrysler AG for the business publication *Across the Board* showed that 73 per cent of international mergers failed.

Ironically, when Daimler-Benz and Chrysler announced that they were merging, competitors were quick to predict failure because of the inevitable clash of German and North American cultures. Whilst it has suffered some problems since integration – mixing process-led German engineering with US risk-taking was always going to be fraught with danger – the combined group remains together. It appears that it has survived by recognising its cultural differences rather than trying to suppress them. So much so that the chairman famously announced: 'We have a clear understanding: one company, one vision, two cultures'.

Clearly this is not going to work in most cases. So how should potential culture clashes be addressed? In our experience there are four key elements:

Do not ignore potential culture clashes

(i)   Assess cultural compatibility pre-deal

(ii) Identify the differences, promote the similarities

(iii) Define, promote and reinforce the desired behaviours

(iv) Select and deploy role models

(i) Assess cultural compatibility pre-deal

Often important questions about the people aspects of a deal are overlooked during due diligence. A company's approach to bringing people together affects productivity, quality of output, staff retention rates, customer service and also the speed at which an integration proceeds.

Whilst cultural effects can be difficult to quantify, understanding the target's style, traditions, values and unwritten rules is essential. This should be done as part of the due diligence process in order to identify any potential risks to the deal. It should, where possible, include:

- an evaluation of the target's history and reputation;
- interviewing company management and staff; and
- studying the company's degree of focus on profitability, customers and employees.

(ii) Identify the differences, promote the similarities

Following completion of the deal, it is essential that differences in the operating style are identified and their impact on the business as a whole and the integration process considered. This requires a detailed analysis of behaviours across all aspects of the business – an assessment should be made as to the magnitude and importance of differences or gaps in policies and practices in the areas of:

- *performance metrics* – emphasis on individual or team accomplishment;
- *procedural compliance* – emphasis on following policies and procedures;
- *supervisory structure* – the extent of supervisory intensity;
- *selection process* – the rigour with which candidates are selected;
- *decisionmaking* – the extent to which decisionmaking is centralised;
- *demographics* – gaps in age, tenure, experience, unionisation, gender;
- *recruiting and training* – degree of skills development/acquisition;
- *incentive structure* – competitiveness and risk of the pay structure; and

– *employee engagement* – the extent to which employees are directly involved in company decisions and processes.

Once this is done, major differences can be tackled. Meanwhile, in communiqués to staff and other stakeholders, positive examples of similarities should be published and promoted to give stakeholders a feeling of common ground between the parties. This helps to maintain a stable environment during the period when differences are being addressed.

(iii) Define, promote and reinforce the desired behaviours

To move two cultures into one, the process must begin with changing behaviour at the individual level. The desired behaviours must first be defined. At GE Capital, cultural workout sessions are conducted to address cultural integration issues and define a set of behaviours – a blueprint of how the company should move forward.

Once the behaviours are defined, they must be consistently reinforced – this leads to a kind of behavioural memory that takes over and drives desired behaviours.

In our experience, driving core behaviours cannot be achieved simply by promoting a series of vision and value statements. Such statements need to be translated into straightforward examples of how people are expected to behave and operate in the post-deal environment.

(iv) Select and deploy role models

The most effective way of reinforcing desired behaviour is through role models – they should be deployed in visible positions of authority. This also requires generous public praise and recognition of their performance – making it clear that if people want to succeed in the new company, they need to emulate these behaviours. This message is further reinforced if other employees who engage in the desired behaviours are quickly and visibly promoted, recognised and rewarded.

So in summary, identify the culture clashes early, establish what impact they could have on the new organisations and quickly seek to address them. Accentuate the similarities and overlaps and drive the desired behaviour changes by visibly promoting and recognising role models.

Speed makes the difference

4. Appoint the top team as quickly as possible

There are two facets to this dilemma. The first is: what should the organisation look like now that it is increased dramatically in size and scope because of this acquisition? The second is: who shall form the executive top team?

This usually is one of the most difficult areas to deal with in post-merger integration and typically the area which keeps the CEO awake at night the longest as he wrestles with a new organisational structure. Questions such as 'With an increase in critical mass in some areas, is it now time to rationalise the organisation? Should the new entity be product/brand driven, geographically structured or aligned along with customer needs?'

Then once the design has been crafted, there is the tricky task of how to fill the top positions from the list of directors of both companies. For any CEO this is something they cannot necessarily share with too many people – this is a CEO's job and largely his alone. The difficulty connected with this part of the integration is the need to balance speed against the desire to get the right person in the right job. A CEO will argue that it takes time to get to know the new executives from the acquired company – to understand them and appreciate their strengths and weaknesses – how can that be done with speed? It needs careful thought and consideration. Get it wrong and the consequences could be disastrous.

It is difficult to argue against this approach. However, be dilatory, overconsiderate, overdeliberate and the entire success of the integration could be undermined. With any delay of announcement of the new structure, executives become distracted from their current role and start vying for perceived jobs on offer whilst not committing to any integration initiatives for fear of being sidelined into a permanent position that they believe is not for them. The inertia that results slows down the integration to a snail's pace. Projects and actions are delayed because responsibilities cannot be assigned; middle managers lose patience with the top-tier politics and strutting that they witness and the momentum created in the initial days after completion evaporates.

There are three key features to appointing the top team as quickly as possible:

Appoint the top team as quickly as possible

(i)   Identify and retain top talent (before they receive other offers)

(ii) Define roles and responsibilities for top layers of management

(iii) Announce new structure quickly to stakeholders

(i) Identify and retain top talent (before they receive other offers)

One of the most difficult tasks a CEO faces during a merger or acquisition is ensuring that the key people necessary to the success of the new organisation do not leave. Nearly half of senior executives in acquired companies walk out the door in the first year; moreover three-quarters leave in the first three years. Successful integrators evaluate the talent pool in both companies, decide whom to keep and then act quickly.

It is therefore extremely important that a clearly defined process for identifying and retaining the top talent is put in place. This process must be seen as fair and consistent. Any suggestion that the process is not robust will harm the remainder of the business.

Employees who see inconsistency and perceive that the process is a sham could become disillusioned, and this creates the real risk that key people will be lost. The importance of creating a clear, visible process cannot be overstated. This can be done using tools such as talent identification inventories, succession plan reviews, special bonuses, plus options and incentive programmes. Each individual should be assessed against a set of clearly defined competencies which are appropriate for the needs of the new entity. Further, senior executives should meet with selected employees to tell them what the integration plans are, how they fit into the new structure, and, most importantly how much their talent is appreciated and how they will be rewarded through a retention bonus and new career opportunities.

(ii) Define roles and responsibilities for top layers of management
Mark L Feldman and Michael F Spratt, in their no-nonsense mergers and acquisition guide *Five Frogs on a Log* cite preoccupation with organisation charts as a major contribution to delays to an integration. Often organisation charts are published without the associated reporting lines or defined roles and responsibilities. Charts with just boxes and lines cannot alone clarify complex roles, interrelationships or how decisions are made. As Fred Graver, co-chairman of Barclays Global Investors once stated: 'You can no more create role clarity by drawing an organisation chart than you can make it rain by washing your car'.

So the key message here is to accompany organisation announcements and charts with the accountability and decision authority for each box on the chart. Further, roles and interdependencies should also be clarified. This should ensure that on announcement, employees, suppliers and other stakeholders are not left with more questions than answers regarding how the new entity is to be organised. Consequently, this has a very positive effect on the stability of the organisation.

Once the direct reports to the senior executives have been agreed and announced, it is important that these newly appointed individuals quickly set about appointing their teams. Again, it is essential to have a robust process as it is likely that the middle managers will be watching what happens intently. Clearly, if the process from the top of the organisation has been transparent and fair then it is much easier to replicate a similar process down through the business with positive results.

(iii) Announce the new structure quickly to stakeholders
One of the most frequently encountered issues in deciding on the top team is when senior executives are not certain which of the candidates is most suited to the role. Understandably, the natural reaction is to appoint the person they already know or to delay in making the appointment. Putting the right process in place at the outset will certainly help provide sufficient independent information to help make the decision. Where the

decision is still not clear and, given the prevailing atmosphere of uncertainty that surrounds integrations, it is better to make a decision and move on it than take no decision at all. After all, businesses do not always make the right decisions in other operational matters. Recognition that the decision may need to be carefully monitored is an important way of helping senior executives make the decision and then communicate it. Too often the whole organisational structure communiqué is delayed because senior executives are unable to agree about one post. As Percy Barnevik, former CEO of ABB once said: 'I'd prefer to do something and make a mistake over doing the right thing too late.' Universal Music Group certainly subscribed to this view. Formed in 1998, when Seagram acquired Polygram Records, the new management structure and associated reporting lines were announced less than a month after Seagram's tender offer for the remaining shares of Polygram had closed.

Further, the announcement of the new organisation should be handled with care. The CEO should be particularly sensitive when it is possible that one company is perceived to be taking over the other simply because it has an undue number of its legacy employees in significant positions in the new organisation structure, or that directors in one of the companies involved in the merger have not been given a fair opportunity to apply for the senior jobs.

In summary, instigate a process which is robust and appropriate enough to allow for a fair assessment of directors' skills, experiences and capabilities. Then, manage the announcement of the top jobs carefully, so that those directors who may not be in their ideal job but nevertheless have a crucial role in their appointed position, are not alienated or encouraged to look elsewhere. Finally, do not just put names in boxes on an organisation chart – define roles and responsibilities so that all senior management are clear about what they should be focusing on in the new organisation. So the message is, of course get the organisational structure right and appoint the right people for the right jobs – but do not take too long over it. Ideally this should all be completed and announced within two months of deal-completion.

5. Integrate quickly – tailor the integration to match the deal rationale

It has already been said that integrations should be carried out quickly: speed really does makes the difference. In a 2000 PricewaterhouseCoopers survey, we asked top executives who had experienced a recent integration what the effect of speed has on an integration. The conclusions were stark. When asked what they would do differently if they were to do it all over again, over 85 per cent of respondents stated that they would move faster. Moreover, companies that reported an accelerated integration following deal completion also reported achieving over 80 per cent of their integration objectives. More tellingly, they noted a favourable effect on gross margins, cash flow, productivity and profitability.

Exhibit 14.1: Integration approach

	Current product/service	New product/service
Current geography	• Rationalise fast and efficiently • Implement processes early • Do not lose key resources too soon • Watch out for merger of equals A	• Take time to evaluate target's business processes • Understand target's key competencies and relationships • Use strong, reliable executives to manage speed of process appropriately • Watch out for culture mismatch – use carrots not sticks C
New geography	• Do not leave alone • Implement processes early • Integrate operations more slowly • Focus on key employee and customer retention • Balance time between people management and integration B	• High risk acquisition and integration ie, Do not buy it? D

The evidence is clear – do not delay an integration – a prolonged process delays the effect of change, adds cost and slows growth, prolonging the payback.

Having said that any integration should be done with pace, the second key message is to tailor the integration approach to match the deal rationale. This requires careful planning, ideally in advance of day one, so that the integration can begin with speed immediately. Exhibit 14.1 summarises how the integration approach should be varied according to the situation.

Scenario A – The integration involves similar products/services in similar territories
Undoubtedly the most straightforward situation, the key here is to move quickly. There may be a number of painful decisions about employees that need to be taken but speed removes uncertainty. Lack of speed leaves the businesses open to the threat that key resources leave, because the best employees are typically the most mobile.

Scenario B – The integration involves similar products/services but in different territories
The key for successful integration under this scenario is that the businesses are not left alone. Such an approach will only reinforce existing behaviours and will make attempts at future integration more difficult. Therefore, a balance has to be achieved between understanding each other's business and ways of operating and implementing the steps that you know must be made to make progress in the integration. Typically, this will involve implementing processes early but taking slightly more time than under scenario A to integrate operations. The challenge is to understand the cultural differences, why they exist

and how important they are before deciding on how the new merged business will operate. Cultural change cannot be achieved over night and is much more likely to succeed by using incentives to drive behaviour.

Scenario C – The integration involves different products/services in the same territory
Under this scenario, care must be taken to evaluate the different processes used by each business. It is imperative under this scenario that management is strong and able to judge the pace of the integration. Speed is always important but it must not be at the expense of understanding key competencies and relationships. People management is crucial.

Scenario D – The integration involves different products/services in different territories
In our experience this is very high risk. Different operating styles and cultures with different products or services are a recipe for disaster – far too much management time will be spent getting to know the business (if not travelling) and understanding the cultural differences before any benefits can be realised – few synergies will exist – they will mainly be back office which will be difficult to realise if the geographical spread is large. In short, given the difficulty in making integrations work, the advice is: do not buy the business in the first place.

Focus on the value driving actions

6. Plan, then manage the integration

As has already been mentioned, any integration is typically a large-scale change programme. Typical workstreams include plant or site rationalisations, back office consolidation and harmonisation of employees' terms and conditions. These all involve significant change to systems, processes and particularly people. Consequently, these workstreams need coordinating, managing and monitoring. This involves putting a simple programme management structures in place to ensure it occurs in a coordinated manner. When we work with businesses on integrations we begin with a structure as shown in Exhibit 14.2 as a working template.

It is important to begin integration planning as early as possible – ideally before deal completion. Both GE Capital and Johnson & Johnson base success in the acquisition arena to a well-planned integration process which begins during the pre-deal phase.

The premise of the structure in Exhibit 14.2 is based on experience of what works and what does not. Looking briefly at each element:

Executive board sponsorship
All change programmes require a sponsor and an integration is no different. We strongly advise this person to be an executive member of the board, ideally the CEO. This effec-

Exhibit 14.2: Template integration structure

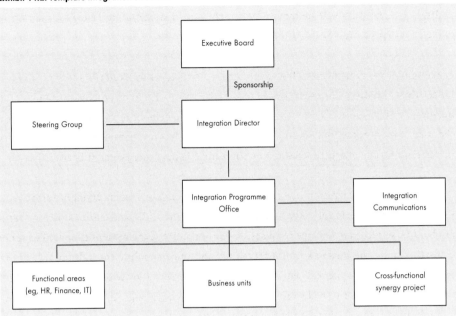

tively ensures that the integration has the required visibility with the executive so that issues can be solved quickly and effectively without any delay to the integration.

The role of the sponsors is to:

- ultimately approve priorities and major expenditure/changes to plan;
- adjudicate major conflicts raised by the Steering Group (see below);
- provide broad strategic direction for the project teams; and
- be the change champion(s)/monitor overall progress.

Steering Group

In our experience, an integration rarely suffers like other change projects sometimes do from lack of executive interest and sponsorship. It is largely safe to say that an integration is the single most important thing that is going on in a company at any one time so the CEO and the board tend to want to get involved. In fact, the challenge is to keep the board out of the day-to-day integration issues without upsetting them. Setting up a Steering Group allows this to occur. As the name suggests, the Steering Group's job is to steer the integration in the right direction and make sure it is on track. The group should comprise one or two executives who can act as the executive board's representatives, plus two or three more personnel. One of these two executives should assume overall responsibility as

Integration Director. It should also ideally have representation from both parties being integrated to ensure an element of balance to proceedings is maintained. We recommend that a Steering Group should consist of no more than six or seven people. Such a group would meet regularly to review progress of the Programme Office (see below) and prepare brief summaries for board meetings. How regular the meetings are will depend on the status of the integration. In the early days of an integration where there is a lot of planning and coordination to do, the group may meet fortnightly. This may move to monthly once the integration workstreams are up and running and then may be as infrequent as every six or eight weeks once the integration is in the final stages of implementation.

The Steering Group's responsibilities are summarised below:

- reviews output/recommends ongoing mandate;
- evaluates strategic implications of project team proposals/interdependencies;
- approves (and if necessary secures) resources for projects – funding, people, facilities;
- monitors performance to plan/approves changes to scope/funding of projects;
- debates and resolves conflicts;
- coordinates communications according to plan;
- ensures projects remain in line with normal business.

Programme Office

Any integration has a number of issues that must be dealt with each day throughout the whole programme. This cannot be done in an ad hoc fashion. Moreover, an issue that surfaces today cannot be left to a week later before it is addressed. This means that a small but dedicated team is required to manage the day-to-day integration issues and coordinate the workstreams. This effectively means taking two or three people away from their day jobs to work exclusively on the integration and run the Programme Office. This may be difficult if the company is resource constrained, but in our view this job cannot be done part-time. Ideally a balance should be maintained in the Programme Office, in terms of sourcing people from both companies in the integration.

At Astra Zeneca, one of the success factors that management cited for the impeccable integration of Astra AB and Zeneca was the unconstrained cooperation by all team members who were drawn from both parties.

The roles of the Programme Office are listed below:

- establishes procedures and processes for monitoring and reporting;
- tracks progress of individual projects against plan;
- coordinates interdependencies across individual projects;
- responsible for meeting agendas, minutes, capturing issues;

- provides informal/ad hoc progress reports to Integration Director on a regular basis (eg, every other day);
- highlights issues to Steering Group (via status reports); and
- evaluates performance to plan and changes to scope/expenditure elevating when necessary to Steering Group.

This role is vital to the success of the integration. The people in the Programme Office (who should have good project management and people skills) will be the only ones in the entire organisation who will know what is going on in all of the project teams – that is their job. Such an overseeing role – essentially an eyes and ears role for the Integration Director cannot be underestimated. It highlights problems as soon as they arise, can identify people issues associated with the integration (particularly culture clash issues) and can communicate and receive feedback on key messages.

In this structure the workstreams all report progress to the Programme Office on a regular basis (eg, fortnightly) normally through some sort of simple reporting template. We normally advise a simple reporting format – it is important here not to create an overly complex monitoring and reporting structure. It is vital that the Programme Office monitors and reports but it must also solve issues and address actions. It cannot do this if it spends all its time reporting so that there is little time left to get things done. We have witnessed one integration where the Programme Office began producing its weekly report on Tuesdays for a Friday afternoon deadline. This meant that there were only Mondays each week where the team could assist the other workstreams and actually drive the achievement of actions.

Communications

We have already talked about the importance of communications throughout an integration programme. With the communication team tied to the Programme Office, integration issues are more easily identified and addressed.

The processes and structures that we recommend are vital to the success of an integration. They help maintain a focus and allow the executive board to get on with what it should do best – run the business and deliver the profits. If there are integration issues that require the board's input or attention then the structure provides for that, but the rest of the integration can proceed with pace without any distractions.

7. Apply scarce resources to where the greatest benefit will be gained

It is more than likely that one of the key reasons behind any merger will be the opportunity to derive either revenue or cost synergies or indeed both. Deals are no longer secured where the synergy number is the balancing figure – these days much more thought is put into what synergies can be achieved before the deal is completed. Nevertheless, once the deal is done significant work remains to turn these high-level synergy ideas and calculations into well defined action plans which will lead to the delivery of the intended value. Not only that, the initiatives that are required to deliver the synergy numbers need to be adequately resourced – this is difficult as the number of available resources will always be less than what is required. This is what drives the focus – resources (time, capital, finance) should only be applied to initiatives where the greatest (quantifiable) benefit will be derived.

To achieve this, PricewaterhouseCoopers' approach of Value Driver Prioritisation includes the following four steps:

Value Driver Prioritisation

(i)   Identify the 20 per cent of actions that will drive 80 per cent of the value (Value Drivers)

(ii) Develop financially-robust business cases for each Value Driver

(iii) Rank all Value Drivers in terms of probability of success

(iv) Launch project teams to prepare detailed plans to deliver the Value Drivers

---

Step (i) Identify the Value Drivers in the transaction – the 20 per cent of actions that will drive 80 per cent of the value in the shortest possible timeframe with the greatest probability of success. These will come from detailed discussions with the key managers in the business, reports and other deal papers produced during due diligence.

Establishing those 20 per cent of actions is not easy. Each executive will have his list of preferences according to his areas of responsibilities. In addition, there will always be a few projects favoured by one or two senior management and will inevitably be aired again at this time. Further, in most instances the synergy numbers developed pre-deal will have been done so at a fairly high level due to the difficulty in getting access to detailed information. The synergies are also unlikely to have been formulated by the parts of the business that will be responsible for delivery of the results. If not handled carefully this can be an area which creates significant problems. A balance must be found whereby employees are not disenfranchised from the numbers they are asked to achieve. This is the process of Value Driver Prioritisation.

Often the focus for achieving synergies is on cost-cutting initiatives such as headcount reduction and plant rationalisation. Whilst revenue generating synergies should not be ignored, the easiest way to achieve value is from trimming annual costs. On the announcement of the merger of Guinness Plc and Grand Metropolitan Plc to form Diageo Plc, management predicted £195 million of savings through sharing distribution channels and reducing the workforce by 2,000. Within nine months, Diageo had cut 3,000 jobs and exceeded expectations by reporting savings of nearly £300 million.

Probability of success is also very important as it is the ultimate determinant of the extent to which actions will yield value and helps flush out those pet projects. In this context, probability of success involves assessing the likelihood of delivering on the actions after taking account of available skilled resources and the interdependencies of other actions.

Step (ii) Develop financially-robust business cases for each Value Driver – work with key managers in each functional area to develop a detailed business case for each major initiative. Here focus should be on the methods of implementation and challenging assumptions:

– assess the resources required – are they available?
– quantify the potential additional revenue or cost savings;
– assess the costs to implement (capital expenditure is important but there may also be training and other hidden costs);
– consider the probability of success of key assumptions and initiatives;
– cross-confirm information between the two businesses; and
– prepare an outline action plan and identify key risks or impediments.

Step (iii) Rank all Value Drivers in terms of probability of success – senior management can now review and debate a ranking table of expected Value Drivers assessing potential initiatives on a common basis right across the organisation. The business cases should be rigorous, financially based and value focused – this allows for a more constructive discussion of priorities because subjective valuation is removed. This way it is clear whether or not the CEO's pet project is a priority Value Driver (see Exhibit 14.3).

The senior management team for the first time can then reach consensus as to the priorities for the new business going forward and the composition of teams to implement the priority Value Drivers. This focuses (inevitably) scarce resources and removes some of the uncertainty in the organisation – it becomes clear what the priorities are – they are the priority projects (shown as bullets in the top right-hand corner of Exhibit 14.3).

Step (iv) Launch project teams to prepare detailed plans to deliver the Value Drivers. These teams, selected by senior management, develop detailed action plans together. Such plans identify:

– responsibilities and timetable;
– information required;
– the level of senior management support required; and
– interdependencies between teams and initiatives.

Exhibit 14.3: Value Driver Prioritisation

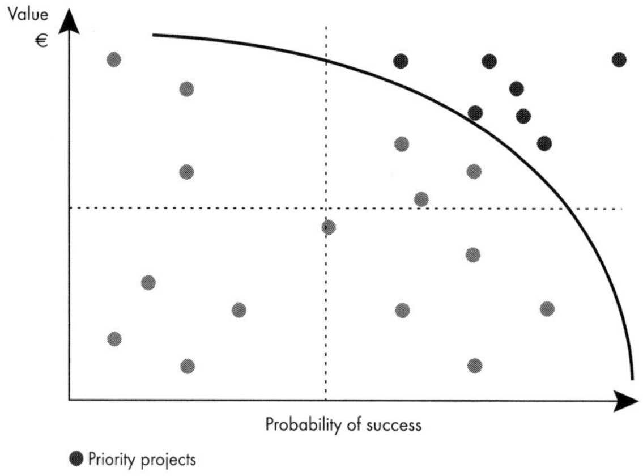

The business now has an overall plan for implementation, with clear accountabilities and responsibilities for each individual manager's contribution to profit improvement.

8. Set clear targets, incentivise and measure

This is a very difficult area and strikes at the heart of how to measure the success of any integration. In many cases, executives believe that measuring success is just too difficult – managers claim savings and synergies that were already built into pre-deal budgets and five-year plans; others make a great play of how much value they can create through the value driving project teams until they are asked to commit to a saving target for next year's budget – miraculously leading to a target at a fraction of the original estimate. One CEO we worked with asked us to track the total synergy savings estimated by the teams over time as they moved close to finalising the budget. The CEO had set a target of £20 million synergies over three years. The total estimate moved from £46 million to £24 million during the month of preparing budget plans.

The solution is to link the Value Driver Prioritisation exercise to the setting of targets and incentives. By attaching a very tangible quantified benefit (in £, US$ or €) to each Value Driver, the project team is essentially setting its own target. This target can then be linked to an individual's incentives. This is important as managers involved in the Value Driver project teams would otherwise find themselves torn between their integration responsibilities and their regular jobs. Having quantified targets allows schemes to be set up which are self-funding and tied to value creation. They can be structured in such a way that the cost of the incentives are paid out of incremental free cash the teams produce over an an18-month or two-year period. Plus, assigning quality people to the integration teams sends a powerful message that integration is important and getting involved can be career enhancing, not limiting.

The important messages are that aligning employees' personal objectives with the integration objectives is critical; and rewarding employees for hitting those targets is well worth the related costs. Ignoring the measurement and incentive question can leave even high-performing managers focused on the wrong tasks or frustrated with the stress of doing two jobs for the same pay. When it comes to incentives, our credo is simple: 'what gets measured gets done'.

Summary

There is inevitably a lot to get right when performing an integration – it is a process which is fraught with problems. Based on our experience at PricewaterhouseCoopers, we have found that companies that follow the eight imperatives described in this chapter have greater success with their implementations. Following these imperatives has allowed them to *stabilise* the business, integrate with *speed* and *focus* on the value driving actions.

15

Exit strategies

Neil Vickers, partner, Denton Wilde Sapte

Introduction

This chapter identifies the main types of exit route available for equity investments in the United Kingdom, explains some of the pitfalls of which investors need to be aware and outlines the main characteristics, merits and disadvantages of each method.

No matter what type of investment is in contemplation, other than perhaps a strategic acquisition made with long-term objectives, investors should at the outset give thought to how their ultimate exit should be structured. With liquid investments, such as listed securities, the means of divestment is straightforward. Matters become more complicated, and more interesting, when considering the private equity markets. The performance of venture capital funds is judged and the future success of their fund managers is determined in large part on the exit rates of return of the underlying securities.

Timing is also critical, particularly for funds. Private equity fund managers typically look for an exit in the period of two to six years from investment, although in practice factors internal to the investee companies, such as the concerns of management, and external ones, such as market conditions, may delay the plans considerably.

Investors in illiquid securities should, depending on their percentage holding and bargaining power, seek to control, or at the least to influence, the preferred form of exit at the outset. Equity investment agreements tend to include expressions of hope or expectation as regards the exit, which to a lawyer's eye are rarely specific enough or certain enough to be enforceable. Accepting that the best laid plans can be blown off course and may need to be changed in the future to deal with events, such provisions should deal specifically with the preferred time of exit, the minimum valuation at which it can be triggered, who is in control of the process and the preferred method.

Types of exit

The most common forms of divestment are as follows:

- *Trade sale* – where the assets of a business or securities in the investee entity are transferred in their entirety to a third party, commonly a participant in the same market as the target entity. This can take the form of a controlled auction.
- *Initial public offering (IPO)* – in which equity securities in the undertaking are listed on a recognised stock exchange and simultaneously offered to the public or otherwise placed with new investors. This method can allow for a partial or total exit.
- *Second round buy-out* – where the existing capital provider is replaced and equity and/or debt is refinanced by fresh venture capital.
- R*etirement of equity* – where profits or the proceeds of a fresh issue of shares are used to repay some of the existing equity.
- *Liquidation* – which for several reasons, including tax, is generally an undesirable means of exit usually to be contemplated only where the investment is unsuccessful.

There are variations on and combinations of the above solutions. A diverse group, for instance, may be groomed for an exit by being restructured and enhanced in order to unlock value by means of a series of sales. The proceeds can subsequently be realised by way of repayment of capital or simple distribution.

This chapter concentrates on the two main forms of exit, the trade sale and the IPO.

Recent trends

Statistics for the year 2002 indicate that in the United Kingdom of 257 exits from buy-outs and buy-ins, 71 were by way of trade sale, 12 by IPO, 62 by secondary buy-out or buy-in and 112 by receivership.[1] This broadly corresponded with the picture in 2001.

Grooming the investee company

Investors will wish early on in the process to condition the business for exit. Typical ways to achieve this are by:

- strengthening and enhancing the management team (often focusing on the finance function) and generally improving corporate governance disciplines;
- focusing the management team's attention on specific and achievable strategic objectives and disposing of non-core assets;

– putting in place proper financial reporting procedures and systems and ensuring that the investors receive adequate financial information on a regular basis;
– adopting appropriate share option and other management incentives; and
– with a view to subsequent due diligence, terminating any questionable practices and improving the record-keeping procedures.

Many of these matters will in any event be necessary on exit, particularly on an IPO, and establishing the correct culture from the outset will repay itself handsomely.

Constructive tension – management versus investors

It is important to recognise that significant differences in interest often exist between the company's executives and its shareholders and to put in place mechanisms as far as possible to minimise these conflicts and align the interests of both parties. Management will have invested time, commitment and effort as well as possibly cash in the business and for them there is not just the financial but also the human issues. On exit they may be expected to give warranties, they may leave or may take on additional responsibilities, and will be subject to restrictive covenants and lock-ins. The means of exit is often a source of tension in itself. Management may prefer an IPO thus enabling them to retain their independence and gain the personal and corporate profile which a listing provides, factors which may have no concern to investors more interested in timing and value.

Conflicts are not limited to those between management and investors. Different investors can have different views on the balance between the timing of an exit and realisable value. This is particularly the case where the equity is held by private equity funds that are approaching maturity. For this reason, it is usually preferable for funds who invest together or in successive rounds to have similar maturity timescales.

Provisions of a typical investment agreement

An investment agreement entered into between investors, the company acquiring or owning the business and its management will ideally, as described in the *Introduction*, contemplate the preferred exit route for the investor. The investment agreement is not solely concerned with the exit strategy, but also regulates the terms on which the investor will subscribe for shares and the ongoing relationship between the investor and the company together with its management during the course of the investment. The investor wishes the provisions of the agreement to give it sufficient control over the business of the target in order to protect its investment and to maximise its return on its eventual exit. There follows a brief summary of the principal provisions found in an investment agreement, though it should be noted that these areas can also be regulated in the target's articles of association.

Conditions

A typical investment agreement will contain a list of conditions precedent which will have to be fulfilled before the investor purchases any shares in the business. For example, the investor will wish to satisfy itself that the business plan, accounts, disclosures, bank facilities and insurance are acceptable and will also require that the management purchases shares in the target. If any of the conditions precedent are not fulfilled prior to the date specified for completion, the investor will not be obliged to purchase shares in the target.

Share rights

Closely linked to the issue of exit routes are the rights attached to the shares owned by the investor. The investment agreement or the articles of association of the target will specify the rights attached to the shares. Typically, the investor will subscribe for shares which give it enhanced rights over other shareholders. In particular, it will have priority in respect of dividends or a return of capital and enhanced voting rights in respect of certain issues. Rights in respect of share transfers will be dealt with below.

Warranties

Prior to purchasing any shares in the target, the investor will seek the comfort of warranties in respect of the business of the target, which will enable it to seek financial compensation in the event that any of the matters warranted later turn out to be untrue.

However, the issue of who should give warranties often gives rise to much debate and negotiation. The seller of the target will generally seek to avoid giving warranties on the basis that the management of the target have been involved in running the business and therefore have a greater knowledge, a claim which the management will seek to refute. The priority of the investor is to ensure that, regardless of who gives the warranty, it will be sufficiently compensated in the event of a breach. This speaks against taking warranties solely from management who will generally not have sufficient resources to meet a liability claim. A compromise is often reached whereby the seller gives warranties in respect of all matters but has no liability for matters of which the management was aware. The investor will seek warranties from the management to cover such cases, but will limit such liability. Alternatively, the investor may accept reduced warranties from the seller in return for a reduced price for the shares.

Supervision

Whilst the investor will not wish to be heavily involved in the day-to-day running of the business in which it holds shares, it will wish to exercise sufficient control to ensure that its investment is protected. The investment agreement can provide for this in a variety of ways. Examples of provisions include (i) the appointment of a director, chairman or observer to the board, (ii) the requirement of consent from the investor before the management or shareholders can take any action which is outside the ordinary course of business and (iii) the provision of regular accounts, reports and budgets to the investor.

Pre-emption rights

To ensure further control over the business, the investor will normally insist on restrictions on the transfer of shares in the target. The identity of the management is often of vital importance to the investor, who will therefore be reluctant to allow any member of management to sell their shareholding freely. Investment agreements may therefore contain provisions which only allow management to transfer their shares if the investor consents and, if such consent is given, to offer their shares to the remaining shareholders. However, if a member of the management does or is required to leave, it is unlikely that the investor will wish him to remain as a shareholder and consequently contractual provisions contained in the investment agreement may force a member of the management to sell their shares upon leaving the business. In addition, such a management member will often be subject to a restrictive covenant preventing him or her from engaging in any activity which may conflict or overlap with the business of the target. The extent of such a clause should be carefully considered to ensure that it is enforcable.

Whereas the investor will wish to control and restrict the ability of the management to leave the target company, it will wish to retain as much freedom as possible for itself to transfer its shares. During the course of the investment, it will not want to be bound by pre-emption, to the extent at least of intra-group transfers and transfers to beneficiaries.

Exit

The investor should also insist on the ability to exit freely from the agreement. Whilst the investment agreement is often vague about the precise timing and the manner of exit, deliberately giving the investor the ability to decide upon the best route, it will generally remove any obstacles to an exit. In particular, the investor may wish to force all other shareholders to sell their shares upon an exit (commonly known as 'drag-along' rights).

Which exit route – advantages and disadvantages

There are inevitably merits and disadvantages, which will depend on the particular circumstances, between the two main exit routes, the IPO and the trade sale. The latter's typical advantages are that it:

–   results in 100 per cent of the investment being disposed of by way of a clean break (save for warranty and indemnity liability);
–   involves negotiations with only a single purchaser rather than a multiplicity of new investors;
–   involves a flexible period of negotiation which enables the vendors to deal with issues of concern from purchasers as they arise; and
–   tends to be simpler and cheaper in terms of fees in that fewer professional advisers need to be involved and the equity market regulators are not involved in the process.

However, on the negative side, greater warranty and indemnity protection is required by purchasers, who will be able to undertake a greater level of due diligence prior to sale. Trade sales also offer a greater level of uncertainty for management, who may expect to lose their jobs or at least their independence once the sale has taken place.

Whilst on an IPO warranties are not given to investors directly, the sponsor and underwriters of the IPO will insist on warranties being given by selling shareholders and management. These warranties are generally not as extensive as those in a typical sale and purchase agreement. However, they will extend to the statements of fact in the prospectus issued as part of the listing process and there will usually also be a tax indemnity. Overall therefore, but with the exceptions described in the next sentence, in practice the difference in the extent of the warranty and indemnity liability on an IPO and on a trade sale is not very significant. Venture capital investors tend to resist giving warranties and indemnities. Management and any non-executive directors are expected to give such warranties although their financial liability for claims is often limited to a multiple of their salary in the case of executives and directors' fees in the case of non-executives. The typical period for the making of warranty claims (18 months to two years for most warranties and six years for tax claims) is frequently the same whether on an IPO or trade sale.

One significant difference in documentation between an IPO and a trade sale is that there is no disclosure letter to accompany and to qualify the warranties in the case of an IPO. This is because the rules of the listing regime will require that all matters relevant for disclosure to investors are stated in the prospectus, which in effect forms the disclosure letter for the purposes of warranties given to underwriters. Note that listing regimes will impose statutory liability for false or misleading statements on persons responsible for a prospectus in addition to the warranties customarily sought by underwriters. In the United

Kingdom this regime is now to be found in Part VI of the Financial Services and Markets Act 2000.

An IPO can provide a route for a partial divestment for investors who wish to retain an interest in the newly floated vehicle (and indeed typically would be required by underwriters to retain their continuing shareholdings for a period of up to two years from IPO, the lock-in period).

The IPO route has its own particular disadvantages. The process is carried out in the glare of publicity which may shed unwanted light on areas of the business, its management and its shareholders. The management will need to be prepared to accept the much greater degree of regulation and responsibilities accompanying their new listed company status. However, management will not be free from shareholder participation. Whilst now having to pay regard to the general body of shareholders, institutional shareholders will continue to wish to be consulted by management. Decisions (including equity raisings and major acquisitions or disposals) will, under the relevant listing rules, require shareholder approval, giving rise to uncertainty and the cost of the preparing and issuing circulars to shareholders and holding shareholder meetings.

Finally, the newly listed company will be expected to satisfy the demands of the public markets as regards dividends and the enhancement of its share price.

The exit process – sale by auction

The sale of a company or business by private treaty is now a well established process and it is not necessary to expand on it in this chapter. Particular considerations, however, apply when it is decided to sell a business or entity by way of a competitive auction. This will only be an option if there are potential buyers willing to compete with each other but, if the right conditions exist or can be created, investors should be able by this method to maximise the price on exit and minimise their ongoing liability. In order not to lose the initiative, it is important for vendors to follow the correct procedures and to maintain them during the course of the bid process.

The main steps of a typical auction process are as follows:

– investors engage the services of a financial adviser who identifies potential bidders and establishes the ground rules of the auction;

– potential bidders who express an initial interest are required to sign a confidentiality undertaking following which they receive an investment memorandum prepared by the company in conjunction with a financial adviser and draft sale documentation;

– those wishing to go forward to the next phase and who are acceptable to the vendors will then be given the opportunity to undertake due diligence under a controlled timetable in a data room prepared and collated by the management and its advisers. The data room should be located away from the premises from the target company and practical steps are taken to ensure that competing bidders do not learn of each other's identity or come into contact with each other;

- bidders are then invited to submit their bids and deliver with them their proposed amendments to the draft sale and purchase agreement, dealing with any matters arising from due diligence (the draft agreement, having been drafted by the vendors, will contain less warranty protection than would otherwise be the case);

- a further round may occur at which a short-list of bidders is interviewed by representatives of the vendors and the financial adviser to clarify issues arising from the bidders' submissions; and

- the preferred bidder is then selected and is either given a period of exclusivity in which to complete the transaction or, if the vendors are in a particularly strong position, is simply given preferred bidder status with secondary bidders being kept informed of progress.

One concern of management will be to restrict the disclosure of sensitive commercial information. It is sometimes the case that the most sensitive information, such as customer lists or key commercial contracts, is only made available once preferred bidder status has been achieved. Clearly, however, such late disclosure of material information may lead to a price adjustment and on the process being partially rewound and so is problematic.

The vendors will wish to have as short an exclusivity period as possible, since in practice the granting of exclusivity can be the point at which the balance of power begins to swing towards the purchaser.

The IPO process

The timetable required for an IPO will vary according to the stock exchange chosen and the manner in which shares are offered. However, companies planning to list should anticipate the procedure lasting about three months and, particularly in the latter stages, the potential distraction inflicted on the management by the exercise should not be underestimated.

Initially, the company will appoint and instruct the appropriate sponsor, broker, lawyers, reporting accountants, media consultants and any industry consultants.

The work involved in preparing the company for listing includes the following:

- planning any reorganisation of the company or its business which is required to make it suitable for listing and drafting the necessary documentation and, in the United Kingdom at least, re-registering it as a public company;

- drafting the prospectus which should then be submitted to the listing authority for its comments and approval. Ancillary marketing documentation, for example presentations to industry analysts, should also be drafted;
- both lawyers and accountants carrying out a due diligence exercise into the company, its business and assets;
- the accountants drafting a long form report based on their due diligence exercise and conducting a working capital review for the purposes of the company's working capital statement in the prospectus;
- the sponsor undertaking a marketing exercise to generate sufficient interest from investors, usually via a bookbuilding process;
- the underwriting agreement being negotiated between lawyers respectively for the company and for the underwriters;
- the connected broker carrying out its research and publishing a report (now recommended to be at least four weeks before the publication of the prospectus); and
- the responsibilities and liabilities of directors of a listed company (together with the continuing obligations on companies under the listing rules) being explained to the directors.

Once the listing authority has given its consent to the relevant documentation, including the prospectus, the sponsor on the company's and the shareholders' behalf will be ready to launch the offer or place the securities being disposed of by the exiting investors together with any new equity being raised by the company. At that point the brokers, the sponsor and the company will agree the price for the securities in the light of market conditions, and the offer or placing will be made.

Conclusion

Whilst the methods of achieving an exit are now well established and investors and their advisers have become increasingly sophisticated in fine-tuning the procedures for such routes, there are no standard solutions to divestment and the most appropriate route will depend on the relative importance of the considerations set out above. It is, however, clear that lawyers are playing an increasingly significant role in influencing these transactions and that the engagement of lawyers practised in these transactions at an early stage of the process should help to ease that process for investors and management alike.

[1] *Sources:* CMBOR; Barclays Private Equity; and Deloitte & Touche.